Better Homes and Gardens®

very merry COOKIES

WILEY

JOHN WILEY & SONS, INC.

For general information on our other products and services or for technical support, please contact our Customer Care Department within the United States at (877) 762-2974, outside the United States at (317) 572-3993, or fax (317) 572-4002.

Wiley also publishes its books in a variety of electronic formats. Some content that appears in print may not be available in electronic books. For more information about Wiley products, visit our web site at www.wiley.com.

Library of Congress Cataloging-in-Publication Data is available upon request.

ISBN: 978-1-118-01603-9 (pbk.), 978-1-118-11944-0 (ebk.), 978-1-118-11945-7 (ebk.), 978-1-118-11946-4 (ebk.)

Printed in the United States of America

10 9 8 7 6 5 4 3 2 1

Meredith Corporation

Editor: Jan Miller

Contributing Editor: Shelli McConnell

Recipe Development and Testing: Better Homes and Gardens Test Kitchen

John Wiley & Sons, Inc.

Publisher: Natalie Chapman

Executive Editor: Anne Ficklen

Editor: Charleen Barila

Production Editor: Abby Saul

Production Director: Diana Cisek

Art Director: Tai Blanche

Interior Design and Layout: Holly Wittenberg

Manufacturing Manager: Tom Hyland

Some design elements © istockphoto.com/crossroadscreative

Our seal assures you that every recipe in *Very Merry Cookies* has been tested in the Better Homes and Gardens® Test Kitchen. This means that each recipe is practical and reliable and meets our high standards of taste appeal. We guarantee your satisfaction with this book for as long as you own it.

contents

Look for these symbols:

 Santa's Little Helper—just right for kids

Quickie Cookie—start with a ready-made dough or cookie mix

10 Steps to Your Best Christmas Cookies *Ever*

Before you tie on an apron and spoon into the flour, take a few minutes to polish up on what it takes to become a cookie-baking pro.

1 Get the Best Goods

First, make sure you have the exact ingredients you need and that they're in top-quality condition. A few words about using and/or storing the most commonly used cookie ingredients:

✳ **Butter vs. margarine?** Choose unsalted butter. Nothing compares to the rich flavor and consistent results that butter brings to cookies. Stick margarine will work if it contains at least 80 percent fat (check the label). Avoid low-fat, liquid, and soft spreads. When a recipe calls for softened butter, allow it to stand about 30 minutes or until it has lost its chill and is spreadable. Never use melted butter when softened butter is called for.

✳ **Baking powder and baking soda:** These ingredients help your cookies rise and become light and tender. Keep both on hand, and never substitute one for the other. Store in airtight containers in a cool, dry place and replace every 6 months or check the "use by" date.

✳ **Eggs:** All recipes were tested using large eggs. Make sure the ones you use are fresh; store in their carton in the coldest part of the refrigerator for up to 5 weeks after the packing date.

✳ **Brown sugar:** Recipes were tested using light brown sugar (unless dark is specified). Light and dark brown sugar may be

used interchangeably in recipes, unless one is specifically called for.

✳ **Granulated and powdered sugars:** These can be stored indefinitely in airtight containers.

✳ **Flour:** Store flour in an airtight container in a cool, dry place for 10 to 15 months; for longer storage, refrigerate or freeze in a moistureproof container.

2 Carefully Choose Your Cookie Sheets

✳ Replace cookie sheets that have become warped or dark from years of baked-on grease.

✳ Purchase shiny, heavy-gauge cookie sheets of light to medium color. Shiny metal helps your cookies brown more evenly.

✳ Look for one- or two-sided cookie sheets. The raised sides make them easier to grasp, while the flat sides allow heat to circulate more effectively.

✳ Avoid dark-color cookie sheets, which can cause cookies to overbrown.

✳ Choose cookie sheets that easily fit in your oven, allowing 1 to 2 inches of space all around the pan.

✳ Use jelly-roll pans (four-sided 15x10x1-inch baking pans) only when called for (usually for bar cookies). Their 1-inch sides prevent other types of cookies from browning evenly.

✳ Perforated cookie sheets (with accompanying perforated silicone mats), insulated cookie sheets, and cookie baking stones do not measure up, performance-wise, to standard cookie sheets. Generally, there's no need to invest in these specialty items.

3 Measure Up

When you correctly measure ingredients, you greatly enhance your chances for success. Some ingredients require a little extra know-how:

Brown sugar: To measure, press into a dry measuring cup or spoon until it holds the shape of the measuring cup or spoon when inverted.

Liquids: Pour liquid in a glass or clear plastic liquid measuring cup placed on a level surface. Read the markings on the cup by bending down so you can view them at eye level.

Flour: First, stir the flour in the bag or canister to fluff it up. Gently spoon the flour into a dry measuring cup or spoon, filling it to overflowing. Level off the top with the straight edges of a spatula. Avoid packing the flour into the cup or tapping the cup to level it. Sifting before measuring is only necessary for cake flour.

Shortening: Measure solid shortening by pressing it into a dry measuring cup or measuring spoon with a rubber scraper. Level off the excess with the straight edge of a knife. Shortening is also sold in sticks with markings on the wrapper that indicate measures.

4 Avoid Sticky Situations

To help cookies glide off the tray after baking, most recipes call for greasing the cookie sheets. A light coating of shortening is best. Butter and margarine often contain salt, which tends to make cookies stick. For a handy way to grease cookie sheets, dip a piece of plastic food wrap into the shortening and spread the shortening thinly across the sheet.

If you bake often, you may wish to invest in silicone baking mats, which can be reused for years and (unlike perforated silicone mats) clean easily. Parchment paper also works well (see "Parchment Paper," page 187). Use all products according to each manufacturer's directions.

For brownies and bars, lining the pan with aluminum foil makes for easy removal and cleanup.

made in France **SILPAT**

5 Space Out

Always remember most cookies expand while they bake. Drop or place dough as many inches apart as the recipe specifies. Otherwise, they may run together. Also see "How to Drop Dough," page 118.

6 Bake Until Done

Minutes matter when baking something as small as cookies. Oven temperature is equally important.

❋ Check your oven temperature before a heavy round of holiday baking. Set the oven at 350°F and let it heat at least 10 minutes. Place an oven thermometer in the oven. Close the door and heat the thermometer for at least 5 minutes. If the thermometer reads higher than 350°F, reduce the oven setting by the number of degrees difference each time you bake. If the thermometer reads lower than 350°F, increase the oven setting by the number of degrees difference. If your oven is more than 50 degrees off, have a service person adjust the thermostat.

❋ When baking cookies, set a kitchen timer and check doneness a few minutes early. Some ovens may over- or underheat, causing cookies to bake faster or slower than the recipe suggests.

❋ For high-altitude baking, start by increasing the oven temperature by 25°F and decreasing the baking time by a minute or two. If further adjustment is necessary, reduce the sugar by a couple tablespoons. If a recipe calls for baking powder or baking soda, you may need to reduce the amount by ⅛ teaspoon. Make only one recipe adjustment at a time.

7 Cool It!

Cool cookie sheets—and correctly cooling the cookies themselves—are key steps in the process.

✳ Always place cookies on cold or room-temperature pans. Warm or hot cookie sheets cause your cookies to spread when the fat in the dough begins to melt. Work with multiple baking sheets so a cool sheet is always ready to go into the oven; always let hot cookie sheets cool completely between batches.

✳ After the cookies have baked, allow them to cool on the cookie sheet for 1 minute before removing them (unless otherwise specified). Hot-from-the-oven cookies are fragile; the standing time allows them to firm up before transfering them to wire racks to cool.

✳ Transfer cookies with a thin metal spatula from the sheet to the cooling rack. Allow cookies to cool completely before frosting or decorating (unless otherwise specified).

8 Store Smartly

Once you've mastered a batch of perfectly baked cookies, make sure you keep them at their best by storing them properly.

✳ Make sure cookies have cooled completely on a wire rack before storing. If they're still warm, they are likely to stick together.

✳ Use storage containers with tight-fitting lids. Never store crisp cookies and soft cookies in the same container; crisp cookies will soften and soft cookies will harden.

✳ For most cookies and bars, layer them between waxed paper in an airtight container. Follow the storage directions that accompany each recipe.

9 Freeze with Ease

In most cases, cookie dough and baked cookies can be frozen. Here's how:

Cookie dough: Most doughs can be frozen for baking later; exceptions include bar cookie batters and meringue or macaron mixtures. Place the dough into freezer containers, cover, and freeze up to 6 months. Before baking, thaw frozen dough in the refrigerator. If it's too stiff to work with, let it stand at room temperature for a few minutes until it's easy to handle. Shape slice-and-bake dough into rolls and wrap in foil before freezing.

Baked cookies: Most drop, sliced, bar, and shaped cookies freeze well. Use only containers and bags intended for freezer storage. Place cookies in layers separated by waxed paper so they don't stick together. Tightly cover and freeze the cookies for up to 3 months. If you plan to frost or glaze cookies, do so after freezing and thawing.

10 Ship with the Greatest of Care

Here's how to make sure shipped cookies arrive intact (and not in crumbs):

* Choose crisp or firm varieties, such as slice-and-bake and most kinds of drop and bar cookies. Avoid moist, frosted, or filled treats.

* Pack cookies when they're fresh but completely cooled. Wrap cookies individually, in back-to-back pairs, or in stacks (especially good for thin, flat cookies).

* Line a sturdy corrugated cardboard box with bubble wrap; add a generous cushion of foam packing peanuts, crumpled tissue paper, or additional bubble wrap.

* Place the sturdiest cookies on the bottom; add a layer of filler and then another layer of cookies. Repeat as necessary, topping off the box with more filler so the cookies won't shift and break.

* Insert a card with the recipient's name and address and mark the outside of the box "Perishable."

* Ship early in the week so that delivery won't be delayed over a weekend and choose a shipping option that will provide quick delivery.

8 Great Decorating Hints

Part of the pleasure of baking Christmas cookies is making them look festive and fun. Here are eight tips to get you started; find more great ideas throughout the book—look for "In a Twinkling" tips with selected recipes.

1 Grab Some Brushes

The quickest way to glaze or ice cookies is with a brush. Use a large pastry brush to lightly apply an egg wash (1 egg beaten with 1 tablespoon water) on smooth-topped unbaked cookies, such as sugar cookies; once baked, the glazed cookies have a nice sheen. Use small, clean paintbrushes for detail work, such as applying thin strokes of frosting or luster dust to cookies.

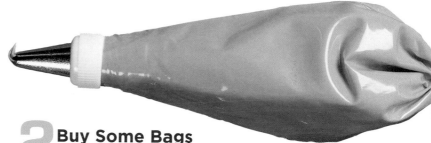

2 Buy Some Bags

Head to the cake decorating aisle of a crafts store or a bakery supply shop and look for decorating bags and tips.

Decorating bags: For ease and convenience, use plastic disposable decorating bags to pipe frosting. When you are finished decorating your cookies, simply discard the bag.

Decorating tips: Interchangeable tips for decorating bags come in several shapes and sizes, but to decorate cookies, you need only three: a round tip, a star, and a leaf. Choose tips with small or medium holes to pipe frosting.

3 Add Some Color

Food coloring adds so much appeal with just a few dabs or drops. Liquid food coloring, usually available in four colors (red, green, yellow, and blue), has a relatively low concentration of dye. Available in a wider variety of colors, paste food coloring is highly concentrated, offering more color intensity. Use less paste coloring than you would liquid.

4 Bring on the Buttercream

Here's a recipe for **Buttercream Frosting,** which looks and tastes great on cookies:

In a medium mixing bowl beat ½ cup softened butter with an electric mixer on medium speed until fluffy. Add 1 teaspoon vanilla. Beat in 1¼ cups powdered sugar. Beat in 1 tablespoon milk. Beat in another 1¼ cups powdered sugar until smooth. Beat in enough additional milk (up to 1 tablespoon more) to make a frosting of spreading consistency. Tint as desired with food coloring. **MAKES ABOUT 1¼ CUPS.**

5 Pipe with Expertise

To pipe Buttercream Frosting, fill a decorator bag about two-thirds full with the frosting. Fold the corners over and roll the bag down to the frosting. With one hand, grip the bag under the roll and above the frosting. Apply pressure with the palm of your hand, forcing frosting toward the tip. Use your other hand to guide the tip of the bag.

To learn how to decorate with royal icing, see "Special Effects," page 18.

Star tip: In addition to stars, a star tip can create shells, zigzags, and decorative lines and borders.

Leaf tip: To form leaves, hold the bag at a 45-degree angle, keeping the tip opening parallel to the surface. Squeeze out some frosting to make the base of a leaf. Continue squeezing but ease up on the pressure as you pull toward the leaf tip. Stop the pressure, then pull away.

Round tip: The round tip is ideal for writing and creating dots, lines, stems, and vines.

Star Tip   **Leaf Tip**   **Round Tip**

6 Sprinkle with Skill

Online, in the baking aisle, and at crafts stores, you'll find a great variety of sprinkle-on embellishments for adding a finishing finesse to cookies. Here are a few to look for:

Sugars: Fine sanding sugar gives cookies a shimmer, while coarse sugar—with granules up to four times larger than those of regular granulated sugar—adds more dramatic sparkle. Colored sugars easily add holiday hues without requiring food coloring. Sprinkle cookies with sugars when the icing is still tacky. If you plan to present cookies without icing, sprinkle before baking.

Edible glitter: Much flakier than sugar, edible glitter makes cookies glisten with color. Sprinkle onto icing while it is still wet.

Candies and nonpareils: Tiny candies, such as sprinkles and confections made in holiday shapes provide eye-catching effects on cookies. Nonpareils are tiny opaque balls that add a beadlike texture. Sprinkle onto iced cookies before the icing sets.

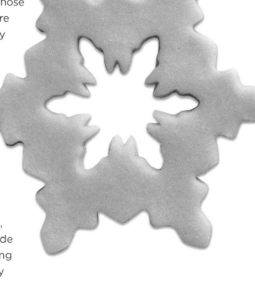

7 Think Outside the Square

To pretty up bar cookies for the season, cut them into triangles. Cut the pan of cookies into 2- or 2½-inch squares. Then cut each square in half diagonally. Triangles work best for bars that are fairly firm. If the bars are crumbly, you're better off with square or rectangles.

8 Choose Chocolate

A dusting of chocolate or a few luscious curls make bar cookies look even more irresistible.

Coarsely grated chocolate: Rub a cool, firm square of chocolate across the large section of a handheld grater.

Chocolate curls: For large curls, draw a vegetable peeler across the broad surface of a bar of room-temperature chocolate (milk chocolate works best). For smaller curls, use the narrow side of the bar.

CANVAS COOKIES, PAGE 14

sugar
sugar

Few cookies
say "Christmas" quite so merrily
as buttery sugar cookies that take on the
shapes, the colors, and the sparkle of the season.
Sugar cookies are a joy to share; each recipe lets
you express your creativity and your affection
your own special way.

★

Canvas Cookies

PREP **1 HOUR**   CHILL **3 HOURS**   BAKE **8 MINUTES PER BATCH**   COOL **1 MINUTE PER BATCH**   OVEN **375°F**

⅓ cup butter, softened
⅓ cup shortening
¾ cup sugar
1 teaspoon baking powder
⅛ teaspoon salt
1 egg
1½ teaspoons vanilla
½ teaspoon almond extract
2 cups all-purpose flour
1 recipe Edible Paint
  Red and green paste food coloring
  Natural sea sponge
  Stencils (optional)
  Small decorative candies (optional)

1 In a large mixing bowl beat butter and shortening with an electric mixer on medium to high speed for 30 seconds. Add sugar, baking powder, and salt. Beat until combined, scraping sides of bowl occasionally. Beat in the egg, vanilla, and almond extract until combined. Beat in as much of the flour as you can with the mixer. Using a wooden spoon, stir in any remaining flour. Divide dough in half. Cover and chill dough about 3 hours or until easy to handle.

2 Preheat oven to 375°F. On a lightly floured surface roll dough halves to ¼-inch thickness. Using a 3- to 4-inch cookie cutter, cut dough into desired shapes. Place cutouts 1 inch apart on an ungreased cookie sheet.

3 Bake for 8 to 10 minutes or until edges are firm and bottoms are very light brown. Cool on cookie sheet for 1 minute. Transfer cookies to a wire rack and let cool.

4 Divide Edible Paint in half; set aside one portion. Ice cookies with a thin layer of Edible Paint. Let cookies stand on waxed paper until paint is dry.

5 Meanwhile, divide the reserved Edible Paint into two portions; tint one portion with red paste food coloring and the other with green paste food coloring. Decorate cookies as desired with the tinted Edible Paint using natural sea sponges, stencils, and the small decorating candies.
MAKES ABOUT 30 COOKIES

Edible Paint: In a large mixing bowl stir together 4 cups powdered sugar, 3 tablespoons meringue powder, and ½ teaspoon cream of tartar. Add ½ cup warm water and 1 teaspoon vanilla. Beat with an electric mixer on low speed until combined, then on high speed for 7 to 10 minutes or until very stiff. Beat in 2 to 4 tablespoons additional water, 1 teaspoon at a time, to make an icing of spreading consistency.

TO MAKE AHEAD AND STORE: Layer cookies between sheets of waxed paper in an airtight container; cover. Store at room temperature for up to 3 days or freeze for up to 3 months.

In a *twinkling*

Use a natural sea sponge to blot alternating colors of the Edible Paint over the cookies.

 # Santa Cutouts

PREP **50 MINUTES**   CHILL **3 HOURS**   BAKE **7 MINUTES PER BATCH**   COOL **1 MINUTE PER BATCH**   OVEN **375°F**

⅓   cup butter, softened
⅓   cup shortening
¾   cup granulated sugar
1   teaspoon baking powder
    Pinch salt
1   egg
1   tablespoon milk
1   teaspoon vanilla
2   cups all-purpose flour
1   recipe Egg Paint
1   recipe Snow Frosting
1   recipe Powdered Sugar Icing
    Flaked coconut
    Small decorative candies

1 In a large mixing bowl beat butter and shortening with an electric mixer on medium to high speed for 30 seconds. Add sugar, baking powder, and salt. Beat until combined, scraping sides of bowl occasionally. Beat in the egg, milk, and vanilla until combined. Beat in as much of the flour as you can with the mixer. Using a wooden spoon, stir in any remaining flour. Cover and chill dough about 3 hours or until easy to handle.

2 Preheat oven to 375°F. On a lightly floured surface roll dough to ⅛-inch thickness. Using a 3-inch triangle-shape cookie cutter, cut out dough. Place cutouts 1 inch apart on an ungreased cookie sheet. Brush coat and hat areas of cutouts with red Egg Paint.

3 Bake for 7 to 8 minutes or until bottoms are light brown. Cool on cookie sheet for 1 minute.

Transfer cookies to a wire rack and let cool.

4 Decorate cookies with Snow Frosting and Powdered Sugar Icing as desired. Sprinkle with coconut and candies, or attach candies with small dabs of frosting. Let stand until frosting and icing are set. **MAKES ABOUT 40 COOKIES**

Egg Paint: In a small bowl stir together 1 egg yolk and 2 drops water. Tint with red paste food coloring.

Snow Frosting: In a small bowl beat ½ cup shortening and ½ teaspoon vanilla with an electric mixer on medium to high speed for 30 seconds. Gradually add 1⅓ cups powdered sugar, beating well. Beat in 1 tablespoon milk. Gradually beat in 1 cup additional powdered sugar. Beat in 3 to 4 teaspoons additional milk, 1 teaspoon at a time, to make a frosting of piping consistency. Spoon frosting into a pastry bag fitted with a medium star tip; pipe frosting in areas on cookies where a textured look is desired.

Powdered Sugar Icing: In a medium bowl stir together 4 cups powdered sugar and 1 teaspoon vanilla. Stir in 3 to 4 tablespoons milk, 1 tablespoon at a time, to make an icing of piping consistency. If desired, tint with paste food coloring. Spoon icing into a pastry bag fitted with a writing tip; pipe icing in areas on cookies where fine details are desired.

TO MAKE AHEAD AND STORE: Layer cookies between sheets of waxed paper in an airtight container; cover. Store at room temperature for up to 3 days or freeze for up to 3 months.

"The Best" Sugar Cookies

PREP **35 MINUTES**   CHILL **30 MINUTES**   BAKE **7 MINUTES PER BATCH**   OVEN **375°F**

⅔   cup butter, softened
¾   cup sugar
1   teaspoon baking powder
¼   teaspoon salt
1   egg
1   tablespoon milk
1   teaspoon vanilla
2   cups all-purpose flour
1   recipe Royal Icing (optional)
    Small decorative candies (optional)

1 In a large mixing bowl beat butter with an electric mixer on medium to high speed for 30 seconds. Add sugar, baking powder, and salt. Beat until combined, scraping sides of bowl occasionally. Beat in the egg, milk, and vanilla until combined. Beat in as much of the flour as you can with the mixer. Using a wooden spoon, stir in any remaining flour. Divide dough in half. Cover and chill dough about 30 minutes or until easy to handle.

2 Preheat oven to 375°F. On a lightly floured surface roll each dough half to ⅛- to ¼-inch thickness. Using a 2½-inch cookie cutter, cut dough into desired shapes. Place cutouts 1 inch apart on an ungreased cookie sheet.

3 Bake for 7 to 10 minutes or until edges are very light brown. Transfer cookies to a wire rack and let cool. If desired, frost with Royal Icing and decorate with decorative candies. **MAKES ABOUT 36 COOKIES**

Royal Icing: In a large mixing bowl stir together 4 cups powdered sugar, 3 tablespoons meringue powder, and ½ teaspoon cream of tartar. Add ½ cup warm water and 1 teaspoon vanilla. Beat with an electric mixer on low speed until combined, then on high speed for 7 to 10 minutes or until very stiff. Beat in 2 to 4 tablespoons additional water, 1 teaspoon at a time, to make an icing of spreading consistency. If desired, tint portions of icing with food coloring.

TO MAKE AHEAD AND STORE: Layer cookies between sheets of waxed paper in an airtight container; cover. Store at room temperature for up to 2 days or freeze for up to 3 months.

gift It

Swathed in Song

Sheet music makes a sweet-looking sleeve for holding cookies. Fold one sheet of music in half crosswise or lengthwise (depending on cookie sizes). Cut the folded sheet in half crosswise (or cut folded sheet in thirds, depending on cookie size). Glue the edges of two of the open sides, leaving one side open to insert cookies. If desired, fold bottom corners diagonally and glue. Wrap cookies in plastic wrap and place in sleeve.

To make a tag, punch a hole in an old game card; string the card and an old key onto butcher's twine. Tie around the cookie sleeve.

Cream Cheese Sugar Cookies

PREP **30 MINUTES** CHILL **1 HOUR** BAKE **8 MINUTES PER BATCH** COOL **1 MINUTE PER BATCH** OVEN **375°F**

½ cup butter, softened
1 3-ounce package cream cheese, softened
1 cup powdered sugar
½ teaspoon baking powder
¼ teaspoon salt
1 egg
1 teaspoon vanilla
1 teaspoon almond extract
2½ cups all-purpose flour
1 recipe Royal Icing

1 In a large mixing bowl beat butter and cream cheese with an electric mixer on medium to high speed for 30 seconds. Add powdered sugar, baking powder, and salt. Beat until combined, scraping sides of bowl occasionally. Beat in the egg, vanilla, and almond extract until combined. Beat in as much of the flour as you can with the mixer. Using a wooden spoon, stir in any remaining flour. Cover and chill dough about 1 hour or until easy to handle.

2 Preheat oven to 375°F. On a lightly floured surface roll dough to ¼-inch thickness. Using a scalloped 4-inch cookie cutter, cut out dough. Place cutouts 1 inch apart on an ungreased cookie sheet.

3 Bake for 8 to 10 minutes or until edges are very light brown. Cool on cookie sheet for 1 minute. Transfer cookies to a wire rack and let cool. Decorate cookies with Royal Icing as desired. **MAKES ABOUT 12 COOKIES**

Royal Icing: In a large mixing bowl stir together 4 cups powdered sugar, 3 tablespoons meringue powder, and ½ teaspoon cream of tartar. Add ½ cup warm water and 1 teaspoon vanilla. Beat with an electric mixer on low speed until combined, then on high speed for 7 to 10 minutes or until very stiff. Beat in 2 to 4 tablespoons additional water, 1 teaspoon at a time, to make an icing of spreading consistency. If desired, tint portions of icing with food coloring.

TO MAKE AHEAD AND STORE: Layer undecorated cookies between sheets of waxed paper in an airtight container; cover. Store at room temperature for up to 2 days or freeze for up to 3 months. Thaw cookies, if frozen. Decorate with Royal Icing as desired.

Special Effects

Royal Icing, a pastry bag, a paintbrush, and some toothpicks are all you need to transform your cookies into holiday masterpieces. Try these tips:

✦ Beautiful Borders: Use a pastry bag and a small round tip to pipe a border of Royal Icing around the cookie edge. Then fill in the piped border by piping a different color of icing into the center. Spread to edges with a clean, new artist's paintbrush. Allow to dry or create marbling (right).

✦ Marvelously Marbled: To create cookies with a wet-on-wet marbled effect, pipe dots of the Royal Icing in additional colors on the still-wet base icing. Use a toothpick to pull swirls of the dots through the first icing. Decorate cookies one at a time so that the icings dry evenly.

Holiday Snowmen

PREP **40 MINUTES**   BAKE **10 MINUTES PER BATCH**   COOL **3 MINUTES PER BATCH**   OVEN **375°F**

1   18-ounce roll refrigerated sugar or chocolate chip cookie dough
1   recipe Royal Icing
    Miniature semisweet chocolate pieces, miniature candy-coated milk chocolate pieces, and/or gumdrops

1 Preheat oven to 375°F. Divide cookie dough into 15 equal pieces. Divide each dough piece into graduated-size balls of about 1 inch, ¾ inch, and ½ inch in diameter. On an ungreased large cookie sheet arrange each set of balls into a snowman shape, placing balls for each snowman ¼ inch apart and spacing snowmen at least 3 inches apart.

2 Bake for 10 to 12 minutes or until edges are light brown. Cool on cookie sheet for 3 minutes. Transfer cookies to a wire rack and let cool. Spread Royal Icing on cookies and decorate as desired with chocolate pieces and/or candies. **MAKES 15 COOKIES**

Royal Icing: In a large mixing bowl stir together 4 cups powdered sugar, 3 tablespoons meringue powder, and ½ teaspoon cream of tartar. Add ½ cup warm water and 1 teaspoon vanilla. Beat with an electric mixer on low speed until combined, then on high speed for 7 to 10 minutes or until very stiff. Beat in 2 to 4 tablespoons additional water, 1 teaspoon at a time, to make an icing of spreading consistency.

TO MAKE AHEAD AND STORE: Layer unfrosted cookies between sheets of waxed paper in an airtight container; cover. Store at room temperature for up to 1 day or freeze for up to 3 months. Thaw cookies, if frozen. Frost and decorate as directed.

gift It

Personalized Package

For a sweet and simple way to say "Merry Christmas" to plenty of people on your list, simply slip pairs of cookies into resealable plastic bags prettied up with a few simple touches. Cut a piece of decorative scrapbooking paper to fit inside a sandwich-size plastic bag. Label the cookies on a sticker tag and affix it to the front of the bag. Wait until the icing is dry, then carefully slide cookies inside the bag and seal the bag.

Eggnog-Frosted Nutmeg Sugar Cookies

PREP **25 MINUTES**   CHILL **1 HOUR**   BAKE **8 MINUTES PER BATCH**   OVEN **375°F**

½ of a vanilla bean, split in
 half lengthwise, or
 2 teaspoons vanilla
1¼ cups butter, softened
1 cup sugar
1½ teaspoons baking powder
1 teaspoon freshly grated
 nutmeg or ½ teaspoon
 ground nutmeg
½ teaspoon salt
1 egg
1 tablespoon eggnog
3¼ cups all-purpose flour
1 recipe Eggnog Icing
 Coarse sugar (optional)

1 Using the tip of a sharp knife, scrape pulp from the vanilla bean; set aside. In a large mixing bowl beat butter with an electric mixer on medium to high speed for 30 seconds. Add sugar, baking powder, nutmeg, and salt. Beat until combined, scraping sides of bowl occasionally. Beat in the egg, eggnog, and vanilla pulp or vanilla until combined. Beat in as much of the flour as you can with the mixer. Using a wooden spoon, stir in any remaining flour. Divide dough in half. Cover and chill dough about 1 hour or until easy to handle.

2 Preheat oven to 375°F. On a lightly floured surface roll each dough half to ¼-inch thickness. Using a fluted round 3-inch cookie cutter, cut out dough. Place cutouts 1 inch apart on an ungreased cookie sheet.

3 Bake for 8 to 10 minutes or until edges are firm and bottoms are light brown. Transfer cookies to a wire rack and let cool. Spread Eggnog Icing on cookies. If desired, sprinkle with coarse sugar. Let stand until icing is dry.
MAKES ABOUT 24 COOKIES

Eggnog Icing: In a medium bowl stir together 3 cups powdered sugar and ½ teaspoon vanilla. Stir in enough eggnog or milk (3 to 4 tablespoons) to make an icing of spreading consistency.

TO MAKE AHEAD AND STORE: Layer unfrosted cookies between sheets of waxed paper in an airtight container; cover. Store at room temperature for up to 3 days or freeze for up to 3 months. Thaw cookies, if frozen. Ice cookies as directed.

Snowflake Cookie Wreath

PREP **25 MINUTES**   BAKE **15 MINUTES**   OVEN **375°F**

1 **16.5-ounce roll refrigerated sugar cookie dough**
½ **cup all-purpose flour**
½ **cup canned white or cream cheese frosting**
2 **to 3 teaspoons milk**
   Snowflake sprinkles, coarse sugar, and/or edible glitter

1 Preheat oven to 375°F. Line a large baking sheet with parchment paper. Draw a 10-inch circle on the paper. Turn paper over. In a medium bowl combine the dough and flour; stir until well mixed.

2 On a lightly floured surface roll dough to ¼-inch thickness. Using a 3½-inch snowflake-shape cookie cutter, cut out 10 snowflakes from dough. Arrange snowflakes around the circle on the parchment paper. Using a 2½-inch snowflake shape cutter, cut out remaining dough. Arrange smaller snowflakes on top of larger stars, filling in open spaces to create a wreath shape.

3 Bake about 15 minutes or until golden. Cool on cookie sheet on a wire rack.

4 In a medium bowl stir together the frosting and milk until frosting is of drizzling consistency. Spoon or pipe frosting over cookie wreath. Decorate with sprinkles. Let stand until frosting is set. **MAKES 1 WREATH (24 SERVINGS)**

TO MAKE AHEAD AND STORE: Wrap unfrosted cookie wreath tightly with foil. Store at room temperature for up to 3 days. Decorate cookie wreath as directed.

gift It

Box It Up

Pretty up a pizza box for a handy way to carry and present this somewhat fragile edible wreath. Use a glue stick to attach paper snowflakes to the top of a 12-inch or larger pizza box. Cut ribbon into four 4-inch pieces and angle-cut the ends. Using crafts glue, attach the ribbon to the top of the box to create a frame. Cut a piece of colored paper to fit inside the frame; write a holiday greeting. Use a decorative furniture tack to attach the greeting in the center of the ribbon frame. To avoid breaking the cookie wreath, leave the wreath on the parchment paper when you transfer it from the baking sheet to the box.

Snickerdoodle Croissant Cookies

PREP **50 MINUTES**   CHILL **1 HOUR**   BAKE **14 MINUTES PER BATCH**   COOL **2 MINUTES PER BATCH**   OVEN **350°F**

½ cup butter, softened

2 3-ounce packages cream cheese, softened

½ cup packed brown sugar

1 teaspoon vanilla

⅛ teaspoon salt

1⅔ cups all-purpose flour
   Milk

½ cup finely chopped toasted pecans

2 tablespoons packed brown sugar

¾ teaspoon ground cinnamon

¼ teaspoon ground nutmeg
   Powdered sugar (optional)

1 In a large mixing bowl beat butter and cream cheese with an electric mixer on medium to high speed for 30 seconds.

Add the ½ cup brown sugar, the vanilla, and salt. Beat until combined, scraping sides of bowl occasionally. Beat in as much of the flour as you can with the mixer. Using a wooden spoon, stir in any remaining flour. Divide dough into thirds. Shape each portion into a disk. Cover and chill dough about 1 hour or until easy to handle.

2 Preheat oven to 350°F. On a lightly floured surface roll each dough portion into a 9-inch circle. Lightly brush each circle with milk. In a small bowl stir together nuts, the 2 tablespoons brown sugar, the cinnamon, and nutmeg. Sprinkle nut mixture evenly over dough circles to within ½ inch of edges. Using a pizza cutter or sharp knife,

cut each circle into 12 wedges. Starting from the wide end, roll up each wedge. Bend rolls to shape them into crescents. Place crescents 1 inch apart on an ungreased cookie sheet.

3 Bake for 14 to 16 minutes or until bottoms are light brown. Cool on cookie sheet for 2 minutes. Transfer cookies to a wire rack and let cool. If desired, sprinkle with powdered sugar before serving. **MAKES 36 COOKIES**

TO MAKE AHEAD AND STORE: Layer plain cookies between sheets of waxed paper in an airtight container; cover. Store at room temperature for up to 3 days or freeze for up to 3 months. Before serving, sprinkle cookies with powdered sugar.

Tender Sugar Cookies

PREP **40 MINUTES**   BAKE **15 MINUTES PER BATCH**   OVEN **300°F**

1   cup butter, softened
1   cup sugar
1   teaspoon baking powder
¼   teaspoon salt
1   egg
1   teaspoon vanilla
2¼   cups all-purpose flour
¼   cup sugar

1 In a large mixing bowl beat butter with an electric mixer on medium to high speed for 30 seconds. Add the 1 cup sugar, the baking powder, and salt. Beat until combined, scraping sides of bowl occasionally. Beat in the egg and vanilla until combined. Beat in as much of the flour as you can with the mixer. Using a wooden spoon, stir in any remaining flour. If necessary, cover and chill dough for 30 to 60 minutes or until easy to handle.

2 Preheat oven to 300°F. Place the ¼ cup sugar in a bowl. Shape dough into 1-inch balls. Roll balls in the sugar to coat. Place balls 2 inches apart on an ungreased cookie sheet. Bake about 15 minutes or until tops are slightly crackled and sides are set (do not let edges brown). Transfer cookies to a wire rack and let cool. **MAKES ABOUT 60 COOKIES**

TO MAKE AHEAD AND STORE: Layer cookies between sheets of waxed paper in an airtight container; cover. Store at room temperature for up to 3 days or freeze for up to 3 months.

In a *twinkling*

Roll the balls in colored sugar to add holiday color and sparkle. Consider using pastel hues, such as light green and pink, to add an up-to-date touch to these old-fashioned favorites.

Soft Maple Sugar Cookies

PREP **30 MINUTES**   BAKE **12 MINUTES PER BATCH**   COOL **2 MINUTES PER BATCH**   OVEN **300°F**

½   cup butter, softened
½   cup shortening
1½   cups granulated sugar
¼   cup packed brown sugar
¼   cup pure maple syrup
1   teaspoon baking soda
1   teaspoon cream of tartar
⅛   teaspoon salt
3   egg yolks
½   teaspoon vanilla
1¾   cups all-purpose flour
1   recipe Maple Icing

1 Preheat oven to 300°F. In large mixing bowl beat butter and shortening with electric mixer on medium to high speed for 30 seconds. Add granulated sugar, brown sugar, maple syrup, baking soda, cream of tartar, and salt. Beat until combined, scraping occasionally. Beat in egg yolks and vanilla until combined. Beat in as much of the flour as you can with mixer. Using a wooden spoon, stir in any remaining flour.

2 Shape dough into 1-inch balls. Place balls 2 inches apart on ungreased cookie sheet. Bake for 12 to 14 minutes or until edges are light brown. Cool on cookie sheet for 2 minutes. Transfer cookies to wire rack and let cool. (Centers will dip as cookies cool.)

Drizzle Maple Icing over cookies. Let stand until icing is set. **MAKES ABOUT 48 COOKIES**

Maple Icing: In a medium bowl stir together ¼ cup whipping cream or milk, ¼ cup melted butter, and 3 tablespoons pure maple syrup. Whisk in 3 to 4 cups powdered sugar to make an icing of drizzling consistency.

TO MAKE AHEAD AND STORE: Layer unfrosted cookies between sheets of waxed paper in an airtight container; cover. Store at room temperature for up to 2 days or freeze for up to 3 months. Thaw cookies, if frozen. Ice cookies as directed.

Browned-Butter Sugar Cookies

PREP **30 MINUTES**   CHILL **2 HOURS 30 MINUTES**   BAKE **9 MINUTES PER BATCH**   COOL **1 MINUTE PER BATCH**   OVEN **375°F**

1   cup butter
1½   cups sugar
2   eggs
1   teaspoon cream of tartar
1   teaspoon baking soda
1   teaspoon ground cardamom
1   teaspoon vanilla
¼   teaspoon salt
2¾   cups all-purpose flour
¼   cup sugar
¼   teaspoon ground cardamom

1 In small heavy saucepan cook and stir butter over medium heat for 10 to 12 minutes or until butter turns light brown. Pour butter into large mixing bowl; cover and chill for 30 minutes, stirring once.

2 Beat chilled browned butter with electric mixer on medium to high speed for 30 seconds. Add the 1½ cups sugar. Beat until combined, scraping occasionally. Beat in eggs, cream of tartar, baking soda, the 1 teaspoon cardamom, the vanilla, and salt until combined. Beat in as much of the flour as you can with mixer. Using a wooden spoon, stir in any remaining flour. Cover; chill dough about 2 hours or until easy to handle.

3 Preheat oven to 375°F. In small bowl combine the ¼ cup sugar and the ¼ teaspoon cardamom. Shape dough into 1-inch balls. Roll balls in sugar mixture to coat. Place balls 2 inches apart on ungreased cookie sheet.

4 Bake for 9 to 12 minutes or until edges are light brown. Cool on cookie sheet for 1 minute. Transfer cookies to a wire rack and let cool. **MAKES ABOUT 48 COOKIES**

TO MAKE AHEAD AND STORE: Layer cookies between sheets of waxed paper in an airtight container; cover. Store at room temperature for up to 3 days or freeze for up to 3 months.

Brown Sugar Shortbreads

PREP **35 MINUTES**   BAKE **12 MINUTES PER BATCH**   OVEN **350°F**

1   **cup butter, softened**
½   **cup packed brown sugar**
½   **teaspoon apple pie spice**
      or pumpkin pie spice
⅛   **teaspoon salt**
2¼   **cups all-purpose flour**
      Nonstick cooking spray
      Granulated sugar

1 Preheat oven to 350°F. Line a cookie sheet with parchment paper. In a large mixing bowl beat butter with an electric mixer on medium to high speed for 30 seconds. Add brown sugar, apple pie spice, and salt. Beat until combined, scraping sides of bowl occasionally. Beat in as much of the flour as you can with the mixer. Using a wooden spoon, stir in any remaining flour.

2 Shape dough into 1-inch balls. Place balls 2 inches apart on the prepared cookie sheet. Lightly coat the bottom of a cookie stamp with cooking spray and dip the stamp in granulated sugar. Flatten a ball of dough, imprinting the pattern onto the cookie. Repeat until all cookies are imprinted.

3 Bake for 12 to 15 minutes or until light brown. Transfer cookies to a wire rack and let cool.

MAKES ABOUT 36 COOKIES

TO MAKE AHEAD AND STORE: Layer cookies between sheets of waxed paper in an airtight container; cover. Store at room temperature for up to 3 days or freeze for up to 3 months.

Cookie Stamp Stand-In

If you don't have special cookie stamps, look through your cupboards and drawers for vessels and utensils that have deeply cut designs. Good options include the bottoms of juice glasses, jelly and jam jars, candy dishes, stemmed glasses, and dessert dishes. A meat mallet or a potato masher also can make interesting designs.

Spray the pressing surface with nonstick cooking spray. Then dip in granulated or colored granulated sugar, and stamp as directed in the recipe to imprint the pattern on the dough.

Look for cookie stamps in specialty bakeware shops, Scandinavian gift shops, and online.

Vanilla Bean Angel Pillows

PREP **30 MINUTES**   BAKE **12 MINUTES PER BATCH**   COOL **5 MINUTES PER BATCH**   OVEN **350°F**

1½ cups all-purpose flour
½   cup powdered sugar
¼   cup cornstarch
¼   teaspoon salt
1   vanilla bean, split in half
    lengthwise
1   cup cold butter, cubed
¼   cup Vanilla Sugar

1 Preheat oven to 350°F. In a food processor combine flour, powdered sugar, cornstarch, and salt. Cover and process until mixed.

2 Using the tip of a sharp knife, scrape pulp from the vanilla bean. Add vanilla pulp and butter to the flour mixture. Cover and process with several on-off pulses until dough starts to cling together. Gather dough into a ball.

3 Shape dough into 1¼-inch balls. Place balls 2 inches apart on an ungreased cookie sheet. Bake about 12 minutes or just until edges start to brown. Transfer cookies to a wire rack; let cool for 5 minutes. Place Vanilla Sugar in a small bowl. Roll warm cookies in Vanilla Sugar to coat. Cool completely on wire rack.

MAKES ABOUT 28 COOKIES

Vanilla Sugar: In a small bowl combine 1 cup sugar and 1 vanilla bean, split in half lengthwise. Cover and let stand at room temperature for 1 week.

TO MAKE AHEAD AND STORE: Layer cookies between sheets of waxed paper in an airtight container; cover. Store at room temperature for up to 3 days or freeze for up to 3 months.

Using Vanilla Beans

Using dried vanilla bean—rather than liquid vanilla extract—may require an extra step or two, but your cookies will gain heightened vanilla flavor, as well as beautiful confetti-like flecks. To use a vanilla bean, cut the pod lengthwise with a paring knife and use the tip of the knife to scrape out the tiny seeds.

The pod itself should not be eaten. Instead, use it to make vanilla sugar to keep on hand for recipes or for flavoring coffee. To make vanilla sugar, simply place the split pod in a small bowl with 1 cup granulated sugar. Cover and let stand at room temperature for 1 week.

Find vanilla beans at specialty spice stores and online sources. Store vanilla beans in a closed (but not airtight) container in a cool, dark, and dry place. Do not refrigerate or freeze.

Almond Spritz

PREP **30 MINUTES**　BAKE **8 MINUTES PER BATCH**　OVEN **350°F**

- 1　cup butter, softened
- 1　3-ounce package cream cheese, softened
- 1　cup sugar
- ¼　teaspoon salt
- 1　egg yolk
- 1　teaspoon vanilla
- ¼　teaspoon almond extract
- 2½　cups all-purpose flour
- 1　recipe Powdered Sugar Icing (optional)
  Small decorative candies (optional)
  Colored sugar (optional)

1 Preheat oven to 350°F. In a large mixing bowl beat butter and cream cheese with an electric mixer on medium to high speed for 30 seconds. Add sugar and salt. Beat until combined, scraping sides of bowl occasionally. Beat in the egg yolk, vanilla, and almond extract until combined. Beat in as much of the flour as you can with the mixer. Using a wooden spoon, stir in any remaining flour.

2 Pack unchilled dough into a cookie press fitted with desired-shape plate. Force dough through the cookie press 2 inches apart onto an ungreased cookie sheet.

3 Bake for 8 to 10 minutes or until edges are firm but not brown. Transfer cookies to a wire rack and let cool. If desired, brush or drizzle cookies with Powdered Sugar Icing and decorate with candies or colored sugars. **MAKES ABOUT 96 COOKIES**

Powdered Sugar Icing: In a small bowl stir together 1 cup powdered sugar, 1 tablespoon milk, and 1 teaspoon vanilla. Stir in additional milk, 1 teaspoon at a time, until icing reaches desired consistency. If desired, tint icing with food coloring.

TO MAKE AHEAD AND STORE: Layer unfrosted cookies between sheets of waxed paper in an airtight container; cover. Store at room temperature for up to 3 days or freeze for up to 3 months. Thaw cookies, if frozen. Frost and decorate as directed.

In a *twinkling*

If you don't wish to frost these cookies, simply sprinkle on some colored sugars, sprinkles, nonpareils, or quins before baking.

Golden Butterscotch Icebox Cookies

PREP **30 MINUTES**   CHILL **2 HOURS**   BAKE **10 MINUTES PER BATCH**   COOL **1 MINUTE PER BATCH**   OVEN **325°F**

1   cup butter, softened
2   cups packed dark brown
     sugar
½   teaspoon baking soda
½   teaspoon salt
2   eggs
1½ teaspoons vanilla
3   cups all-purpose flour
1   cup finely chopped pecans

1 In a large mixing bowl beat butter with an electric mixer on medium to high speed for 30 seconds. Add brown sugar, baking soda, and salt. Beat until combined, scraping sides of bowl occasionally. Beat in the eggs and vanilla until combined. Beat in as much of the flour as you can with the mixer. Using a wooden spoon, stir in any remaining flour and the pecans.

2 Divide dough in half. Shape each half into an 8-inch log. Wrap each log in plastic wrap or waxed paper; chill about 2 hours or until firm.

3 Preheat oven 325°F. Cut logs crosswise into ¼-inch-thick slices. Place slices 1 inch apart on an ungreased cookie sheet. Bake for 10 to 12 minutes or until edges are firm. Cool on cookie sheet for 1 minute. Transfer cookies to a wire rack and let cool. **MAKES ABOUT 60 COOKIES**

TO MAKE AHEAD AND STORE: Layer cookies between sheets of waxed paper in an airtight container; cover. Store at room temperature for up to 3 days or freeze for up to 3 months.

gift It

Antique Angle

An antique baking mold or gelatin dessert mold will offer handy little grooves or ridges that allow these cookies to stand upright. Simply tie with a ribbon and present.

Snickerdoodle Sandwiches

PREP **30 MINUTES**   BAKE **7 MINUTES PER BATCH**   OVEN **375°F**

- 3 tablespoons sugar
- 1 teaspoon ground cinnamon
- 1 16.5-ounce package refrigerated sugar cookie dough
- 1 8-ounce package cream cheese, softened
- 3 tablespoons honey
- ½ teaspoon ground cinnamon
- 3 tablespoons snipped golden raisins or raisins (optional)

1 Preheat oven to 375°F. In a small bowl stir together sugar and the 1 teaspoon cinnamon. Shape dough into ¾- to 1-inch balls. Roll balls in sugar mixture to coat. Place balls 1 inch apart on an ungreased cookie sheet. Bake for 7 to 9 minutes or just until edges are firm. Transfer cookies to a wire rack and let cool.

2 Meanwhile, for filling, in a medium bowl whisk together the cream cheese, honey, and the ½ teaspoon cinnamon until smooth. If desired, stir in raisins.

3 To assemble cookies, spread filling over the bottom of one cookie; lightly press the bottom of a second cookie against the filling. **MAKES ABOUT 24 SANDWICH COOKIES**

TO MAKE AHEAD AND STORE: Layer unfilled cookies between sheets of waxed paper in an airtight container; cover. Store at room temperature for up to 2 days or freeze for up to 3 months. Store filling in an airtight container in the refrigerator for up to 1 week or freeze for up to 3 months. Thaw cookies and filling, if frozen. Assemble sandwich cookies as directed.

CHOCO-MINT BLOSSOMS, PAGE 32

perfectly peppermint

Red and white with flavor
so cool, fresh, and bright, peppermint
reigns as the candy of Christmas. Whether
you stir it into your creations or sprinkle
it on top, the confection makes an
unmistakably merry mark on these bites
of holiday magic.

✳

Choco-Mint Blossoms

PREP **25 MINUTES**   CHILL **1 HOUR**   BAKE **10 MINUTES PER BATCH**   OVEN **350°F**

- ½ cup butter, softened
- ½ cup shortening
- 1 cup sugar
- ¾ cup unsweetened Dutch-process cocoa powder
- 2 teaspoons baking powder
- 1 egg
- 2 tablespoons milk
- 1 teaspoon peppermint extract
- 1½ cups all-purpose flour
- 42 peppermint-swirled candy kisses or milk chocolates, unwrapped
- 1 recipe Minty Chocolate Drizzle (optional)

1 In a large mixing bowl beat butter and shortening with an electric mixer on medium to high speed for 30 seconds. Add sugar, cocoa powder, and baking powder. Beat until combined, scraping sides of bowl occasionally. Beat in the egg, milk, and peppermint extract until combined. Beat in as much of the flour as you can with the mixer. Using a wooden spoon, stir in any remaining flour. Cover and chill dough about 1 hour or until easy to handle.

2 Preheat oven to 350°F. Shape dough into 1-inch balls. Place balls 2 inches apart on an ungreased cookie sheet.

3 Bake for 10 to 12 minutes or until edges are firm. Immediately press a peppermint-swirled candy into the center of each cookie. Transfer cookies to a wire rack and let cool. If desired, drizzle cookies with Minty Chocolate Drizzle. Let stand until drizzle is set. **MAKES ABOUT 42 COOKIES**

Minty Chocolate Drizzle: In a small microwave-safe bowl combine 4 ounces chopped semisweet or bittersweet chocolate, 2 teaspoons shortening, and ½ teaspoon peppermint extract or mint extract. Microwave, uncovered, on 100 percent power (high) for 1 to 2 minutes or until chocolate melts, stirring every 30 seconds.

TO MAKE AHEAD AND STORE: Layer cookies between sheets of waxed paper in an airtight container; cover. Store at room temperature for up to 3 days or freeze for up to 3 months.

Kisses All Year Long

Some candies only make their way onto supermarket shelves during the holiday season. Yet the Choco-Mint Blossoms make lovely treats year-round. In November and December, stock up on mint-flavor candy kisses and other festive candies in a variety of colors that you can use throughout the year—swirled peppermint for Valentine's Day, green for St. Paddy's Day, and other cheerful colors for showers, graduation parties, and celebrations throughout the year. To maintain freshness, store the candies in the freezer and thaw as needed.

Peppermint Munchies

PREP **35 MINUTES**   CHILL **30 MINUTES**   BAKE **9 MINUTES PER BATCH**   COOL **1 MINUTE PER BATCH**
OVEN **375°F**

- 1   recipe Peppermint Filling
- ¾   cup butter, softened
- 1   cup granulated sugar
- 1   teaspoon baking powder
- 1   egg
- 1   tablespoon milk
- 1   teaspoon vanilla
- 2   cups all-purpose flour
- 2   tablespoons coarse white and/or red sugar

1 Prepare Peppermint Filling. Cover and chill for 30 minutes.

2 Preheat oven to 375°F. In a large mixing bowl beat butter with an electric mixer on medium to high speed for 30 seconds. Add sugar and baking powder. Beat until combined, scraping sides of bowl occasionally. Beat in the egg, milk, and vanilla until combined. Beat in as much of the flour as you can with the mixer. Using a wooden spoon, stir in any remaining flour.

3 Shape dough into 1¼-inch balls. Press your thumb into the center of each ball. Spoon ½ teaspoon of the Peppermint Filling into each indentation in cookies. Shape dough around filling to enclose; roll gently to reshape into balls. Place balls 2 inches apart on an ungreased cookie sheet. Dip the bottom of a wet glass in coarse sugar; use glass to flatten each ball until ½ inch thick.

4 Bake for 9 to 12 minutes or until light brown. Cool on cookie sheet for 1 minute. Transfer cookies to a wire rack and let cool.

MAKES ABOUT 32 COOKIES

Peppermint Filling: In a small mixing bowl combine one 3-ounce package cream cheese, softened; 2 tablespoons powdered sugar; 2 tablespoons finely crushed striped round peppermint candies; and ¼ teaspoon peppermint extract. Beat with an electric mixer on low speed until smooth.

TO MAKE AHEAD AND STORE: Layer cookies between sheets of waxed paper in an airtight container; cover. Store at room temperature for up to 3 days or freeze for up to 3 months.

Peppermint Sandies

PREP **25 MINUTES**   BAKE **15 MINUTES PER BATCH**   STAND **45 MINUTES**   OVEN **325°F**

1   cup butter, softened
⅓   cup powdered sugar
¼   cup finely crushed striped round peppermint candies (about 10)
1   tablespoon water
½   teaspoon vanilla
½   teaspoon peppermint extract
2   cups all-purpose flour
1   cup whipping cream
6   ounces white baking chocolate, chopped
     Crushed striped round peppermint candies

1 Preheat oven to 325°F. In a large mixing bowl beat butter with an electric mixer on medium to high speed for 30 seconds. Add powdered sugar and the ¼ cup crushed peppermint candies. Beat until combined, scraping sides of bowl occasionally. Beat in the water, vanilla, and peppermint extract until combined. Beat in as much of the flour as you can with the mixer. Using a wooden spoon, stir in any remaining flour.

2 Shape dough into 1-inch balls. Place balls 1 inch apart on an ungreased cookie sheet.

3 Bake about 15 minutes or until bottoms are light brown. Transfer cookies to a wire rack and let cool.

4 Meanwhile, for glaze, in a medium saucepan bring whipping cream just to boiling over medium-high heat. Remove from heat. Add the white chocolate (do not stir). Let stand for 5 minutes. Stir until smooth. Let stand for 45 to 60 minutes or until glaze starts to thicken.

5 Spread glaze over the top of each cooled cookie. Sprinkle with additional crushed peppermint candies. Let stand until glaze is set. **MAKES ABOUT 48 COOKIES**

TO MAKE AHEAD AND STORE: Layer cookies between sheets of waxed paper in an airtight container; cover. Store at room temperature for up to 3 days. Or freeze unglazed cookies for up to 3 months. Thaw cookies; glaze as directed.

Swirled Peppermint Thumbprints

PREP **30 MINUTES**   BAKE **10 MINUTES PER BATCH**   COOL **1 MINUTE PER BATCH**   CHILL **1 HOUR**   OVEN **350°F**

2 16- or 16.5-ounce rolls refrigerated sugar cookie dough

1 cup all-purpose flour

10 ounces white baking chocolate, chopped

½ cup whipping cream

¼ teaspoon peppermint extract

Several drops red liquid food coloring

1 recipe White Chocolate Drizzle (optional)

1 Preheat oven to 350°F. In a large bowl combine cookie dough and flour; knead until smooth. Shape dough into 1½-inch balls. Place balls 2 inches apart on an ungreased cookie sheet. Press your thumb into the center of each ball.

2 Bake for 10 to 12 minutes or until edges are very light brown. Cool on cookie sheet for 1 minute. Transfer cookies to a wire rack and let cool.

3 In a medium microwave-safe bowl combine white chocolate and cream. Microwave, uncovered, on 100 percent power (high) for 1 to 2 minutes or until chocolate melts, stirring every 30 seconds. Stir in peppermint extract. Divide chocolate mixture in half. Use food coloring to tint one portion pink. Cover and chill both portions for 1 to 2 hours or until spreading consistency.

4 Spoon about 1 teaspoon of the white chocolate mixture and about 1 teaspoon of the pink chocolate mixture into the indentation in each cookie. Gently swirl a knife through mixtures to marble. Let stand until chocolate is set. If desired, drizzle cookies with White Chocolate Drizzle.

MAKES ABOUT 34 COOKIES

White Chocolate Drizzle:

In a small microwave-safe bowl combine 2 to 3 ounces chopped white baking chocolate and 2 teaspoons shortening. Microwave, uncovered, on 100 percent power (high) about 1 minute or until chocolate melts, stirring every 30 seconds. Stir in 1 or 2 drops peppermint extract.

TO MAKE AHEAD AND STORE: Layer cookies between sheets of waxed paper in an airtight container; cover. Store at room temperature for up to 3 days or freeze for up to 3 months.

Butter Mint Cookies

PREP **25 MINUTES**   BAKE **15 MINUTES PER BATCH**   OVEN **325°F**

- 1 **cup butter, softened**
- ¾ **cup finely crushed butter mints (about 1 cup mints)**
- ¼ **cup powdered sugar**
- 1 **tablespoon water**
- 1 **teaspoon vanilla**
- 2 **cups all-purpose flour**

1 In a large mixing bowl beat butter with an electric mixer on medium to high speed for 30 seconds. Add ¼ cup of the crushed mints and the powdered sugar. Beat until combined, scraping sides of bowl occasionally. Beat in the water and vanilla until combined. Beat in as much of the flour as you can with the mixer. Using a wooden spoon, stir in any remaining flour. If necessary, cover and chill dough about 1 hour or until easy to handle.

2 Preheat oven to 325°F. Shape dough into 1-inch balls. Place balls 1 inch apart on an ungreased cookie sheet.

3 Bake about 15 minutes or until bottoms are light brown. Transfer cookies to a wire rack.

Place the remaining crushed mints in a plastic bag. Add warm cookies, a few at a time, shaking gently to coat. Cool completely on wire rack. **MAKES ABOUT 36 COOKIES**

TO MAKE AHEAD AND STORE: Layer cookies between sheets of waxed paper in an airtight container; cover. Store at room temperature for up to 3 days or freeze for up to 3 months.

gift It
Sensational Santa Bag

This jolly box is super-simple if you purchase a white window box featuring one round cut and a handle on top. Look for such boxes at containerstore.com or crafts shops. To create the second cutout for the snowman's head, use a large round scrapbooking punch or a sharp crafts knife.

If your box doesn't have circles, cut 2 circles on the front of the box, with the one on the bottom slightly larger than the one on the top. Cut a piece of clear acrylic the size of the front of the box; attach it to the inside using a glue stick.

Using pinking shears, cut a 6-inch-long piece of red felt, tie in a bow, and glue between the circles with crafts glue. For the hat, cut a 2-inch-long strip of felt and a square piece of felt. Attach the hat pieces above the top circle on the box. Place 3 sticker dots in the middle of the bottom window to resemble buttons.

Cocoa Tassies with Peppermint Cream Filling

PREP **1 HOUR**   CHILL **30 MINUTES**   BAKE **8 MINUTES PER BATCH**   COOL **5 MINUTES PER BATCH**   OVEN **375°F**

1¼   cups all-purpose flour
⅓   cup sugar
¼   cup unsweetened cocoa
        powder
½   cup cold butter
1   egg yolk, lightly beaten
2   tablespoons cold water
1   recipe Peppermint Cream
        Filling
        Crushed striped round
        peppermint candies

1 In a medium bowl stir together flour, sugar, and cocoa powder. Using a pastry blender, cut in the butter until mixture resembles coarse crumbs. In a small bowl whisk together the egg yolk and the cold water. Gradually stir egg yolk mixture into flour mixture. Gently knead the dough just until a ball forms. If necessary, cover and chill dough for 30 to 60 minutes or until easy to handle.

2 Preheat oven to 375°F. Shape dough into 36 balls. Press balls evenly into the bottoms and up the sides of 36 ungreased 1¾-inch muffin cups.

3 Bake for 8 to 10 minutes or until pastry shells are firm. Cool in pan on a wire rack for 5 minutes. Remove shells from cups; cool completely on wire rack.

4 Using a pastry bag fitted with an open star tip, pipe Peppermint Cream Filling into shells. Sprinkle filling with crushed peppermint candies. **MAKES 36 TASSIES**

Peppermint Cream Filling: In a large mixing bowl combine ¼ cup butter, softened; one 7-ounce jar marshmallow creme; and ½ teaspoon peppermint extract. Beat with an electric mixer on medium speed until smooth. Gradually beat in 1½ cups powdered sugar. Beat in 1 tablespoon milk. Beat in 1 cup

powdered sugar. Using a wooden spoon, stir in 1 cup powdered sugar. If necessary, stir in enough additional milk, 1 teaspoon at a time, to make a filling of piping consistency.

TO MAKE AHEAD AND STORE: Layer unfilled shells between sheets of waxed paper in an airtight container; cover. Store at room temperature for up to 3 days or freeze for up to 3 months. Thaw shells, if frozen. Fill as directed.

Tassies Tip

When pressing the pastry into the bottoms and sides of the muffin cups, make sure the pastry is spread as evenly as possible. It helps to flatten each piece of pastry with the palm of your hand or a rolling pin before you place it in the cup. Then, use your fingers to press and spread the dough evenly up the sides.

You can also use a mini tart shaper tool specifically designed for this step. Reminiscent of a mini barbell, the ends of this tool have wide, flat bases and round sides that help you evenly pat pastry into muffin cups. Find them at kitchen supply stores.

Star Mint Meringues

PREP **20 MINUTES**   BAKE **1 HOUR 30 MINUTES**   OVEN **200°F**

3   **egg whites**
¼   **teaspoon cream of tartar**
¼   **teaspoon peppermint extract**
⅛   **teaspoon salt**
¾   **cup sugar**
     Red paste food coloring

1 Preheat oven to 200°F. Line a cookie sheet with parchment paper. In a large mixing bowl combine egg whites, cream of tartar, peppermint extract, and salt. Beat with an electric mixer on medium speed until soft peaks form (tips curl). Gradually add sugar, about 1 tablespoon at a time, beating on high speed until stiff peaks form (tips stand straight).

2 With a clean small paintbrush, brush stripes of red paste food coloring on the inside of a pastry bag fitted with a ½-inch open star tip. Carefully transfer meringue into the bag. Pipe 2-inch stars 1 inch apart onto the prepared cookie sheet.

3 Bake for 1½ hours or until meringues appear dry and are firm when lightly touched. Transfer cookies to a wire rack and let cool. **MAKES ABOUT 24 COOKIES**

TO MAKE AHEAD AND STORE:
Layer meringues between sheets of waxed paper in an airtight container; cover. Store at room temperature for up to 3 days or freeze for up to 3 months.

In a *twinkling*

To dress up your cookie platter, create meringues with different extract flavors and shades of food coloring.

Peppermint Sandwich Cremes

PREP **30 MINUTES**   FREEZE **2 HOURS**   BAKE **10 MINUTES PER BATCH**   OVEN **350°F**

½ cup butter, softened
1 cup sugar
¼ teaspoon baking soda
¼ teaspoon salt
1 egg
2 teaspoons vanilla
1 teaspoon peppermint
    extract
1¾ cups all-purpose flour
1 recipe Peppermint–Cream
    Cheese Filling
    Finely crushed striped
    round peppermint
    candies or sprinkles

1 In a large mixing bowl beat butter with an electric mixer on medium to high speed for 30 seconds. Add sugar, baking soda, and salt. Beat until combined, scraping sides of bowl occasionally. Beat in the egg, vanilla, and peppermint extract until combined. Beat in as much of the flour as you can with the mixer. Using a wooden spoon, stir in any remaining flour.

2 Divide dough into four portions. Shape each portion into an 8-inch log. Wrap and freeze logs for 2 to 3 hours or until firm.

3 Preheat oven to 350°F. Cut logs into ⅜-inch-thick slices. Place slices 1 inch apart on an ungreased cookie sheet. Bake for 10 to 12 minutes or just until firm. Transfer cookies to a wire rack and let cool.

4 To assemble, spread a little Peppermint–Cream Cheese Filling onto the bottom of one cookie; press the bottom of a second cookie against the filling just until filling comes slightly out over the edges. Roll edges of cookies in crushed candies or sprinkles. Repeat with the remaining cookies, filling, and candies. **MAKES ABOUT 35 SANDWICH COOKIES**

Peppermint–Cream Cheese Filling: In a large mixing bowl combine one 3-ounce package cream cheese, softened, and ¼ cup butter, softened. Beat with an electric mixer on medium speed until smooth. Beat in 1 teaspoon vanilla and ½ teaspoon peppermint extract. Gradually beat in 3 cups powdered sugar. If necessary, beat in milk, 1 teaspoon at a time, to make a filling of spreading consistency.

TO MAKE AHEAD AND STORE: Layer filled cookies between sheets of waxed paper in an airtight container; cover. Store at room temperature for up to 3 days or freeze for up to 3 months.

Edible Embellishments

Sprinkle-on garnishes come in many forms—from colored sugars, sprinkles, and nonpareils to quins, those mini sugar confections made in shapes such as Christmas trees, stars, and snowflakes. Such products make for an easy way to add just a little something extra to your cookies. If you plan to present the cookies unfrosted, add the sprinkles before baking. Otherwise, spread icing on cooled cookies and immediately top with the sprinkles before the icing sets.

Find decorative sprinkles in baking supply stores; for a good online source, go to fancyflours.com.

Chocolate-Glazed Peppermint Cookies

PREP **45 MINUTES**   CHILL **1 HOUR**   BAKE **6 MINUTES PER BATCH**   OVEN **375°F**

1   **cup butter, softened**
1   **cup sugar**
½   **cup unsweetened cocoa powder**
1½   **teaspoons baking powder**
½   **teaspoon salt**
1   **egg**
1   **teaspoon vanilla**
2½   **cups all-purpose flour**
1   **recipe Chocolate-Peppermint Coating**

1 In a large mixing bowl beat butter with an electric mixer on medium to high speed for 30 seconds. Add sugar, cocoa powder, baking powder, and salt. Beat until combined, scraping sides of bowl occasionally. Beat in the egg and vanilla until combined. Beat in as much of the flour as you can with the mixer. Using a wooden spoon, stir in any remaining flour.

2 Divide dough in half. Shape each half into a 10-inch log. Wrap and chill logs about 1 hour or until firm.

3 Preheat oven to 375°F. Cut logs into ¼-inch-thick slices. Place slices 1 inch apart on an ungreased cookie sheet. Bake for 6 to 8 minutes or until edges are firm. Transfer cookies to a wire rack and let cool.

4 Dip each cookie into Chocolate-Peppermint Coating, turning to coat all sides of cookie. Using a thin metal spatula, scrape off excess coating so cookie is covered with a thin layer. (Reheat coating as necessary.) Place cookies on cookie sheets lined with waxed paper. Chill until coating is set. **MAKES ABOUT 68 COOKIES**

Chocolate-Peppermint Coating: In a medium saucepan combine two 12-ounce packages (4 cups) semisweet chocolate pieces, ¼ cup shortening, and ½ teaspoon peppermint extract. Cook and stir over low heat until chocolate melts.

TO MAKE AHEAD AND STORE: Layer cookies between sheets of waxed paper in an airtight container; cover. Store in the refrigerator for up to 3 days or freeze for up to 3 months.

In a *twinkling*

Sprinkle crushed peppermint candies on top of the cookies while the coating is still wet. You'll add seasonal color, along with a tempting flavor cue.

Peppermint Pinwheels

PREP **40 MINUTES**   CHILL **2 HOURS**   BAKE **6 MINUTES PER BATCH**   OVEN **375°F**

- 1 cup butter, softened
- 1 cup granulated sugar
- 1 teaspoon baking powder
- ¼ teaspoon salt
- 1 egg
- 1 teaspoon vanilla
- 2¼ cups all-purpose flour
- 2 ounces semisweet chocolate, melted and slightly cooled＊
- 1 cup layered chocolate-mint candy baking pieces＊＊
- ¼ teaspoon peppermint extract
- White edible glitter, coarse sugar, or granulated sugar (optional)

1 In a large mixing bowl beat butter with an electric mixer on medium to high speed for 30 seconds. Add the I cup granulated sugar, the baking powder, and salt. Beat until combined, scraping sides of bowl occasionally. Beat in the egg and vanilla until combined. Beat in as much flour as you can with the mixer. Using a wooden spoon, stir in any remaining flour.

2 Divide dough in half. Stir melted chocolate into one portion of dough. Stir chocolate-mint baking pieces and peppermint extract into the remaining portion of dough. Divide each dough portion in half. Wrap dough portions in plastic wrap; chill about 1 hour or until easy to handle.

3 On waxed paper roll each peppermint dough portion into a 9½x6-inch rectangle. On waxed paper roll each chocolate dough portion into a 9½x6-inch rectangle. Use the waxed paper to invert one chocolate dough rectangle on top of one peppermint dough rectangle; remove top sheet of waxed paper. Roll up dough, jelly-roll style, starting from a long side and using the bottom sheet of waxed paper to help lift and roll the dough. Discard waxed paper. Pinch dough edges to seal; wrap roll in plastic wrap. Repeat with remaining chocolate and peppermint dough rectangles. Chill rolls for 1 to 2 hours or until very firm.

4 Preheat oven to 375°F. Lightly grease a cookie sheet. Unwrap dough rolls; reshape, if necessary. Cut rolls into ¼-inch-thick slices. Place slices about 2 inches apart on the prepared cookie sheet. If desired, sprinkle with edible glitter, coarse sugar, or granulated sugar.

5 Bake for 6 to 8 minutes or until edges are firm and just starting to brown. Transfer cookies to a wire rack and let cool. **MAKES ABOUT 72 COOKIES**

＊*note* To melt the semisweet chocolate, chop chocolate and place it in a small microwave-safe bowl. Microwave, uncovered, on 50 percent power (medium) for 1 to 2 minutes or until chocolate melts, stirring once.

＊＊*note* If chocolate-mint candy pieces aren't available, use one 4.67-ounce package of individually wrapped layered chocolate-mint candies. Unwrap candies and finely chop.

TO MAKE AHEAD AND STORE: Layer cookies between sheets of waxed paper in an airtight container; cover. Store at room temperature for up to 2 days or freeze for up to 3 months.

Skillful Slicing

With slice-and-bake cookies, to get the cleanest slices possible be sure to refrigerate the dough for the time directed in the recipe. Warm or room-temperature dough simply won't slice as neatly as well-chilled dough. Use a sharp, thin-blade knife to cut across the dough into slices of the width specified in each recipe.

Chocolate-Peppermint Biscotti

PREP **45 MINUTES**   CHILL **30 MINUTES**   BAKE **24 MINUTES PER BATCH**   COOL **1 HOUR**   OVEN **375/325°F**

½   **cup butter, softened**
⅔   **cup sugar**
¼   **cup unsweetened cocoa powder**
2   **teaspoons baking powder**
½   **teaspoon salt**
2   **eggs**
1   **teaspoon peppermint extract**
1¾   **cups all-purpose flour**
4   **ounces bittersweet chocolate, chopped**
8   **ounces vanilla-flavor candy coating, melted**
¼   **cup crushed striped round peppermint candies (about 10)**

1 In a large mixing bowl beat butter with an electric mixer on medium to high speed for 30 seconds. Add sugar, cocoa powder, baking powder, and salt. Beat until combined, scraping sides of bowl occasionally. Beat in the eggs and peppermint extract until combined. Beat in as much of the flour as you can with the mixer. Using a wooden spoon, stir in any remaining flour and the bittersweet chocolate.

2 Divide dough into four portions. Wrap each portion in plastic wrap or waxed paper. Chill dough for 30 to 60 minutes or until easy to handle.

3 Preheat oven to 375°F. Lightly grease two cookie sheets.

Shape each dough portion into a 7-inch roll. Place rolls 4 inches apart on the prepared cookie sheets; flatten rolls slightly until about 2 inches wide.

4 Bake, one sheet at a time, for 14 to 16 minutes or until a wooden toothpick inserted near centers comes out clean. Cool on cookie sheets on wire racks for 1 hour.

5 Reduce oven to 325°F. Transfer rolls to a cutting board. Using a serrated knife, cut rolls diagonally into ½-inch-thick slices. Place slices, cut sides down, on cookie sheets. Bake for 5 minutes. Turn slices over; bake for 5 to 7 minutes more or until crisp. Transfer cookies to a wire rack and let cool.

6 Dip one long side of each cookie into melted candy coating. Place cookies on waxed paper. Sprinkle with crushed candies while coating is still wet. Let stand until coating is set.
MAKES ABOUT 42 BISCOTTI

TO MAKE AHEAD AND STORE: Layer biscotti between sheets of waxed paper in an airtight container; cover. Store at room temperature for up to 1 week or freeze for up to 3 months.

White Chocolate Candy Cane Drops

PREP **40 MINUTES**   BAKE **8 MINUTES PER BATCH** OVEN **375°F**

- 4 ounces white baking chocolate, chopped
- ½ cup butter, softened
- 1 cup sugar
- 1 teaspoon baking powder
- ½ teaspoon salt
- 2 eggs
- 1 teaspoon vanilla
- 2¾ cups all-purpose flour
- 4 ounces white baking chocolate, chopped
- ⅔ cup finely crushed chocolate-filled peppermint candy canes or peppermint candy canes

1 Preheat oven to 375°F. Line a cookie sheet with parchment paper; set aside. In a small heavy saucepan cook and stir 4 ounces white chocolate over low heat until chocolate melts. Set aside to cool slightly.

2 In a large mixing bowl beat butter with an electric mixer on medium to high speed for 30 seconds. Add sugar, baking powder, and salt. Beat until combined, scraping sides of bowl occasionally. Beat in the eggs and vanilla until combined. Beat in melted white chocolate. Beat in as much of the flour as you can with the mixer. Using a wooden spoon, stir in any remaining flour, 4 ounces white chocolate, and the crushed candy canes.

3 Drop dough by rounded teaspoons 2 inches apart onto the prepared cookie sheet. Bake for 8 to 10 minutes or until cookies are light brown around edges. Transfer cookies to a wire rack and let cool. **MAKES ABOUT 50 COOKIES**

TO MAKE AHEAD AND STORE: Layer cookies between sheets of waxed paper in an airtight container; cover. Store at room temperature for up to 3 days or freeze for up to 3 months.

Crushing Candy Canes

A food chopper makes quick work of transforming peppermint candies and candy canes into beautiful tidbits for topping your cookies. However, if you don't have a chopper, you can do it by hand. Place the candies in a heavy resealable plastic bag. On a steady surface, use a meat mallet or rolling pin to crush the candies into pieces. Whether you use a chopper or the bag method, shake the candies in a sifter or strainer and discard any dust or small pieces.

Red Velvet Whoopie Pies with Peppermint Filling

PREP **45 MINUTES**   BAKE **7 MINUTES PER BATCH**   COOL **2 MINUTES PER BATCH**   OVEN **375°F**

½   cup butter, softened

1   cup packed brown sugar

2   tablespoons unsweetened cocoa powder

½   teaspoon baking soda

¼   teaspoon salt

1   egg

1   teaspoon vanilla

2   cups all-purpose flour

½   cup buttermilk

1   1-ounce bottle red food coloring (2 tablespoons)

1   recipe Peppermint and Cream Cheese Filling

Striped round peppermint candies, finely chopped (optional)

1 Preheat oven to 375°F. Line a cookie sheet with parchment paper. In a large mixing bowl beat the ½ cup butter with an electric mixer on medium to high speed for 30 seconds. Add the brown sugar, cocoa powder, baking soda, and salt. Beat until combined, scraping sides of bowl occasionally. Beat in the egg and vanilla until combined. Alternately add the flour and buttermilk, beating on low speed after each addition just until combined. Stir in the red food coloring.

2 Drop dough by rounded teaspoons 2 inches apart onto the prepared cookie sheet. Bake for 7 to 9 minutes or until edges are set. Cool on cookie sheet for 2 minutes. Transfer cookies to a wire rack and let cool.

3 To assemble, spread a little of the Peppermint and Cream Cheese Filling onto the bottom of one cookie; press the bottom of a second cookie against the filling. Repeat with the remaining cookies and filling.

4 Serve cookies immediately or chill. If chilled, let cookies stand at room temperature for 15 minutes before serving. If desired, sprinkle each cookie with some chopped peppermint candies before serving. **MAKES ABOUT 40 SANDWICH COOKIES**

Peppermint and Cream Cheese Filling: In a large mixing bowl combine two 3-ounce packages cream cheese, softened; 3 tablespoons butter, softened; and ½ teaspoon peppermint extract. Beat with an electric mixer on medium speed until light and fluffy. Gradually beat in 3 cups powdered sugar. If necessary, beat in milk, 1 teaspoon at a time, to make a filling of spreading consistency.

TO MAKE AHEAD AND STORE: Layer filled cookies between sheets of waxed paper in an airtight container; cover. Store in the refrigerator for up to 3 days.

gift It

Good Things in Small Packages

Fresh berries may be long out of season, but the wooden pint-size boxes they're sold in make cute containers for your cookies (find them inexpensively online). Tie a red velvet ribbon around the top edge of the box. Place folded holiday-themed parchment paper inside the box. Arrange the whoopie pies inside.

Peppermint Sandwiches

PREP **1 HOUR** CHILL **1 HOUR 30 MINUTES** BAKE **7 MINUTES PER BATCH** OVEN **350°F**

¾ cup butter, softened
1 cup granulated sugar
½ teaspoon baking powder
1 egg
2 cups all-purpose flour
¼ cup butter, softened
2 cups powdered sugar
1 to 2 tablespoons milk
½ teaspoon peppermint extract

1 In a large mixing bowl beat the ¾ cup butter with an electric mixer on medium to high speed for 30 seconds. Add granulated sugar and baking powder. Beat until combined, scraping sides of bowl occasionally. Beat in the egg until combined. Beat in as much of the flour as you can with the mixer. Using a wooden spoon, stir in any remaining flour.

2 Divide dough in half. Roll each half of the dough between sheets of waxed paper into a 12x10-inch rectangle. Chill dough rectangles for 30 minutes.

3 Preheat oven to 350°F. Remove top sheets of waxed paper. Using a fluted pastry wheel or pizza cutter, cut each dough rectangle lengthwise into 10 strips and crosswise into 6 strips to make sixty 2x1-inch rectangles per dough half (120 rectangles total). Place rectangles 1 inch apart on an ungreased cookie sheet. Bake for

7 to 9 minutes or until edges are very light brown. Transfer cookies to a wire rack and let cool.

4 In a medium mixing bowl beat the ¼ cup butter on medium to high speed for 30 seconds. Add 1 cup of the powdered sugar, 1 tablespoon of the milk, and the peppermint extract; beat until smooth. Beat in the remaining 1 cup powdered sugar and enough of the remaining milk to make a frosting of spreading consistency.

5 To assemble, spread a little of the frosting over the bottom of one cookie; press the bottom of a second cookie against the frosting. Spread more of the frosting on top; press the bottom of a third cookie against the frosting. Repeat with the

remaining cookies and frosting.
MAKES 40 SANDWICH COOKIES

note To decorate the assembled sandwich cookies with chocolate, fill a heavy resealable plastic bag with melted bittersweet chocolate and snip a small hole in one corner of the bag. Squeeze the bag, piping the chocolate over the cookies in dots or drizzles.

TO MAKE AHEAD AND STORE: Layer unfilled cookies between sheets of waxed paper in an airtight container; cover. Store at room temperature for up to 3 days or freeze for up to 3 months. Thaw cookies, if frozen. Up to 4 hours before serving, prepare frosting as directed. Assemble and decorate cookies as directed.

Peppermint Cream Bars

PREP **30 MINUTES**   BAKE **27 MINUTES**   COOL **1 HOUR**   CHILL **1 HOUR 30 MINUTES**   OVEN **350°F**

- 1 **17.5-ounce package sugar cookie mix**
- 2 **tablespoons all-purpose flour**
- ½ **cup butter**
- 4 **egg yolks**
- 1 **14-ounce can sweetened condensed milk**
- ½ **teaspoon peppermint extract**
- ½ **cup crushed striped round peppermint candies (about 20)**
- 1 **recipe White Chocolate Ganache**

1 Preheat oven to 350°F. Line a 13x9x2-inch baking pan with foil, extending the foil over the edges of the pan. Lightly grease foil.

2 For crust, in a large bowl stir together cookie mix and flour. Using a pastry blender, cut in the butter until mixture resembles fine crumbs. Press the mixture evenly onto the bottom of the prepared baking pan. Bake for 12 to 15 minutes or until edges are light brown.

3 Meanwhile, for filling, in a medium bowl whisk together the egg yolks, sweetened condensed milk, and peppermint extract. Stir in crushed candies. Carefully pour filling over hot crust, spreading evenly.

4 Bake for 15 to 20 minutes or until filling is set. Cool in pan on a wire rack for 1 hour. Cover and chill about 30 minutes or until completely cool.

5 Pour White Chocolate Ganache over the bars, spreading evenly. Cover and chill about 1 hour or until ganache is firm. Use the foil to lift the uncut bars out of the pan. Place on a cutting board; cut into bars.

MAKES 36 BARS

White Chocolate Ganache: In a medium saucepan bring ¼ cup whipping cream just to boiling over medium-high heat. Remove from heat. Add 6 ounces chopped white baking chocolate (do not stir). Let stand for 5 minutes. Stir until smooth. Cool about 5 minutes.

TO MAKE AHEAD AND STORE: Layer bars between sheets of waxed paper in an airtight container; cover. Store at room temperature for up to 3 days or freeze for up to 3 months.

In a *twinkling*

Spread the white chocolate ganache over bars as directed. After the ganache cools but before it completely sets, score the bars into slices, and place a trio of white baking chips in the center of each bar.

Swirls-of-Peppermint Cheesecake Bars

PREP **35 MINUTES**   BAKE **30 MINUTES**   COOL **1 HOUR**   CHILL **4 HOURS**   OVEN **350°F**

2 cups finely crushed chocolate wafer cookies (about 35 cookies)

2 tablespoons sugar

⅓ cup butter, melted

2 8-ounce packages cream cheese, softened

1 cup sugar

1 teaspoon vanilla

¼ cup milk

5 eggs, lightly beaten

½ teaspoon peppermint extract

Red food coloring

½ cup crushed striped round peppermint candies (about 20)

1 Preheat oven to 350°F. Grease the bottom of a 13x9x2-inch baking pan.

2 In a medium bowl combine crushed cookies, the 2 tablespoons sugar, and the melted butter; stir until coated. Press cookie mixture evenly onto the bottom of the prepared pan. Bake for 10 minutes.

3 Meanwhile, in a large mixing bowl beat cream cheese, the 1 cup sugar, and the vanilla with an electric mixer on medium speed until smooth. Beat in milk until combined. Stir in eggs.

4 Transfer 1 cup of the cream cheese mixture to a small bowl; stir in peppermint extract and enough red food coloring to make desired color. Spoon the plain cream cheese mixture over the partially baked crust, spreading evenly. Drizzle red cream cheese mixture over plain cream cheese mixture. Use a thin metal spatula to gently swirl the mixtures.

5 Bake about 20 minutes or until set. Cool in pan on a wire rack for 1 hour. Cover and chill for 4 to 24 hours. Cut into bars. Before serving, sprinkle bars with crushed candies. **MAKES 32 BARS**

TO MAKE AHEAD AND STORE: Place bars in a single layer in an airtight container; cover. Store in the refrigerator for up to 3 days or freeze for up to 3 months.

MAPLE-NUT PIE BARS, PAGE 52

nutty for nuts

Crazy about cashews?
Mad for macadamias? Wacky about
walnuts? If you're nuts about nuts in general—
and the texture, flavor, and richness they bring
to your holiday cookies—you're going to love
these nut-filled recipes.

★

Maple-Nut Pie Bars

PREP **25 MINUTES**   BAKE **40 MINUTES**   OVEN **350°F**

1¼   cups all-purpose flour
½   cup powdered sugar
¼   teaspoon salt
½   cup butter, cut up
2   eggs, lightly beaten
1   cup chopped mixed nuts
     or pecans
½   cup packed brown sugar
½   cup pure maple syrup
2   tablespoons butter,
     melted
½   teaspoon maple flavoring
     or 1 teaspoon vanilla
½   cup white baking pieces
     (optional)
1   teaspoon shortening
     (optional)
24   pecan halves (optional)

1 Preheat oven to 350°F. Line a 11x7x1½-inch baking pan with foil, extending the foil over the edges of the pan. Lightly grease foil.

2 For crust, in a medium bowl stir together the flour, powdered sugar, and salt. Using a pastry blender, cut in the ½ cup butter until the mixture resembles coarse crumbs. Press flour mixture evenly onto the bottom of the prepared baking pan. Bake about 20 minutes or until light brown.

3 Meanwhile, for filling, in a medium bowl stir together the eggs, mixed nuts, brown sugar, maple syrup, the 2 tablespoons melted butter, and the maple flavoring. Pour filling over hot crust, spreading evenly.

4 Bake about 20 minutes more or until filling is set. Cool in pan on a wire rack. Use the foil to lift the uncut bars out of the pan. Place on a cutting board; cut into bars.

5 If desired, in a medium microwave-safe bowl combine the white baking pieces and shortening. Microwave, uncovered, on 100 percent power (high) about 1 minute or until pieces melt, stirring every 30 seconds. Drizzle over bars; top each bar with a pecan half. Let stand until set. **MAKES 24 BARS**

TO MAKE AHEAD AND STORE: Place bars in a single layer in an airtight container; cover. Store in the refrigerator for up to 2 days. Do not freeze.

Gooey Mixed-Nut Bars

PREP **25 MINUTES**   BAKE **45 MINUTES**   OVEN **350°F**

1   package 2-layer-size
       yellow cake mix
½   cup butter, cut up
4   eggs, lightly beaten
1   cup packed brown sugar
½   cup light corn syrup
⅓   cup butter, melted
1   teaspoon vanilla
½   teaspoon ground
       cinnamon
2   cups mixed nuts, coarsely
       chopped

1 Preheat oven to 350°F. Line
a 13x9x2-inch baking pan
with foil, extending the foil over
the edges of the pan. Lightly
grease foil.

2 Place cake mix in a large bowl.
Using a pastry blender, cut
the ½ cup butter into the cake mix
until mixture resembles coarse
crumbs. Press dough evenly onto
the bottom of the prepared pan.
Bake for 15 to 20 minutes or until
light brown and set.

3 Meanwhile, in a large bowl
whisk together the eggs,
brown sugar, corn syrup, the
⅓ cup melted butter, the vanilla,
and cinnamon. Stir in nuts. Pour
nut mixture over warm crust,
spreading evenly.

4 Bake about 30 minutes more
or until bubbly around the
edges and golden brown. Cool in
pan on a wire rack. Use the foil to
lift the uncut bars out of the pan.
Place on a cutting board; cut into
bars. **MAKES 32 BARS**

TO MAKE AHEAD AND STORE: Layer
bars between sheets of waxed
paper in an airtight container;
cover. Store in the refrigerator for
up to 1 week or freeze for up to
3 months.

In a *twinkling*

Turn these gooey-good bars
into a spectacular dessert by
placing them on dessert plates
and drizzling the plate and the
bar with melted semisweet
chocolate. A scoop of ice
cream or a dollop of whipped
cream adds a finishing touch.

Baklava

PREP **45 MINUTES**   BAKE **35 MINUTES**   OVEN **325°F**

3   cups walnuts, finely chopped
½   cup sugar
1   teaspoon ground cinnamon
¾   cup butter, melted
½   of a 16-ounce package frozen phyllo dough (14x9-inch rectangles), thawed
1   cup sugar
¾   cup water
3   tablespoons honey
½   teaspoon finely shredded lemon peel
1   tablespoon lemon juice
2   inches stick cinnamon

1 Preheat oven to 325°F. In a large bowl stir together walnuts, the ½ cup sugar, and the ground cinnamon.

2 Brush the bottom of a 13x9x2-inch baking pan with some of the melted butter. Unroll phyllo dough; cover with plastic wrap. (As you work, keep the phyllo covered to prevent it from drying out.) Layer five or six sheets of the phyllo in the prepared baking pan, brushing each sheet generously with some melted butter. Sprinkle with about 1 cup of the nut mixture. Repeat layering phyllo sheets and sprinkling with the nut mixture two more times, brushing each sheet with butter.

3 Layer the remaining phyllo sheets on top of filling, brushing each sheet with more butter. Drizzle with any remaining butter. Using a sharp knife, cut stacked layers into 24 to 48 diamond-, rectangle-, or square-shaped pieces.

4 Bake for 35 to 45 minutes or until golden brown. Cool slightly in pan on a wire rack.

5 Meanwhile, in a medium saucepan stir together the 1 cup sugar, the water, honey, lemon peel, lemon juice, and stick cinnamon. Bring to boiling; reduce heat. Simmer, uncovered, for 20 minutes. Remove cinnamon. Pour syrup over warm baklava in the pan. Cool completely.
MAKES 24 TO 48 BAKLAVA

TO MAKE AHEAD AND STORE: Layer baklava between sheets of waxed paper in an airtight container; cover. Store in the refrigerator for up to 3 days or freeze for up to 3 months.

Get to Know Phyllo

Flaky and delicate treats made with frozen phyllo dough are easier to make than they look—that is, once you learn a few tricks:

✦ Allow frozen phyllo dough to thaw while it is still wrapped and sealed. Once unwrapped, the sheets can dry out quickly and crumble.

✦ Each time you remove a sheet of phyllo to work with, keep the remaining phyllo covered with plastic wrap or a moist cloth. This will help keep it from drying out.

✦ Brush each sheet you layer with melted butter, margarine, or (in the case of a savory dish) olive oil. Brush the edges of the sheet first. Once the edges are brushed, begin in the middle and brush outward to the edges.

✦ Tightly rewrap any remaining sheets of dough and return them to the freezer.

Macadamia Bars with Eggnog Drizzle

PREP **25 MINUTES**   BAKE **25 MINUTES**   OVEN **350°F**

2   cups sugar

⅔   cup butter, cut up

2   eggs

1   teaspoon vanilla

2   cups all-purpose flour

1   teaspoon baking powder

½   teaspoon ground nutmeg

1   cup chopped macadamia
     nuts

1   recipe Eggnog Drizzle
     Freshly grated nutmeg
     (optional)

1 Preheat oven to 350°F. Line a 13x9x2-inch baking pan with foil, extending the foil over the edges of the pan. Lightly grease foil.

2 In a medium saucepan cook and stir the sugar and butter over medium heat until butter melts. Remove from heat. Cool slightly. Stir in the eggs and vanilla until combined. Stir in flour, baking powder, and the ½ teaspoon nutmeg. Stir in nuts. Spoon batter into the prepared baking pan, spreading evenly.

3 Bake for 25 to 30 minutes or until edges just begin to pull away from the sides of the pan. Cool in pan on a wire rack. Use the foil to lift the uncut bars out of the pan. Place on a cutting board; cut into bars. Drizzle Eggnog Drizzle over bars. If desired, sprinkle with freshly grated nutmeg. Let stand until drizzle is set. **MAKES ABOUT 36 BARS**

Eggnog Drizzle: In a small bowl stir together 1 cup powdered sugar, ¼ teaspoon vanilla, and 1 tablespoon eggnog. Stir in additional eggnog, 1 teaspoon at a time, to make icing of drizzling consistency.

TO MAKE AHEAD AND STORE: Layer bars between sheets of waxed paper in an airtight container; cover. Store at room temperature for up to 3 days. Or freeze unfrosted bars for up to 3 months. Thaw bars; frost as directed.

Butterscotch-Toffee Bars

PREP **15 MINUTES**   BAKE **15 MINUTES**   OVEN **350°F**

1 package 2-layer-size yellow cake mix
½ cup packed brown sugar
½ cup butter, melted
2 eggs
1 cup cashews or toasted pecans, chopped
1 8-ounce package toffee pieces

1 Preheat oven to 350°F. Grease a 15x10x1-inch baking pan; set aside.

2 In a large mixing bowl combine cake mix, brown sugar, melted butter, and eggs. Beat with an electric mixer on medium speed about 1 minute or until combined, scraping sides of bowl occasionally. Stir in the cashews.

3 Pat the dough evenly onto the bottom of the prepared pan.

Sprinkle with toffee pieces. Bake for 15 to 20 minutes or until a wooden toothpick inserted in the center comes out clean. Cool in pan on a wire rack. Cut into bars. **MAKES 32 BARS**

TO MAKE AHEAD AND STORE: Layer bars between sheets of waxed paper in an airtight container; cover. Store at room temperature for up to 1 week or freeze for up to 2 months.

Cookie-Friendly Nuts

These varieties are bakers' favorites for bringing nutty-good effects to their creations:

+ Almonds: These originally hail from Asia but are now grown mainly in California and the Mediterranean. They have pale, smooth meat and a delicate flavor.

+ Cashews: Originally from Brazil, these rich, buttery nuts now also grow in Vietnam and India. For baking, use unsalted roasted cashews unless otherwise specified.

+ Hazelnuts: Also known as filberts, these sweet, rich nuts are grown in temperate climate zones around the world. It's best to remove their bitter brown skin before adding the nuts to recipes (see tip, page 115).

+ Macadamia nuts: Originally discovered in Australia, these rich, sweet, buttery nuts now also grow in Hawaii, Africa, and South America. Substitute them for cashews in baking, if you like.

+ Pecans: Related to the walnut and harvested mostly in the southern United States, these nuts have a sweet, buttery flavor and may be used in place of walnuts in recipes.

+ Pistachios: Grown in the Middle East, the Mediterranean, and California, these are sweet and mild like almonds. The two can be used interchangeably in recipes.

+ Walnuts: These meaty nuts are grown mainly in California, France, and India. English walnuts are great for all kinds of baking; black walnuts are more intense and can have a somewhat bitter flavor.

Cashew Crunch Bars

PREP **20 MINUTES**   BAKE **20 MINUTES**   OVEN **350°F**

¾   cup butter, melted
¾   cup packed brown sugar
1½ teaspoons vanilla
½   teaspoon baking powder
2   eggs, lightly beaten
2   cups all-purpose flour
½   cup toffee pieces
1   14-ounce package vanilla caramels, unwrapped
2   tablespoons milk or whipping cream
2   cups salted dry-roasted cashews, coarsely chopped

1 Preheat oven to 350°F. Line a 13x9x2-inch baking pan with foil, extending the foil over the edges of the pan. Lightly grease foil.

2 For crust, in a large bowl stir together the melted butter, brown sugar, vanilla, and baking powder. Stir in eggs until combined. Stir in the flour just until moistened. Stir in toffee pieces. Spoon crust mixture into the prepared baking pan, spreading evenly. Bake for 20 to 25 minutes or until the entire top is light brown and the center is set.

3 In a large microwave-safe bowl combine the caramels and milk. Microwave, uncovered, on 100% power (high) for 1¼ to 2 minutes or until melted and smooth, stirring every 30 seconds. Carefully spoon caramel mixture over warm crust, spreading evenly. Immediately sprinkle cashews over top, lightly pressing into the warm caramel. Cool completely in pan on a wire rack. Use the foil to lift the uncut bars out of the pan. Place on a cutting board; cut into bars. **MAKES 24 BARS**

TO MAKE AHEAD AND STORE: Place bars in a single layer in an airtight container; cover. Store in the refrigerator for up to 3 days. Do not freeze.

Frosted Walnut Cookies

PREP **40 MINUTES**   BAKE **10 MINUTES PER BATCH**   OVEN **375°F**

½ cup shortening
1½ cups packed brown sugar
1 teaspoon baking soda
½ teaspoon baking powder
½ teaspoon salt
2 eggs
1 teaspoon vanilla
2½ cups all-purpose flour
1 8-ounce carton sour cream
⅔ cup chopped walnuts
1 recipe Butter Frosting

1 Preheat oven to 375°F. Grease a cookie sheet. In a large mixing bowl beat shortening with an electric mixer on medium to high speed for 30 seconds.

Add brown sugar, baking soda, baking powder, and salt. Beat until combined, scraping sides of bowl occasionally. Beat in the eggs and vanilla until combined. Alternately add flour and sour cream, beating until combined after each addition. Stir in the nuts.

2 Drop dough by rounded teaspoons 2 inches apart onto the prepared cookie sheet. Bake for 10 to 12 minutes or until edges are light brown. Transfer cookies to a wire rack and let cool. Spread Butter Frosting on cooled cookies. Let stand until frosting is set.
MAKES ABOUT 60 COOKIES

Butter Frosting: In a medium mixing bowl beat ⅓ cup softened butter with 2 cups powdered sugar. Beat in ¼ cup milk and 1½ teaspoons vanilla until smooth. Gradually beat in 2 cups additional powdered sugar. If necessary, beat in additional milk, 1 teaspoon at a time, to make a frosting of spreading consistency.

TO MAKE AHEAD AND STORE: Layer unfrosted cookies between sheets of waxed paper in an airtight container; cover. Store at room temperature for up to 3 days or freeze for up to 3 months. Thaw cookies, if frozen. Frost cookies as directed.

Storing Nuts

Because of their high fat content, nuts can go rancid if not stored properly; common culprits include light, heat, moisture, and metal, which can all cause nuts to spoil. Use nuts as soon as possible after purchasing. For longer storage, place the nuts in resealable plastic freezer bags or containers and freeze for up to 8 months.

Pignoli Cookies

PREP **25 MINUTES**   BAKE **15 MINUTES PER BATCH**   COOL **3 MINUTES PER BATCH**   OVEN **350°F**

1   **8-ounce can almond paste (made without syrup or liquid glucose)**
1   **cup sugar**
2   **egg whites**
¼   **cup pine nuts**

1 Preheat oven to 350°F. Line a large cookie sheet with parchment paper or foil; set aside.

2 Break almond paste into small pieces and place in a food processor. Cover and process until nearly smooth. With the food processor running, gradually add sugar through the feed tube, processing until combined. Add egg whites; process until combined.

3 Drop dough by slightly rounded teaspoons onto the prepared cookie sheet. Press a few pine nuts onto each cookie. Bake about 15 minutes or until edges are firm and tops are light brown. Cool on cookie sheet for 3 minutes. Transfer cookies to a wire rack and let cool. (If the cookies stick to the parchment paper or foil, use a spatula dipped in hot water to remove the cookies.) **MAKES ABOUT 24 COOKIES**

TO MAKE AHEAD AND STORE: Layer cookies between sheets of waxed paper in an airtight container; cover. Store in the refrigerator for up to 3 days or freeze for up to 3 months.

Almond Cookie Bites

PREP **25 MINUTES**   BAKE **13 MINUTES PER BATCH**   COOL **5 MINUTES PER BATCH**   OVEN **375°F**

1   cup packed brown sugar
⅓   cup butter
1   egg
½   teaspoon almond extract
½   teaspoon vanilla
1   cup all-purpose flour
½   teaspoon baking powder
⅛   teaspoon baking soda
½   cup chopped almonds
1   recipe Almond Glaze

1 Preheat oven to 325°F. Line thirty-six 1¾-inch muffin cups with paper bake cups; set aside.

2 In a small saucepan combine the brown sugar and butter. Cook and stir over medium heat until smooth. Remove from heat; cool slightly. Stir in the egg, almond extract, and vanilla.

3 In a small bowl stir together the flour, baking powder, and baking soda. Add the flour mixture to the butter mixture; stir just until combined. Stir in ⅓ cup of the chopped almonds. Spoon batter into paper bake cups, filling each half full. Sprinkle the remaining chopped almonds evenly over tops.

4 Bake for 13 to 15 minutes or until tops are light brown. Cool in pan on a wire rack for 5 minutes. Carefully transfer cookies to a wire rack and let cool. Drizzle Almond Glaze over cooled cookies. **MAKES 36 COOKIES**

Almond Glaze: In a small bowl stir together ¾ cup powdered sugar, ¼ teaspoon almond extract, and enough milk (2 to 3 teaspoons) to make a glaze of drizzling consistency.

TO MAKE AHEAD AND STORE: Layer cookies between sheets of waxed paper in an airtight container; cover. Store at room temperature for up to 3 days or freeze for up to 3 months.

gift It

Cookie Carryall

Look for vintage metal containers at flea markets, thrift stores, and collectibles shops. If desired, spray-paint them in a holiday color; let dry. Fill the container with shredded paper and line with parchment paper.

To make the tag, cut fabric to desired size. (If desired, fold over edges and apply iron-on adhesive to all four edges.) Spray tag with starch. Using letter stamps and an inkpad, stamp a message onto the tag. Iron the tag to set the ink. Attach tag to a ribbon with a scrapbooking clip; tie the ribbon onto the closure of the box.

Almond Shortbread Wedges

PREP **1 HOUR** BAKE **25 MINUTES** OVEN **325°F**

- ¾ cup butter, softened
- 1 cup powdered sugar
- ¼ teaspoon salt
- 2 teaspoons vanilla
- 1¾ cups all-purpose flour
- 1 recipe Almond-Butter Frosting
- 1¼ cups sliced almonds, toasted

1 Preheat oven to 325°F. In a large mixing bowl beat butter with an electric mixer on medium to high speed for 30 seconds. Add powdered sugar and salt. Beat until combined, scraping sides of bowl occasionally. Beat in the vanilla until combined. Beat in as much of the flour as you can with the mixer. Using a wooden spoon, stir in any remaining flour. Divide dough in half.

2 On an extra-large ungreased cookie sheet pat each dough half into a 6-inch circle about ½ inch thick; leaving 3 inches between the dough circles. Cut each circle into 10 wedges, leaving wedges in place.

3 Bake for 25 to 30 minutes or until centers are just firm and edges are light brown. Cut circles into wedges again while warm. Transfer cookies to a wire rack and let cool. Spread Almond-Butter Frosting over cookies. Press sliced almonds into frosting. Let stand until frosting is set. **MAKES 20 COOKIES**

Almond-Butter Frosting:
In a medium mixing bowl beat ¼ cup softened butter with an electric mixer on medium to high speed for 30 seconds. Gradually beat in 2 cups powdered sugar, ¼ teaspoon vanilla, ¼ teaspoon almond extract, and enough milk (3 to 5 teaspoons) to make a frosting of spreading consistency.

TO MAKE AHEAD AND STORE: Layer cookies between sheets of waxed paper in an airtight container. Store at room temperature for up to 3 days or freeze for up to 3 months.

Cashew Icebox Cookies

PREP **30 MINUTES**   CHILL **4 HOURS**   BAKE **8 MINUTES PER BATCH**   OVEN **375°F**

- ½ cup shortening
- ½ cup butter, softened
- 1¼ cups packed brown sugar
- ½ teaspoon baking soda
- ¼ teaspoon salt
- 1 egg
- 1 teaspoon vanilla
- 2½ cups all-purpose flour
- ¾ cup honey-roasted cashews or honey-roasted peanuts, ground
- ⅔ cup finely chopped honey-roasted cashews or honey-roasted peanuts
- 1 cup butterscotch-flavor pieces
- 2 tablespoons shortening
  Honey-roasted cashew halves (optional)

1 In a large mixing bowl beat the ½ cup shortening and the butter with an electric mixer on medium to high speed for 30 seconds. Add brown sugar, baking soda, and salt. Beat until combined, scraping sides of bowl occasionally. Beat in the egg and vanilla until combined. Beat in as much of the flour as you can with the mixer. Using a wooden spoon, stir in any remaining flour and the ground nuts.

2 Divide dough in half. Shape each portion into a 10-inch log. Roll logs in the finely chopped nuts to coat. Wrap each log in plastic wrap or waxed paper; chill about 4 hours or until firm.

3 Preheat oven to 375°F. Cut logs crosswise into ¼-inch-thick slices. Place slices 1 inch apart on an ungreased cookie sheet. Bake for 8 to 10 minutes or until edges are firm. Transfer cookies to a wire rack and let cool.

4 In a small microwave-safe bowl combine butterscotch pieces and the 2 tablespoons shortening. Microwave, uncovered, on 50 percent power (medium) about 2 minutes or until pieces melt, stirring every 30 seconds. Spoon butterscotch mixture into a heavy resealable plastic bag. Seal bag and snip a small hole in one corner. Drizzle butterscotch mixture over cookies. If desired, top each cookie with a cashew half. Let stand until butterscotch is set. **MAKES 72 COOKIES**

TO MAKE AHEAD AND STORE: Layer cookies between sheets of waxed paper in an airtight container; cover. Store at room temperature for up to 3 days or freeze for up to 3 months.

In a *twinkling*

Get some chocolate in on the action by substituting either semisweet chocolate or white chocolate for half of the butterscotch-flavor pieces in the finishing drizzle. Use ½ cup butterscotch-flavor pieces and ½ cup semisweet or white baking pieces; melt with the shortening and continue as directed.

Chocolate-Pistachio Trees

PREP **45 MINUTES**   CHILL **30 MINUTES**   BAKE **9 MINUTES PER BATCH**   OVEN **350°F**

1	cup butter
⅔	cup packed brown sugar
1	teaspoon vanilla
1	egg, beaten
2¼	cups all-purpose flour
¼	cup unsweetened cocoa powder
¾	cup finely chopped pistachios
¾	cup semisweet chocolate pieces
1	tablespoon shortening
½	cup ground pistachios

1 In a medium saucepan combine the butter and brown sugar; cook and stir over low heat until butter melts. Remove from heat; stir in vanilla. Let cool for 15 minutes. Stir in the egg, flour, and cocoa powder until combined. Stir in the ¾ cup pistachios. Divide dough in half. Cover and chill dough about 30 minutes or until easy to handle.

2 Preheat oven to 350°F. On a lightly floured surface roll dough halves to ¼-inch thickness. Using a tree-shaped cookie cutter, cut out dough. Place cutouts 1 inch apart on an ungreased cookie sheet. Bake about 9 minutes or until edges are firm. Transfer cookies to a wire rack and let cool.

3 In a small heavy saucepan combine chocolate pieces and shortening. Cook and stir over low heat until chocolate melts. Dip one-third of each cookie into melted chocolate; roll dipped edges in ground pistachios. Let stand until chocolate is set.

MAKES ABOUT 48 COOKIES

TO MAKE AHEAD AND STORE: Layer cookies between sheets of waxed paper in an airtight container; cover. Store at room temperature for up to 3 days or freeze for up to 3 months.

Prepping the Pistachios

To prepare the pistachio nuts for these cookies, start with 2 cups whole shelled pistachios; place them into a food processor and pulse until finely chopped. Remove ¾ cup of the finely chopped nuts to be used in the dough. Then, continue pulsing the remaining nuts until finely ground. Use these for the garnish.

gift It

Eye-Catching Canister

An empty coffee can provides a surprisingly elegant receptacle for presenting these cookies. Cut a piece of decorative paper to fit and wrap it around the can, securing it with double-sided tape. Trim overhanging edges with a crafts knife. Attach a wide ribbon around the center of the can with double-sided tape or a glue stick. Tie another ribbon around the wide ribbon. Fill the can with Chocolate-Pistachio Trees.

Hazelnut Cookie Sandwiches

PREP **35 MINUTES**   CHILL **1 HOUR**   BAKE **9 MINUTES PER BATCH**   OVEN **350°F**

½   **cup hazelnuts (filberts), toasted**

2   **cups all-purpose flour**

1   **teaspoon baking powder**

⅔   **cup butter, softened**

2   **tablespoons cream cheese, softened**

⅔   **cup sugar**

1   **egg**

¾   **cup chocolate-hazelnut spread**

1 Preheat oven to 350°F. In a food processor combine hazelnuts and ½ cup of the flour. Cover and process until nuts are very finely ground. Add the remaining 1½ cups flour and the baking powder. Cover and process with one on-off pulse to mix.

2 In a large mixing bowl beat butter and cream cheese with an electric mixer on medium to high speed for 30 seconds. Add the ⅔ cup sugar. Beat until light and fluffy, scraping sides of bowl occasionally. Beat in the egg until smooth. Add the flour mixture; beat on low speed until combined.

3 Divide dough into quarters. Shape each portion into an 8-inch log. Wrap each log in plastic wrap or waxed paper; chill about 1 hour or until firm.

4 Line a cookie sheet with parchment paper. Cut logs crosswise into ½-inch-thick slices. Place slices 2 inches apart on the prepared cookie sheet. Place cookie sheet on the center rack in the oven. Bake about 9 minutes or until just golden brown around the edges. Transfer cookies to a wire rack and let cool.

5 To assemble cookies, spread about 1 teaspoon chocolate-hazelnut spread onto the bottom of one cookie; press the bottom of a second cookie against the spread. Repeat with the remaining cookies and chocolate-hazelnut spread. **MAKES ABOUT 32 SANDWICH COOKIES**

TO MAKE AHEAD AND STORE: Layer unfilled cookies between sheets of waxed paper in an airtight container; cover. Store at room temperature for up to 3 days or freeze for up to 3 months. Thaw cookies, if frozen. Assemble cookies as directed.

Hazelnut-Cocoa Coins

PREP **1 HOUR**   CHILL **1 HOUR**   BAKE **6 MINUTES PER BATCH**   OVEN **375°F**

1 cup butter, softened
½ cup sugar
¼ teaspoon salt
1 egg
3 tablespoons unsweetened cocoa powder
1¾ cups all-purpose flour
¾ cup finely chopped toasted hazelnuts (filberts)
6 ounces dark chocolate, chopped
½ teaspoon shortening

1 In a large mixing bowl beat butter with an electric mixer on medium to high speed for 30 seconds. Add sugar and salt. Beat until combined, scraping sides of bowl occasionally. Beat in the egg and cocoa powder until combined. Beat in as much of the flour as you can with the mixer. Using a wooden spoon, stir in any remaining flour and the hazelnuts.

2 Divide dough in half. Shape each portion into an 11-inch log. Wrap logs in plastic wrap or waxed paper; chill for 1 to 2 hours or until firm.

3 Preheat oven to 375°F. Cut logs crosswise into ¼-inch-thick slices. Place slices 1 inch apart on an ungreased cookie sheet. Bake for 6 to 8 minutes or just until tops are firm to the touch. Transfer cookies to a wire rack and let cool.

4 In a small saucepan combine the chocolate and shortening. Cook and stir over low heat until chocolate melts. Generously drizzle melted chocolate over cookies. Let stand until chocolate is set. **MAKES ABOUT 60 COOKIES**

TO MAKE AHEAD AND STORE: Layer cookies between sheets of waxed paper in an airtight container; cover. Store at room temperature for up to 3 days or freeze for up to 3 months.

Almond Breton Biscuits

PREP **25 MINUTES**   CHILL **3 HOURS**   BAKE **12 MINUTES PER BATCH**   OVEN **350°F**

1   cup butter, softened
½   cup granulated sugar
¼   cup powdered sugar
¼   teaspoon salt
2   egg yolks
1½   cups all-purpose flour
½   cup finely ground almonds
     Coarse plain and/or
     colored sugar
1   egg white, lightly beaten

1 In a large mixing bowl beat butter with an electric mixer on medium to high speed for 30 seconds. Add granulated sugar, powdered sugar, and salt. Beat until combined, scraping sides of bowl occasionally. Beat in the egg yolks until combined. Beat in as much of the flour as you can with the mixer. Using a wooden spoon, stir in any remaining flour and the almonds.

2 Divide dough in half. Shape each portion into an 8-inch log. Wrap logs in plastic wrap or waxed paper; chill about 3 hours or until firm.

3 Preheat oven to 350°F. Line a cookie sheet with parchment paper. Place coarse sugar in a shallow dish. Brush logs with egg white, then roll in sugar to coat. Cut logs crosswise into ¼-inch-thick slices. Place slices 2 inches apart on the prepared cookie sheet. Bake about 12 minutes or until edges start to brown. Transfer cookies to a wire rack and let cool.
MAKES ABOUT 54 COOKIES

TO MAKE AHEAD AND STORE: Layer cookies between sheets of waxed paper in an airtight container; cover. Store at room temperature for up to 3 days or freeze for up to 3 months.

gift It

Presents by the Panful

A simple, inexpensive cake pan makes a sturdy vessel for presenting the Almond Breton Biscuits. Place the cookies in paper cupcake liners to keep them from sliding around in the pan. Tie with ribbon and attach a gift tag, and your gift is presentable.

Sandies

PREP **35 MINUTES**   CHILL **30 MINUTES**   BAKE **15 MINUTES PER BATCH**   OVEN **325°F**

1   cup butter, softened
½   cup powdered sugar
1   tablespoon water
1   teaspoon vanilla
2   cups all-purpose flour
1½ cups finely chopped
    pecans, toasted
1   cup powdered sugar

1 In a large mixing bowl beat butter with an electric mixer on medium to high speed for 30 seconds. Add the ½ cup powdered sugar. Beat until combined, scraping sides of bowl occasionally. Beat in the water and vanilla until combined.

Beat in as much of the flour as you can with the mixer. Using a wooden spoon, stir in any remaining flour and the pecans. Cover and chill dough for 30 to 60 minutes or until easy to handle.

2 Preheat oven to 325°F. Shape dough into 1-inch balls. Place balls 1 inch apart on an ungreased cookie sheet. Bake for 15 minutes or until bottoms are light brown. Transfer cookies to a wire rack and let cool.

3 Place the 1 cup powdered sugar in a large resealable plastic bag. Add cooled cookies to bag in batches. Seal bag; shake gently to coat. MAKES ABOUT 55 COOKIES

Chocolate-Covered Sandies: Prepare cookies as directed through Step 2. Decrease the 1 cup powdered sugar to ¾ cup and add ¼ cup unsweetened cocoa powder. Shake cooled cookies in cocoa powder mixture.

TO MAKE AHEAD AND STORE: Layer cookies between sheets of waxed paper in an airtight container; cover. Store at room temperature for up to 3 days or freeze for up to 3 months.

gift It

Tempting Towel of Treats

Head to collectibles shops and find charming vintage towels you adore. Then, simply make a copy of it (you get to keep the towel). Here's how:

Using heavy copy paper, make a photocopy of the towel. Position the paper copy, printed side up, on top of a piece of scrapbooking paper placed printed side down. Using scallop-edge scissors, cut a stocking shape that is approximately 9 inches long and 5 inches wide. Cut accent pieces from another pattern of scrapbooking paper, including toe pieces and two 3x5-inch strips for the top bands on the front and back. Using crafts glue, run a bead down both sides of the stocking, creating a pocket at the top. Attach the top bands and the toe pieces using a glue stick. Add a ribbon to the band and the toe for added accents. Let the glue dry completely before filling the stocking with cookies.

Cherry-Pistachio Cremes

PREP **50 MINUTES**   CHILL **1 HOUR**   BAKE **8 MINUTES PER BATCH**   OVEN **350°F**

¾ cup butter, softened
¾ cup powdered sugar
1 egg
1½ cups all-purpose flour
¼ teaspoon salt
½ cup finely chopped pistachios
  Granulated sugar
1¼ cups powdered sugar
¼ cup butter, softened
½ teaspoon vanilla
1 to 2 tablespoons maraschino cherry juice
  Maraschino cherries with stems * (optional)

1 In a large mixing bowl beat the ¾ cup butter and the ¾ cup powdered sugar with an electric mixer on medium speed until combined, scraping sides of bowl occasionally. Beat in the egg until combined. Gradually beat in flour and salt on low speed until combined. Cover and chill dough about 1 hour or until easy to handle.

2 Preheat oven to 350°F. Place pistachios in a small bowl. Shape dough into ½-inch balls. Roll balls in the nuts to coat. Place balls 1 inch apart on an ungreased cookie sheet. Using the bottom of a wet glass dipped in granulated sugar, slightly flatten each ball. Bake for 8 to 9 minutes or just until edges are golden brown. Transfer cookies to a wire rack and let cool.

3 In a small mixing bowl beat the 1¼ cups powdered sugar, the ¼ cup butter, and the vanilla with an electric mixer on medium speed until smooth. Beat in enough maraschino cherry juice to make a filling of desired consistency. Reserve about one-quarter of the filling for decorating the sandwich cookies.

4 To assemble, spread about 1 teaspoon of the remaining filling onto the bottom of one cookie; press the bottom of a second cookie against the filling. Repeat with the remaining cookies and filling. Before serving, spoon a small amount of the reserved filling on top of each sandwich cookie. If desired, press a maraschino cherry into the filling. **MAKES ABOUT 21 SANDWICH COOKIES**

note Drain maraschino cherries on paper towels and pat dry to remove any excess liquid.

TO MAKE AHEAD AND STORE: Layer cookies between sheets of waxed paper in an airtight container; cover. Store in the refrigerator for up to 3 days or freeze for up to 3 months.

Top-Notch Topper

Maraschino cherries add beautiful, seasonally colored accents to frosted cookies. Just be sure that the cherries are well drained before pressing them into the topping. It helps to blot them dry with clean paper towels.

Pistachio Cookie Cups

PREP **25 MINUTES**   BAKE **25 MINUTES**   COOL **5 MINUTES**   OVEN **350°F**

½   cup butter, softened
1   3-ounce package cream cheese, softened
2   tablespoons granulated sugar
1   cup all-purpose flour
½   teaspoon finely shredded orange peel
1   cup powdered sugar
½   cup finely chopped pistachios
⅓   cup dried cranberries, chopped
1   egg, lightly beaten

1 Preheat oven to 350°F. In a medium mixing bowl beat butter, cream cheese, and granulated sugar with an electric mixer on medium speed until combined.

Beat in the flour and orange peel on low speed just until combined. Shape dough into 24 balls. Press each ball into the bottoms and up the sides of 24 ungreased 1¾-inch muffin cups.

2 For filling, in a medium bowl combine the powdered sugar, ⅓ cup of the pistachios, the dried cranberries, and egg; mix well. Spoon filling into muffin cups, filling each about three-quarters full. Sprinkle the remaining pistachios evenly over tops.

3 Bake for 25 to 28 minutes or until crust is golden brown and filling puffs. Cool in pan on a wire rack for 5 minutes. Carefully transfer cookies to a wire rack and let cool. **MAKES 24 CUPS**

TO MAKE AHEAD AND STORE: Layer cups between sheets of waxed paper in an airtight container; cover. Store at room temperature for up to 3 days or freeze for up to 3 months.

Pecan Tassies

PREP **30 MINUTES**   BAKE **25 MINUTES**   COOL **5 MINUTES**   OVEN **325°F**

½   cup butter, softened
1   3-ounce package cream cheese, softened
1   cup all-purpose flour
1   egg, lightly beaten
¾   cup packed brown sugar
1   tablespoon butter, melted
½   cup coarsely chopped pecans
     Powdered sugar (optional)

1 Preheat oven to 325°F. For pastry, in a medium mixing bowl beat the ½ cup butter and

the cream cheese with an electric mixer on medium speed until combined. Stir in the flour. Shape dough into 24 balls. Press each ball into the bottoms and up the sides of 24 ungreased 1¾-inch muffin cups.

2 For filling, in a small bowl stir together the egg, brown sugar, and the 1 tablespoon melted butter. Stir in pecans. Spoon about 1 heaping teaspoon filling into each pastry-lined muffin cup.

3 Bake for 25 to 30 minutes or until pastry is golden brown and filling puffs. Cool in pan on a wire rack for 5 minutes. Carefully transfer tassies to a wire rack and let cool. If desired, sprinkle tassies with powdered sugar. **MAKES 24 TASSIES**

TO MAKE AHEAD AND STORE: Layer tassies between sheets of waxed paper in an airtight container; cover. Store at room temperature for up to 3 days or freeze for up to 3 months.

TROPICAL MACAROONS, PAGE 80

crazy for coconut

With its nutty-sweet intrigue
and snowflake-like look, coconut works
its magic in holiday cookies in so many
ways. Star it solo or pair it with nuts,
chocolate, citrus, and more in all kinds of
creations—from light airy meringues
to candy-like bars.

✦

Giant Coconut Macaroons

PREP **30 MINUTES**   BAKE **20 MINUTES**   STAND **30 MINUTES**   OVEN **325°F**

- 4   egg whites
- 1   teaspoon vanilla
- ¼   teaspoon cream of tartar
- ⅛   teaspoon salt
- 1⅓ cups sugar
- 1   14-ounce package flaked coconut

1 Preheat oven to 325°F. Line two extra-large cookie sheets with parchment paper. In an extra-large mixing bowl beat egg whites, vanilla, cream of tartar, and salt with an electric mixer on high speed until soft peaks form (tips curl). Add sugar, 1 tablespoon at a time, beating on high speed until stiff peaks form (tips stand straight). Gently fold in coconut, half at a time.

2 Using a 2-inch-diameter ice cream scoop,* drop coconut mixture into mounds 1 inch apart onto prepared cookie sheets. Place cookie sheets on separate racks in the oven. Bake for 20 minutes. Turn off oven. Let cookies dry in oven with door closed for 30 minutes. Transfer cookies to a wire rack and let cool. **MAKES ABOUT 28 COOKIES**

*note *If you do not have a 2-inch diameter scoop (a #20 scoop), use a ¼-cup dry measuring cup. Scoop a scant ¼ cup coconut mixture for each mound. Use a spoon to form rounded mounds.*

For smaller cookies: Drop mixture by rounded teaspoons onto prepared cookie sheets. Bake for 20 to 25 minutes or until cookies are light brown. Cool as above. **MAKES ABOUT 60 COOKIES**

TO MAKE AHEAD AND STORE: Layer cookies between sheets of waxed paper in an airtight container; cover. Store at room temperature for up to 3 days or freeze for up to 3 months.

In a *twinkling*

For chocolate-dipped macaroons, stir 2 ounces semisweet chocolate and ½ teaspoon shortening over low heat until chocolate melts. Dip bottoms of macaroons in melted chocolate. Place on wire rack, bottom sides up, until chocolate is set.

Coconut-Lime Meringues

PREP **50 MINUTES**   BAKE **10 MINUTES**   STAND **30 MINUTES**   OVEN **300°F**

2   egg whites
1   tablespoon coconut-flavor rum or ¼ teaspoon coconut flavoring
½   teaspoon vanilla
¼   teaspoon cream of tartar
⅔   cup sugar
1   cup flaked coconut
1   teaspoon finely shredded lime peel

1 Place egg whites in medium mixing bowl; let stand at room temperature for 30 minutes.

2 Preheat oven to 300°F. Line two cookie sheets with parchment paper or foil; set aside.

3 Add rum, vanilla, and cream of tartar to the egg whites. Beat with an electric mixer on medium speed until soft peaks form (tips curl). Gradually add the sugar, 1 tablespoon at a time, beating on high speed until stiff peaks form (tips stand straight). Gently fold in coconut and lime peel.

4 Drop coconut mixture by teaspoons into 1-inch mounds 1½ inches apart onto the prepared cookie sheets. Place cookie sheets on separate racks in the oven. Bake about 10 minutes or until set. Turn off oven. Let cookies dry in oven with door closed for 30 minutes. Transfer cookies to a wire rack and let cool. **MAKES ABOUT 36 COOKIES**

TO MAKE AHEAD AND STORE: Layer cookies between sheets of waxed paper in an airtight container; cover. Store at room temperature for up to 3 days or freeze for up to 3 months.

gift It

Peek-a-Boo!

Every cook could use another mixing bowl. Offer these meringues in a contemporary-color bowl. Cover with cellophane and tie with a ribbon for a dramatic presentation.

Toffee and Toasted-Coconut Cookies

PREP **30 MINUTES**   BAKE **6 MINUTES PER BATCH**   OVEN **375°F**

½   cup butter, softened
½   cup shortening
1¼ cups packed brown sugar
¾   teaspoon baking soda
¼   teaspoon salt
3   eggs
2   teaspoons vanilla
3⅓ cups all-purpose flour
1   cup chocolate-covered English toffee bits
1   cup flaked coconut, toasted
¾   cup chopped macadamia nuts or almonds
    Granulated sugar

1 Preheat oven to 375°F. In a large mixing bowl beat butter and shortening with an electric mixer on medium to high speed for 30 seconds. Add brown sugar, baking soda, and salt. Beat until combined, scraping sides of bowl occasionally. Beat in the eggs and vanilla until combined. Beat in as much of the flour as you can with the mixer. Using a wooden spoon, stir in any remaining flour, the toffee, coconut, and nuts.

2 Drop dough by rounded teaspoons 2 inches apart onto an ungreased cookie sheet. Using the bottom of a wet glass dipped in granulated sugar, slightly flatten dough mounds. Bake for 6 to 8 minutes or until edges are light brown. Transfer cookies to a wire rack and let cool. **MAKES 72 COOKIES**

TO MAKE AHEAD AND STORE: Layer cookies between sheets of waxed paper in an airtight container; cover. Store at room temperature for up to 3 days or freeze for up to 3 months.

White Chocolate Snowflakes

PREP **30 MINUTES**   CHILL **1 HOUR**   BAKE **8 MINUTES PER BATCH**   OVEN **375°F**

2   ounces white baking chocolate
1   18-ounce roll refrigerated sugar cookie dough
¼   cup all-purpose flour
1   cup canned white frosting
1   to 2 tablespoons milk
    Flaked coconut

1 In a small saucepan cook and stir chocolate over low heat until chocolate melts; cool. Place cookie dough in a large bowl; add melted chocolate and flour. Mix until combined. Divide dough in half. Cover and chill dough about 1 hour or until easy to handle.

2 Preheat oven to 375°F. On a lightly floured surface roll each dough half to ⅛-inch thickness. Using a 2½- to 3-inch snowflake cookie cutter, cut out dough. Place cutouts 2 inches apart on an ungreased cookie sheet. Bake for 8 to 10 minutes or until light brown around the edges. Transfer cookies to a wire rack and let cool.

3 In a small bowl stir together the frosting and enough milk to make a thin glaze. Spread glaze over cookies. While still wet, sprinkle coconut on cookies. Let stand until glaze is set. **MAKES ABOUT 36 COOKIES**

TO MAKE AHEAD AND STORE: Layer cookies between sheets of waxed paper in airtight container; cover. Store at room temperature for up to 3 days. Or freeze unglazed cookies for up to 3 months. Thaw cookies; glaze and decorate as directed.

Macadamia-Coconut Shortbread Coins

PREP **20 MINUTES**   BAKE **18 MINUTES PER BATCH**   OVEN **325°F**

¾ cup butter, softened
¾ cup powdered sugar
1 teaspoon baking powder
¼ teaspoon salt
1 cup macadamia nuts,
   finely chopped
1 cup flaked coconut,
   toasted
2 cups cake flour
   Chopped macadamia nuts

1 Preheat oven to 325°F. In a large mixing bowl beat butter with an electric mixer on medium to high speed for 30 seconds. Add powdered sugar, baking powder, and salt. Beat until combined, scraping sides of bowl occasionally. Beat in the 1 cup macadamia nuts and the coconut until combined. Beat in as much of the flour as you can with the mixer. Using a wooden spoon, stir in any remaining flour (dough will be sticky).

2 Using lightly floured hands, shape dough into 1-inch

balls. Place balls 2 inches apart on an ungreased cookie sheet; flatten balls slightly. Lightly press additional chopped nuts onto the tops of the cookies. Bake for 18 to 20 minutes or until light golden brown. Transfer cookies to a wire rack and let cool. **MAKES ABOUT 32 COOKIES**

TO MAKE AHEAD AND STORE: Layer cookies between sheets of waxed paper in an airtight container; cover. Store at room temperature for up to 3 days or freeze for up to 3 months.

Toasting Coconut

Toasting coconut gives it a toasty and more intense flavor. To toast coconut, spread it in a shallow baking pan. Bake in a 350°F oven for 5 to 10 minutes, stirring the coconut once or twice to ensure an even golden color. Watch the coconut closely so that it does not burn—it can go from golden to brown to black quickly.

Note that if you toast a large amount of coconut at one time, be sure to turn your head away as you open the oven door. Coconut gives off volatile fumes as it toasts. The fumes collect in the oven and can cause severe watering and burning of the eyes.

Coconut Bonbons

PREP **40 MINUTES**   CHILL **4 HOURS 15 MINUTES**   FREEZE **20 MINUTES**   STAND **10 MINUTES**

3¾ cups powdered sugar
1½ cups flaked coconut
¾ cup sweetened condensed milk
½ teaspoon almond extract
¼ teaspoon coconut flavoring
10 ounces bittersweet or semisweet baking chocolate, chopped
2 teaspoons shortening
Toasted flaked coconut (optional)∗

1 In a food processor combine powdered sugar, the 1½ cups coconut, the sweetened condensed milk, almond extract, and coconut flavoring. Cover and process until well combined. Transfer to a medium bowl. Cover and chill coconut mixture about 4 hours or until firm.

2 Line a baking sheet with waxed paper. Shape coconut mixture into 1-inch balls. Place balls on the prepared baking sheet. Cover and freeze about 20 minutes or until very firm.

3 In a medium microwave-safe bowl combine chocolate and shortening. Microwave, uncovered, on 50 percent power (medium) for 2 to 3 minutes or until chocolate melts, stirring every minute. Let stand at room temperature for 10 minutes.

4 Remove half the coconut balls from the freezer. Using a fork, dip balls, one at a time, into melted chocolate. Let excess chocolate drip back into bowl. Place bonbons on the prepared baking sheet. If desired, sprinkle bonbons with toasted coconut. Repeat with the remaining coconut balls and melted chocolate. Chill bonbons about 15 minutes or until chocolate is set. **MAKES 42 COOKIES**

∗*note* To toast coconut, spread coconut in a single layer in a shallow baking pan. Bake in a preheated 350°F oven for 5 to 10 minutes or until coconut is light golden brown, watching carefully and stirring once or twice so coconut doesn't burn.

Coconut Coins: Prepare Coconut Bonbons as directed, except after shaping coconut mixture into balls, flatten the balls into patties. Dip patties in melted chocolate as directed.

TO MAKE AHEAD AND STORE: Place bonbons in a single layer in an airtight container; cover. Store in the refrigerator for up to 1 week or freeze for up to 3 months. Before serving, let cookies stand at room temperature for 30 minutes.

Cocoa-Hazelnut Macarons

PREP **35 MINUTES**   STAND **30 MINUTES**   BAKE **9 MINUTES PER BATCH**   OVEN **325°F**

1¼   cups powdered sugar
1   cup finely ground
     hazelnuts (filberts)
2   tablespoons unsweetened
     cocoa powder
3   egg whites
½   teaspoon vanilla
     Pinch salt
¼   cup granulated sugar
¾   cup chocolate-hazelnut
     spread

1 Line two large cookie sheets with parchment paper; set aside. In a medium bowl stir together powdered sugar, hazelnuts, and cocoa powder; set aside.

2 In a large bowl combine egg whites, vanilla, and salt. Beat with an electric mixer on medium speed until frothy. Gradually add granulated sugar, about 1 tablespoon at a time, beating on high speed just until soft peaks form (tips curl). Stir in nut mixture.

3 Spoon mixture into a large decorating bag fitted with a large (about ½-inch) round tip.* Pipe 1½-inch circles 1 inch apart onto the prepared cookie sheets. Let stand for 30 minutes before baking.

4 Meanwhile, preheat oven to 325°F. Bake in the preheated oven for 9 to 10 minutes or until set. Cool on cookie sheets on wire racks. Carefully peel cookies off parchment paper.

5 Spread chocolate-hazelnut spread on bottoms of half of the cookies. Top with the remaining cookies, bottom sides down. **MAKES 20 TO 24 SANDWICH COOKIES**

*note If you don't own a decorating bag, spoon mixture into a large resealable plastic bag and snip a ½-inch hole in one corner of the bag.

TO STORE: Layer unfilled cookies between sheets of waxed paper in an airtight container; cover. Store in the refrigerator for up to 3 days or freeze for up to 3 months. To serve, thaw cookies if frozen. Fill as directed in Step 5.

Piping Perfection

To determine when the macaron batter is ready for piping, lift a spoonful of batter about 2 inches above the surface and slowly streak it across the batter in the bowl. When it's the perfect consistency, the batter will fall from the spoon into a thick ribbon—the consistency of cold molasses or honey—and sit on the surface about 30 seconds before disappearing into the rest of the batter.

Use a pencil to trace circles on parchment paper about 1 inch apart, using a cookie cutter as a guide. Flip paper over before piping.

Once the macarons are piped onto the parchment paper, let them rest for 30 minutes before baking. This step is the key to creating the delicate, airy base—known as the pied or feet—of the macarons. Don't rush this step!

Toasted Coconut Wafers

PREP **25 MINUTES**   CHILL **4 HOURS**   BAKE **10 MINUTES PER BATCH**   COOL **1 MINUTE PER BATCH**   OVEN **375°F**

1	cup butter, softened
1¼	cups powdered sugar
½	teaspoon almond extract or vanilla
⅛	teaspoon salt
1	egg yolk
2¼	cups all-purpose flour
1	cup shredded coconut, toasted
1	egg white, lightly beaten
1	cup shredded coconut

1 In a large mixing bowl beat butter with an electric mixer on medium to high speed for 30 seconds. Add powdered sugar, almond extract, and salt. Beat until combined, scraping sides of bowl occasionally. Beat in the egg yolk until combined. Beat in as much of the flour as you can with the mixer. Using a wooden spoon, stir in any remaining flour and the 1 cup toasted coconut.

2 Divide dough in half. Shape each dough half into an 8-inch log. Brush logs with egg white, then roll in the 1 cup shredded coconut to coat. Wrap each log in plastic wrap or waxed paper. Chill logs for 4 to 24 hours or until firm.

3 Preheat oven to 375°F. Cut logs crosswise into ¼-inch-thick slices. Place slices 1 inch apart on an ungreased cookie sheet. Bake for 10 to 12 minutes or until edges are light brown. Cool on cookie sheet for 1 minute. Transfer cookies to a wire rack and let cool. **MAKES ABOUT 60 COOKIES**

TO MAKE AHEAD AND STORE: Layer cookies between sheets of waxed paper in an airtight container; cover. Store at room temperature for up to 3 days or freeze for up to 3 months.

Tropical Macaroons

PREP **25 MINUTES**   BAKE **20 MINUTES PER BATCH**   OVEN **325°F**

2	cups flaked coconut
¾	cup coarsely chopped macadamia nuts
⅔	cup granulated sugar
⅓	cup all-purpose flour
¼	teaspoon salt
3	egg whites, lightly beaten
1	teaspoon finely shredded lemon peel
1	tablespoon lemon juice
	Powdered sugar (optional)

1 Preheat oven to 325°F. Line a large cookie sheet with parchment paper.

2 In a large bowl combine coconut, macadamia nuts, granulated sugar, flour, and salt. Add egg whites, lemon peel, and lemon juice. Stir until combined. Drop dough by rounded teaspoons 2 inches apart onto the prepared cookie sheet.

3 Bake for 20 to 25 minutes or until edges are light brown. Transfer cookies to a wire rack and let cool. If desired, sprinkle with powdered sugar. **MAKES ABOUT 30 COOKIES**

TO MAKE AHEAD AND STORE: Layer cookies between sheets of waxed paper in an airtight container; cover. Store in the refrigerator for up to 2 days or freeze for up to 3 months.

Coconut-Date Bars

PREP **30 MINUTES**   BAKE **30 MINUTES**   OVEN **350°F**

- 2 cups all-purpose flour
- 1½ cups sugar
- 2 teaspoons baking powder
- ¼ teaspoon salt
- 1 cup butter
- ¾ cup canned unsweetened coconut milk
- 2 eggs
- 1 teaspoon vanilla
- 1 cup flaked coconut, toasted
- 1 8-ounce package chopped dates (1⅓ cups)
- 1 recipe Coconut Frosting
- ½ cup flaked coconut, toasted

1 Preheat oven to 350°F. Grease and flour a 15x10x1-inch baking pan. In a large mixing bowl stir together the flour, sugar, baking powder, and salt.

2 In a small saucepan combine butter and coconut milk. Bring just to boiling, stirring occasionally. Add butter mixture to flour mixture; beat with an electric mixer on medium speed until well combined. Add the eggs and vanilla; beat for 1 minute. Fold in the 1 cup coconut and the dates. Spoon batter into the prepared baking pan, spreading evenly.

3 Bake about 30 minutes or until a wooden toothpick inserted near the center comes out clean. Cool in pan on a wire rack. Spread Coconut Frosting evenly over bars. Sprinkle with the ½ cup coconut. Cut into bars.
MAKES 36 BARS

Coconut Frosting: In a medium mixing bowl beat one 3-ounce package cream cheese, softened, and 2 tablespoons butter, softened, with an electric mixer on medium to high speed until combined. Beat in 2 tablespoons canned unsweetened coconut milk and ½ teaspoon vanilla. Gradually add 4 cups powdered sugar, beating until smooth.

TO MAKE AHEAD AND STORE: Cover bars and store in the refrigerator for up to 3 days. Or freeze unfrosted bars for up to 3 months. Thaw bars; frost as directed.

In a *twinkling*

Top cookies with white chocolate snowflakes. Melt 2 ounces white baking chocolate; cool slightly. Place in a heavy resealable plastic bag. Cut a small hole in one corner; pipe snowflake designs onto a baking sheet lined with waxed paper. Let stand in a cool, dry place until snowflakes are firm. Place snowflakes on top of bars.

Coconut Candy Bars

PREP **30 MINUTES**   BAKE **22 MINUTES**   OVEN **350°F**

2   cups graham cracker crumbs

1½ cup whole almonds, toasted

⅓   cup packed brown sugar

⅔   cup butter, melted

1   14-ounce package flaked coconut

1   14-ounce can sweetened condensed milk

18 ounces dark chocolate pieces, melted

1 Preheat oven to 350°F. In a food processor combine graham cracker crumbs, ½ cup of the almonds, and the brown sugar. Cover and process until almonds are finely chopped. Add butter; cover and pulse with on-off turns until well combined. Press the crumb mixture evenly onto the bottom of an ungreased 13x9x2-inch baking pan. Bake for 12 minutes.

2 In a medium bowl stir together coconut and sweetened condensed milk. Spread coconut mixture evenly over crust. Sprinkle the remaining almonds evenly over the coconut layer. Bake for 10 minutes.

3 Spoon melted chocolate over top of warm bars, spreading evenly. Cool in pan on a wire rack. (If desired, chill until the chocolate is set.) Cut into bars. **MAKES 36 BARS**

TO MAKE AHEAD AND STORE: Place bars in a single layer in an airtight container; cover. Store in the refrigerator for up to 1 week or freeze for up to 3 months. Before serving, let cookies stand at room temperature for 30 minutes.

Holiday Layer Bars

PREP **25 MINUTES**   BAKE **25 MINUTES**   OVEN **350°F**

½   cup butter
1½ cups finely crushed gingersnaps (about 25)
6   ounces white baking chocolate, chopped, or white baking pieces
⅔   cup dried cranberries or dried tart red cherries, snipped
⅓   cup diced candied orange peel
1   cup pistachios, chopped
1   14-ounce can sweetened condensed milk
1⅓ cups flaked coconut

1 Preheat oven to 350°F. Place butter in a 13x9x2-inch baking pan. Place pan in the oven until the butter melts. Tilt pan to coat bottom of pan with butter. Sprinkle cookie crumbs evenly over bottom of pan.

2 Layer the white baking chocolate, cranberries, candied orange peel, and pistachios evenly over cookie crumbs. Pour sweetened condensed milk evenly over fruit and nut layers. Sprinkle with coconut.

3 Bake about 25 minutes or until coconut is light golden brown. Cool in pan on a wire rack. Loosen edges from pan and cut into bars.
MAKES 42 BARS

TO MAKE AHEAD AND STORE: Place bars in a single layer in an airtight container; cover. Refrigerate for up to 3 days or freeze for up to 3 months.

Crushing Gingersnaps

For a mess-free way to crush gingersnaps, place them in a heavy resealable plastic bag. Seal the bag and roll a rolling pin over the bag until the cookies are finely crushed.

Macaroon-Chocolate Bars

PREP **30 MINUTES**   BAKE **33 MINUTES**   OVEN **350°F**

2 cups crushed chocolate sandwich cookies with white filling (about 20 cookies)
½ cup sugar
⅓ cup unsweetened cocoa powder
½ cup butter, melted
1 teaspoon vanilla
⅔ cup all-purpose flour
⅓ cup sugar
¼ teaspoon salt
2¾ cups flaked coconut
3 egg whites, lightly beaten
½ teaspoon vanilla

1 Preheat oven to 350°F. Line a 13x9x2-inch baking pan with foil, extending the foil over the edges of the pan. Lightly grease foil.

2 In a large bowl stir together crushed cookies, the ½ cup sugar, and the cocoa powder. Add melted butter and the 1 teaspoon vanilla; stir until combined. Press cookie mixture evenly onto the bottom of the prepared baking pan. Bake for 8 minutes.

3 Meanwhile, in a second large bowl stir together flour, the ⅓ cup sugar, and the salt. Stir in coconut. Add egg whites and the ½ teaspoon vanilla; stir until combined. Spoon coconut mixture over crust. Using wet hands, carefully press the coconut filling to the edges of the pan.

4 Bake for 25 to 28 minutes or until coconut layer is set and light brown. Cool in pan on a wire rack. Use the foil to lift the uncut bars out of the pan. Place on a cutting board; cut into 24 bars. Cut each bar diagonally to make 48 triangles. **MAKES 48 BARS**

TO MAKE AHEAD AND STORE: Layer bars between sheets of waxed paper in an airtight container; cover. Store at room temperature for up to 3 days or freeze for up to 3 months.

Coconut Options

While whole coconuts are available in the produce aisles of supermarkets, the most common and easy-to-use forms for baking are found in bags or cans. Here's what you'll find:

✦ Flakes or Shreds? Coconut flakes are short, flat pieces of coconut meat, while shreds are typically longer or wider. Coconut flakes and shreds can be used interchangeably in recipes. Find them in the baking aisle of the supermarket.

✦ Sweetened or unsweetened? Most shredded and flaked coconut is sold sweetened. If you want an unsweetened version, check the organic section at the supermarket or a health foods store.

In a *twinkling*

For a holiday presentation, cut the bars into diamonds. Place some bars on a serving plate. Stir ½ cup semisweet chocolate pieces and 1 teaspoon shortening over low heat until chocolate melts. Drizzle over cookies. Chill about 30 minutes or until chocolate is set.

PEANUT BUTTER BLOSSOMS, PAGE 88

packed with
peanut butter

Peanut butter brings sweet,
nutty satisfaction to cookies. Here, you'll
discover classic and new ways to spread this
ingredient around during the season—from Peanut
Butter Blossoms kids will love to toffee bars
and truffles designed for a more
sophisticated crowd.

Peanut Butter Blossoms

PREP **25 MINUTES**   BAKE **10 MINUTES PER BATCH**   OVEN **350°F**   *PICTURED ON PAGE 86*

- ½ cup shortening
- ½ cup peanut butter
- ½ cup granulated sugar
- ½ cup packed brown sugar
- 1 teaspoon baking powder
- ⅛ teaspoon baking soda
- 1 egg
- 2 tablespoons milk
- 1 teaspoon vanilla
- 1¾ cups all-purpose flour
- ¼ cup granulated sugar
- About 60 milk chocolate stars or candy kisses, unwrapped

1 Preheat oven to 350°F. In a large mixing bowl beat shortening and peanut butter with an electric mixer on medium to high speed for 30 seconds. Add the ½ cup granulated sugar, the brown sugar, baking powder, and baking soda. Beat until combined, scraping bowl occasionally. Beat in egg, milk, and vanilla until combined. Beat in as much of the flour as you can with the mixer. Using a wooden spoon, stir in any remaining flour.

2 Shape dough into 1-inch balls. Roll balls in the ¼ cup granulated sugar to coat. Place balls 2 inches apart on an ungreased cookie sheet.

3 Bake for 10 to 12 minutes or until edges are firm and bottoms are light brown. Immediately press a chocolate star into center of each cookie. Transfer cookies to a wire rack and let cool. **MAKES ABOUT 60 COOKIES**

Milk Chocolate Chunk–Peanut Butter Cookies: Prepare as directed, except stir 1½ cups chopped milk chocolate (about 8 ounces) in with the flour. Shape and bake as directed. Omit milk chocolate kisses or stars.

TO MAKE AHEAD AND STORE: Layer cookies between sheets of waxed paper in an airtight container; cover. Store at room temperature for up to 3 days or freeze for up to 3 months.

 # Peanut Butter Bites

PREP **40 MINUTES**   BAKE **8 MINUTES PER BATCH**   OVEN **375°F**

- ¾ cup butter, softened
- ½ cup creamy peanut butter
- 1 cup sugar
- ½ teaspoon baking powder
- ⅛ teaspoon salt
- 1 egg
- 1 teaspoon vanilla
- 2 cups all-purpose flour
- About 21 bite-size chocolate-covered peanut butter cups, halved
- Unsweetened cocoa powder (optional)

1 Preheat oven to 375°F. In a large mixing bowl combine butter and peanut butter. Beat with an electric mixer on medium to high speed for 30 seconds. Add sugar, baking powder, and salt. Beat until combined, scraping bowl occasionally. Beat in egg and vanilla until combined. Beat in as much of the flour as you can with the mixer. Using a wooden spoon, stir in any remaining flour. If necessary, cover and chill dough about 30 minutes or until easy to handle.

2 Shape dough into 1½-inch balls. Press a peanut butter cup half into each ball and shape dough around peanut butter cup to enclose; roll gently to reshape into balls. Place balls 2 inches apart on an ungreased cookie sheet.

3 Bake for 8 to 10 minutes or until edges are firm and bottoms are very light brown. Transfer cookies to a wire rack and let cool. If desired, sprinkle cookies with cocoa powder. **MAKES ABOUT 42 COOKIES**

TO MAKE AHEAD AND STORE: Layer cookies between sheets of waxed paper in an airtight container; cover. Store at room temperature for up to 3 days or freeze for up to 3 months.

Peanut Crunch Blossoms

PREP **35 MINUTES**   CHILL **1 HOUR**   BAKE **10 MINUTES PER BATCH**   COOL **2 MINUTES PER BATCH**
OVEN **350°F**

½   **cup shortening**
½   **cup peanut butter**
1   **cup packed brown sugar**
¼   **cup unsweetened cocoa
      powder**
1   **teaspoon baking powder**
⅛   **teaspoon baking soda**
1   **egg**
2   **tablespoons milk**
1   **teaspoon vanilla**
1½ **cups all-purpose flour**
1   **cup finely ground peanuts**
48 **milk chocolate stars
      or candy kisses,
      unwrapped**

1 In a large mixing bowl combine
shortening and peanut butter.
Beat with an electric mixer on
medium to high speed for
30 seconds. Add brown sugar,
cocoa powder, baking powder,
and baking soda. Beat until
combined, scraping sides of bowl
occasionally. Beat in the egg, milk,
and vanilla until combined. Beat
in as much of the flour as you can

with the mixer. Using a wooden
spoon, stir in any remaining flour.
Cover and chill dough about
1 hour or until easy to handle.

2 Preheat oven to 350°F. Line a
cookie sheet with parchment
paper.

3 Place finely ground peanuts
in a small bowl. Shape dough
into 1-inch balls. Roll balls in
peanuts to coat. Place balls
2 inches apart on the prepared
cookie sheet. Bake for 10 to
12 minutes or until bottoms are
light brown. Immediately press a
chocolate star into the center of
each cookie. Cool on cookie sheet
for 2 minutes. Transfer cookies to
a wire rack and let cool. **MAKES
ABOUT 48 COOKIES**

TO MAKE AHEAD AND STORE: Layer
cookies between sheets of waxed
paper in an airtight container;
cover. Store at room temperature
for up to 3 days or freeze for up to
3 months.

Peanut Butter Truffles

PREP **50 MINUTES**   COOK **12 MINUTES**   CHILL **45 MINUTES**   FREEZE **15 MINUTES**

2   cups sugar
1   5-ounce can evaporated milk
½   cup butter
2   cups tiny marshmallows
¾   cup creamy peanut butter
½   teaspoon vanilla
12 ounces dark or bittersweet chocolate, chopped
2   teaspoons shortening
    Finely chopped peanuts (optional)

1 In a medium saucepan combine sugar, evaporated milk, and butter. Cook and stir over medium-high heat until boiling; reduce heat to medium.

Continue boiling at a moderate, steady rate for 12 minutes, stirring occasionally. Remove from heat.

2 Stir in the marshmallows, peanut butter, and vanilla. Transfer to a large bowl. Chill for 45 minutes to 1 hour or until mixture is firm.

3 Line a large cookie sheet with waxed paper or parchment paper. Shape the chilled peanut butter mixture into 1-inch balls; place on the prepared cookie sheet. Freeze for 15 minutes.

4 In a medium saucepan combine chocolate and shortening. Cook and stir over low heat until the chocolate melts. Using a fork, dip balls, one at a time, into melted chocolate, allowing excess chocolate to drip off. Place on a wire rack set over waxed paper. If desired, sprinkle with peanuts. Let stand until chocolate is set. ✳ **MAKES ABOUT 50 TRUFFLES**

✳*note If desired, when dark chocolate is set, drizzle truffles with a little melted milk chocolate. Let stand until milk chocolate is set.*

TO MAKE AHEAD AND STORE: Layer truffles between sheets of waxed paper in an airtight container; cover. Store in the refrigerator for up to 2 weeks.

Chocolate Bites

Though chocolate comes in many forms, all true chocolate starts with the fermented, dried, roasted, and cracked beans of the cacao tree. This process produces cocoa butter and an intensely flavored brown paste called chocolate liquor, or pure chocolate (cacao). The percentage of pure chocolate helps determine the flavor of the chocolate and how it is used. Here are some of the most common forms used for baking:

✦ Unsweetened chocolate: Also called baking chocolate, this is pure chocolate and cocoa butter with no added sugar. Use it only for baking.

✦ Bittersweet and semisweet chocolate: These two types of chocolate range between 35 percent and 70 percent pure chocolate, with added cocoa butter and sugar. You can use them interchangeably.

✦ Milk chocolate: This creamy and mild chocolate is made with 10 percent to 35 percent pure chocolate, with dry milk solids added. Do not use milk chocolate if a recipe calls for unsweetened, bittersweet, or semisweet chocolate.

✦ Unsweetened cocoa powder: This is pure chocolate with most of the cocoa butter removed. Dutch-process or European-style cocoa powder has been treated to neutralize acids, making it mellower in flavor.

Chocolate-PB Mini Sandwiches

PREP **45 MINUTES**   BAKE **7 MINUTES PER BATCH**   STAND **1 HOUR**   OVEN **350°F**

½   cup butter, softened
½   cup packed brown sugar
½   cup granulated sugar
½   teaspoon baking soda
½   teaspoon salt
¾   cup creamy peanut butter
¼   cup dry-roasted peanuts,
      finely chopped
1   egg
½   teaspoon vanilla
1½ cups all-purpose flour
¼   cup butter, softened
1½ cups creamy peanut
      butter
⅓   cup powdered sugar
3   tablespoons milk
2   tablespoons packed
      brown sugar
½   teaspoon vanilla
8   ounces bittersweet
      chocolate, coarsely
      chopped

1 Preheat oven to 350°F. In a large mixing bowl beat the ½ cup butter with an electric mixer on medium to high speed for 30 seconds. Add the ½ cup brown sugar, the granulated sugar, baking soda, and salt. Beat until combined, scraping sides of bowl occasionally. Beat in the ¾ cup peanut butter, the ¼ cup peanuts, the egg, and ½ teaspoon vanilla until combined. Beat in as much of the flour as you can with the mixer. Using a wooden spoon, stir in any remaining flour.

2 Shape dough into ¾-inch balls. Place balls 2 inches apart on an ungreased cookie sheet. Flatten balls by making crisscross marks with the tines of a sugared fork.

3 Bake for 7 to 9 minutes or until bottoms are light brown. Transfer cookies to a wire rack and let cool.

4 For filling, in a medium mixing bowl beat the ¼ cup butter with an electric mixer on medium to high speed for 30 seconds. Add the 1½ cups peanut butter, the powdered sugar, milk, the 2 tablespoons brown sugar, and ½ teaspoon vanilla. Beat until smooth and creamy.

5 To assemble, spread 1 teaspoon of the filling over the bottom of one cookie; press the bottom of a second cookie against the filling. Repeat with the remaining cookies and filling. Place sandwich cookies on a wire rack set over waxed paper.

6 In a small saucepan cook and stir chocolate over low heat until chocolate melts; cool slightly. Drizzle melted chocolate over sandwich cookies, allowing excess to drip down sides of cookies. Let stand about 1 hour or until chocolate is set. **MAKES ABOUT 72 SANDWICH COOKIES**

TO MAKE AHEAD AND STORE: Layer unfilled cookies between sheets of waxed paper in an airtight container; cover. Store at room temperature for up to 3 days or freeze for up to 3 months. To serve, thaw cookies if frozen. Prepare filling as directed. Assemble and decorate as directed.

PB Candy Shortbread

PREP **30 MINUTES**   BAKE **20 MINUTES PER BATCH**   COOL **2 MINUTES PER BATCH**   OVEN **325°F**

1   cup butter, softened
½   cup packed brown sugar
1   teaspoon vanilla
¼   teaspoon salt
2½ cups all-purpose flour
½   cup finely chopped chocolate-covered peanut butter cups (3 ounces)
1   recipe Semisweet Chocolate Drizzle (optional)
1   recipe Peanut Butter Drizzle (optional)
    Chopped chocolate-covered peanut butter cups or mini peanut butter cups (optional)*

1 Preheat oven to 325°F. In a large mixing bowl beat butter with an electric mixer on medium to high speed for 30 seconds. Add brown sugar, vanilla, and salt. Beat until combined, scraping sides of bowl occasionally. Beat in as much of the flour as you can with the mixer. Using a wooden spoon, stir in any remaining flour and the chopped candy. If necessary, gently knead dough until it clings together.

2 On a lightly floured surface roll dough to ½-inch thickness. Using 1½-inch cookie cutters, cut dough into desired shapes. Place cutouts 1 inch apart on an ungreased cookie sheet.

3 Bake about 20 minutes or until bottoms just start to brown. Cool on cookie sheet for 2 minutes. Transfer cookies to a wire rack and let cool. If desired, drizzle with Semisweet Chocolate Drizzle and/or Peanut Butter Drizzle and garnish with additional chopped peanut butter cups or mini cups. **MAKES 30 COOKIES**

Semisweet Chocolate Drizzle: In a small saucepan combine ¾ cup semisweet chocolate pieces and 1 teaspoon shortening. Cook and stir over low heat until chocolate melts.

Peanut Butter Drizzle: In a small bowl combine 1 cup powdered sugar; 2 tablespoons creamy peanut butter; 1 teaspoon butter, softened; and ½ teaspoon vanilla. Stir in enough milk (2 to 3 tablespoons) to reach drizzling consistency.

*note Chocolate-covered peanut butter cups are available in three sizes: regular, bite-size, and miniature. Look for the mini cups in the baking or candy aisle of your supermarket.

TO MAKE AHEAD AND STORE: Layer undecorated cookies between sheets of waxed paper in an airtight container; cover. Store at room temperature for up to 3 days or freeze for up to 3 months. To serve, thaw cookies if frozen. If desired, top with Semisweet Chocolate Drizzle and/or Peanut Butter Drizzle and peanut butter cups.

Smaller Is Better

When garnishing cookies with chocolate-covered peanut butter cups, look for bite-size and mini versions of candies that are sold in bags in the supermarket's candy aisle. Cut the bite-size cups in halves or fourths; each bite will offer more of the handsomely ridged chocolate sides than if you used chopped regular-size cups. The mini versions need not be cut—they're just the right size to top your cookies in one scrumptious piece.

Ultimate Tassies

PREP **40 MINUTES**   CHILL **1 HOUR**   BAKE **6 MINUTES PER BATCH**   COOL **5 MINUTES**   OVEN **375°F**

½   cup butter, softened
1   3-ounce package cream cheese, softened
3   tablespoons unsweetened cocoa powder
1   tablespoon granulated sugar
1   cup all-purpose flour
½   cup peanut butter
⅓   cup butter, softened
1   teaspoon vanilla
2   cups powdered sugar
1   to 2 tablespoons milk
2   tablespoons unsweetened cocoa powder

1 In a medium mixing bowl beat the ½ cup butter and cream cheese with an electric mixer on medium to high speed for 30 seconds. Add the 3 tablespoons cocoa powder and the granulated sugar. Beat until combined, scraping sides of bowl occasionally. Beat in as much of the flour as you can with the mixer. Using a wooden spoon, stir in any remaining flour (dough will be crumbly). Form dough into a ball. Cover and chill dough about 1 hour or until easy to handle.

2 Preheat oven to 375°F. Shape dough into 24 balls. Press balls evenly into the bottoms and up the sides of 24 ungreased 1¾-inch muffin cups. Gently prick dough with a fork. Bake for 6 to 8 minutes or until pastry shells are set and dry (shells will puff during baking). Cool in pan on a wire rack for 5 minutes. Gently remove shells from cups; cool completely on wire rack.

3 For fillings, in a large mixing bowl beat peanut butter, the ⅓ cup butter, and the vanilla with an electric mixer on medium speed for 30 seconds. Gradually beat in the powdered sugar. Beat in enough milk to make a filling of piping consistency.

4 Place half of the peanut butter mixture into a medium bowl. Add the 2 tablespoons cocoa powder; whisk until combined. If necessary, whisk in additional milk to reach piping consistency.

5 In a large pastry bag fitted with a star tip, spoon the cocoa filling down one half of the bag. Spoon the peanut butter filling down the other half of the bag. Pipe swirls of the fillings into pastry shells. **MAKES 24 TASSIES**

TO MAKE AHEAD AND STORE: Place tassies in a single layer in an airtight container; cover. Store in the refrigerator for up to 3 days or freeze for up to 3 months.

In a *twinkling*

After the baked cups have cooled, stir 4 ounces bittersweet chocolate with 1 teaspoon shortening over low heat until chocolate melts. Dip the bottoms and halfway up the sides in melted mixture. Place the cups on a wire rack, bottom sides up, and allow the chocolate to dry before filling as directed.

Chocolate–Peanut Butter Shortbread Bites

PREP **35 MINUTES**   BAKE **20 MINUTES PER BATCH**   COOL **5 MINUTES PER BATCH**   OVEN **350°F**

1½   cups all-purpose flour

⅓   cup sugar

¼   cup unsweetened cocoa powder

⅔   cup butter, cut up

¼   cup creamy peanut butter

½   cup semisweet chocolate pieces

3   teaspoons shortening

½   cup peanut butter–flavor pieces

1 Preheat oven to 325°F. In a food processor combine flour, sugar, and cocoa powder. Cover and process with on-off pulses until combined. Add butter and peanut butter. Cover and process with on-off pulses just until

mixture starts to cling. Remove dough from processor and form into a ball.

2 On a lightly floured surface roll dough to ½-inch thickness. Using 1- to 2-inch cookie cutters, cut dough into desired shapes. Place cutouts 1 inch apart on an ungreased cookie sheet.

3 Bake for 20 to 25 minutes or until set. Cool on cookie sheet for 5 minutes. Transfer cookies to a wire rack set over waxed paper and let cool.

4 In a small microwave-safe bowl combine chocolate pieces and 1½ teaspoons of the shortening. Microwave, uncovered,

on 50 percent power (medium) about 2 minutes or until chocolate melts, stirring once. In another small microwave-safe bowl, combine peanut butter pieces and the remaining 1½ teaspoons shortening. Microwave, uncovered, on 50 percent power (medium) about 2 minutes or until peanut butter pieces melt, stirring once. Drizzle both mixtures over tops of cookies. Let stand until drizzle is set. **MAKES ABOUT 32 COOKIES**

TO MAKE AHEAD AND STORE: Layer cookies between sheets of waxed paper in an airtight container; cover. Store at room temperature for up to 3 days or freeze for up to 3 months.

Two-Tone Peanut Butter Slices

PREP **40 MINUTES**   CHILL **2 HOURS**   BAKE **8 MINUTES PER BATCH**   OVEN **375°F**

- ¾ cup creamy peanut butter
- ½ cup butter, softened
- ½ cup granulated sugar
- ½ cup packed brown sugar
- ½ teaspoon baking powder
- ½ teaspoon baking soda
- 1 egg
- 1 teaspoon vanilla
- 1½ cups all-purpose flour
- 1½ ounces unsweetened chocolate, melted and slightly cooled

1 In a large mixing bowl beat peanut butter and butter with an electric mixer on medium to high speed for 30 seconds. Add granulated sugar, brown sugar, baking powder, and baking soda. Beat until combined, scraping sides of bowl occasionally. Beat in the egg and vanilla until combined. Beat in as much of the flour as you can with the mixer. Using a wooden spoon, stir in any remaining flour.

2 Divide dough in half. Stir melted chocolate into one portion of the dough. Divide each dough portion in half. On a lightly floured surface roll each portion of dough into a 10-inch log. Wrap and chill logs for 1 to 2 hours or until firm.

3 Cut logs in half lengthwise. Place the cut side of one peanut butter log and the cut side of one chocolate log together; press to seal. Roll the log lightly to smooth seams.

Repeat with remaining log halves. Wrap and chill logs for 1 to 2 hours or until firm.

4 Preheat oven to 375°F. Cut two-tone logs into ¼-inch-thick slices. Place slices 1 inch apart on an ungreased cookie sheet. Bake about 8 minutes or until edges are light brown and slightly firm. Transfer cookies to a wire rack and let cool. **MAKES ABOUT 120 COOKIES**

TO MAKE AHEAD AND STORE: Layer cookies between sheets of waxed paper in an airtight container; cover. Store at room temperature for up to 3 days or freeze for up to 3 months.

In a *twinkling*

To underscore the peanutty flavor of the peanut butter side, sprinkle that side of each cookie with chopped cocktail peanuts before baking.

Peanut Butter and Banana Drops

PREP **30 MINUTES**   BAKE **8 MINUTES PER BATCH**   OVEN **375°F**

1   16.5-ounce package refrigerated peanut butter cookie dough
1   cup dried banana chips, coarsely crushed
1   cup semisweet chocolate pieces
¼   cup turbinado sugar, demerara sugar, or colored coarse sugar

1 Preheat oven to 375°F. In a large resealable plastic bag combine cookie dough, banana chips, and chocolate pieces. Seal bag; knead with your hands until dough is well mixed. Remove dough from bag.

2 Place sugar in a small bowl. Shape dough into 1-inch balls. Roll balls in sugar to coat. Place balls 2 inches apart on an ungreased cookie sheet. Flatten balls slightly.

3 Bake for 8 to 10 minutes or until edges are golden brown. Transfer cookies to a wire rack and let cool. **MAKES ABOUT 40 COOKIES**

TO MAKE AHEAD AND STORE: Layer cookies between sheets of waxed paper in an airtight container; cover. Store at room temperature for up to 3 days or freeze for up to 3 months.

Pick a Peanut Butter

A few tips to help you choose which peanut butter to bake with:

+ In testing these recipes, the test kitchen used regular (hydrogenated) peanut butter—the popular, time-honored, easily spreadable product that has been making its way into PB&J sandwiches for generations.

+ Chunky versions of peanut butter, which contain small bits of crushed peanuts, may be used interchangeably with creamy versions.

+ Natural peanut butters can be a bit tricky as a baking ingredient. These products are nonhydrogenated, which results in the oil separating and rising to the top of the jar. If using natural peanut butter, be sure to stir it vigorously before adding it to recipes. Also note that the test kitchen has found that natural peanut butter can sometimes result in drier cookies.

Über-Doober Peanut Butter Brownies

PREP **30 MINUTES**   BAKE **30 MINUTES**   OVEN **350°F**

4   ounces bittersweet chocolate, coarsely chopped

¼   cup butter, cut up

¼   cup peanut butter

1   cup packed brown sugar

2   eggs

1   teaspoon vanilla

⅔   cup all-purpose flour

¼   teaspoon baking soda

⅛   teaspoon salt

1   cup chopped chocolate-covered peanut butter cups

1   recipe Nutty Frosting

1 In a medium saucepan combine bittersweet chocolate, butter, and peanut butter. Cook and stir over low heat until melted. Cool.

2 Preheat oven to 350°F. Line an 8x8x2-inch baking pan with foil, extending the foil over the edges of the pan. Grease foil.

3 Stir brown sugar into cooled chocolate mixture. Add eggs, one at a time, beating with a wooden spoon after each addition. Stir in vanilla. In a small bowl stir together flour, baking soda, and salt. Add flour mixture to chocolate mixture; stir just until combined. Stir in chopped peanut butter cups. Spoon the batter into the prepared baking pan, spreading evenly.

4 Bake about 30 minutes or until set. Cool in pan on a wire rack. Spread Nutty Frosting evenly over brownies. Use the foil to lift the uncut brownies out of the pan. Place on a cutting board; cut into brownies. MAKES 24 BROWNIES

Nutty Frosting: In a medium mixing bowl combine ½ cup peanut butter, ½ cup softened butter, 1 tablespoon milk, and 1 teaspoon vanilla. Beat with an electric mixer on medium speed until combined. Gradually beat in 2 cups powdered sugar.

TO MAKE AHEAD AND STORE: Layer brownies between sheets of waxed paper in an airtight container; cover. Store in the refrigerator for up to 3 days or freeze for up to 3 months.

In a *twinkling*

After frosting, sprinkle with additional chopped chocolate-covered peanut butter cups.

Peanut Butter and Toffee Bars

PREP **20 MINUTES**   BAKE **15 MINUTES**   OVEN **350°F**

1½   **cups quick-cooking oats**
¾   **cup all-purpose flour**
⅔   **cup packed brown sugar**
¼   **teaspoon baking soda**
⅓   **cup butter**
⅓   **cup creamy peanut butter**
16   **ounces dark chocolate, chopped**
⅔   **cup creamy peanut butter**
1   **cup toffee pieces**

1 Preheat oven to 350°F. Line a 13x9x2-inch baking pan with foil, extending the foil over the edges of the pan.

2 In a large bowl stir together the oats, flour, brown sugar, and baking soda. In a small saucepan combine the butter and the ⅓ cup peanut butter. Cook over low heat until smooth, stirring occasionally. Add the melted peanut butter mixture to the oats mixture. Stir until well combined. Press the oats mixture evenly onto the bottom of the prepared baking pan. Bake about 15 minutes or until golden brown. Place pan on a wire rack.

3 In a large saucepan combine the dark chocolate and the ⅔ cup peanut butter. Cook over low heat until smooth, stirring occasionally. Spread the chocolate mixture evenly over the warm crust. Sprinkle toffee pieces evenly over the chocolate mixture. Cool in pan on a wire rack until chocolate is set. Use the foil to lift the uncut bars out of the pan. Place on a cutting board; cut into bars. **MAKES 24 BARS**

TO MAKE AHEAD AND STORE: Place bars in a single layer in an airtight container; cover. Store in the refrigerator for up to 3 days.

gift It

Make the Cut

Use decorative scissors found at crafts and scrapbooking supply stores to cut pretty papers into wide strips. Wrap each bar individually and tie with string for darling last-minute gifts.

Buckeye Bars

PREP **20 MINUTES**   BAKE **25 MINUTES**   OVEN **350°F**

- 1   **19.5-ounce package brownie mix**
- 2   **eggs**
- ⅓   **cup vegetable oil**
- 1   **cup chopped peanuts**
- 1   **14-ounce can sweetened condensed milk**
- ½   **cup peanut butter**

1 Preheat oven to 350°F. Line a 13x9x2-inch baking pan with foil, extending the foil over the edges of the pan. Lightly grease foil.

2 In a large mixing bowl combine brownie mix, eggs, and oil. Beat with an electric mixer on medium speed until combined. Stir in peanuts. Spoon half of the brownie mixture into the prepared baking pan, spreading evenly.

3 In a medium bowl whisk together the sweetened condensed milk and peanut butter until smooth. Spoon over brownie mixture in pan, spreading evenly. Flatten spoonfuls of the remaining brownie mixture with your fingers and place on top of the peanut butter mixture in the pan.

4 Bake for 25 to 30 minutes or until the top is set and edges are light brown. Cool in pan on a wire rack. Use the foil to lift the uncut bars out of the pan. Place on a cutting board; cut into bars. **MAKES 32 BARS**

TO MAKE AHEAD AND STORE: Layer bars between sheets of waxed paper in an airtight container; cover. Store at room temperature for up to 3 days or freeze for up to 3 months.

Yummy No-Bake Bars

PREP **30 MINUTES** CHILL **1 HOUR**

1 cup granulated sugar
1 cup light corn syrup
2 cups peanut butter
3 cups crisp rice cereal
3 cups cornflakes
¾ cup butter, cut up
4 cups powdered sugar
2 4-serving-size packages vanilla instant pudding mix
¼ cup milk
1 12-ounce package (2 cups) semisweet chocolate pieces
½ cup butter, cut up

1 Line a 15x10x1-inch baking pan with foil, extending the foil over the edges of the pan.

2 In a large saucepan combine granulated sugar and corn syrup; cook and stir over medium-high heat just until mixture boils around edges. Cook and stir for 1 minute more. Remove from heat. Stir in peanut butter until melted. Using a wooden spoon, stir in rice cereal and cornflakes until coated. Press cereal mixture evenly onto the bottom of the prepared baking pan.

3 For pudding layer, in a medium saucepan melt the ¾ cup butter. Stir in the powdered sugar, pudding mix, and milk. Spread pudding mixture evenly over cereal layer in pan.

4 For frosting, in a small saucepan combine chocolate pieces and the ½ cup butter; cook and stir over low heat until chocolate melts. Spread frosting evenly over pudding layer. Loosely cover and chill about 1 hour or until frosting is set.

5 To serve, use the foil to lift the uncut bars out of the pan. Place on a cutting board; cut into bars. **MAKES 64 BARS**

TO MAKE AHEAD AND STORE: Layer bars between sheets of waxed paper in an airtight container; cover. Store in the refrigerator for up to 2 days.

No-Stick Trick

When baking bar cookies, lining the pan with foil helps keep the bars from sticking to the pan; it also allows you to easily lift the cooled bars out of the pan before cutting them. Here's how to do it:

+ Turn the pan upside down and shape foil over the outside bottom of the pan and up its sides. You'll want to use a piece of foil that is large enough to extend 1 inch past the pan's shortest sides. These extra inches of foil will work as "handles," allowing you to lift the bars out of the pan once they're baked and cooled.

+ Gently lift the shaped foil off the pan.

+ Turn the pan over and fit the shaped foil into it. Grease and flour the foil if directed.

TRIPLE-DECKER DECADENCE, PAGE 116

rich, dark
& chocolate

Need some sure-fire crowd-pleasers on your Christmas cookie platter? You can't go wrong with chocolate! Whether rich and creamy, or chewy, nutty, or crispy, each recipe stars this all-time favorite ingredient in irresistible ways.

★

Minty Fudge Sandwich Cookies

PREP **30 MINUTES**   CHILL **1 HOUR**   BAKE **7 MINUTES PER BATCH**   OVEN **350°F**

3½   cups all-purpose flour
⅔   cup unsweetened Dutch-process cocoa powder
2   teaspoons baking powder
1⅓   cups butter, softened
1½   cups sugar
¼   cup vegetable oil
2   eggs
1   tablespoon vanilla
Sugar
1   14-ounce can sweetened condensed milk
1   10-ounce package mint-flavor semisweet chocolate pieces
2   ounces unsweetened chocolate, chopped

1 In a medium bowl stir together the flour, cocoa powder, and baking powder. In a large mixing bowl beat butter with an electric mixer on medium to high speed for 30 seconds. Add the 1½ cups sugar and the oil. Beat until combined, scraping sides of bowl occasionally. Beat in the eggs and vanilla until combined. Beat in as much of the flour mixture as you can with the mixer. Using a wooden spoon, stir in any remaining flour mixture. Cover and chill about 1 hour or until dough is easy to handle.

2 Preheat oven to 350°F. Shape dough into 1-inch balls. Place balls 2 inches apart on an ungreased cookie sheet. Using the bottom of a wet glass dipped in additional sugar, slightly flatten each ball.

3 Bake for 7 to 9 minutes or just until firm. Transfer cookies to a wire rack and let cool.

4 For filling, in a small saucepan cook and stir the sweetened condensed milk, chocolate pieces, and unsweetened chocolate over medium heat until melted and smooth. Remove from heat; cool completely.

5 To assemble, spread a rounded measuring teaspoon of the filling onto the bottom of one cookie; lightly press the bottom of a second cookie against the filling. Repeat with the remaining cookies and filling. **MAKES ABOUT 36 SANDWICH COOKIES**

TO MAKE AHEAD AND STORE: Place sandwich cookies in a single layer in an airtight container; cover. Store at room temperature for up to 3 days or freeze for up to 3 months.

Mint Chips in a Minute

Look for mint-flavor semisweet chocolate pieces in the baking aisle of the supermarket to use in the filling for the Minty Cocoa Fudge Sandwich Cookies. If they're not available, substitute 1½ cups regular semisweet chocolate pieces and stir ¼ teaspoon mint extract into the melted chocolate mixture.

Super-Duper Chocolate Kisses

PREP **40 MINUTES**   BAKE **8 MINUTES PER BATCH**   OVEN **375°F**

1 **16.5-ounce package refrigerated chocolate chip cookie dough**

⅓ **cup unsweetened cocoa powder**

⅔ **cup chocolate-flavor sprinkles**

2 **tablespoons milk**

About 40 dark chocolate candy kisses, unwrapped

1 Preheat oven to 375°F. Lightly grease a cookie sheet. In a large resealable plastic bag combine cookie dough and cocoa powder. Seal bag; knead with your hands until well mixed. Remove dough from bag.

2 Place chocolate sprinkles in a shallow dish. Place milk in a second shallow dish. Shape dough into 1-inch balls. Dip balls in milk, then roll in sprinkles to coat. Place balls 2 inches apart on the prepared cookie sheet.

3 Bake about 8 minutes or until edges are firm. Immediately press a dark chocolate candy into the center of each cookie. Transfer cookies to a wire rack and let cool.
MAKES ABOUT 40 COOKIES

TO MAKE AHEAD AND STORE: Layer cookies between sheets of waxed paper in an airtight container; cover. Store at room temperature for up to 3 days or freeze for up to 3 months.

Dough Dos

When making the Super-Duper Chocolate Kisses, work with small amounts of the dough at a time during the shaping, dipping, and rolling stages. Leave the rest of the dough covered with plastic wrap to help prevent it from drying out.

Chocolate Blooms

PREP **40 MINUTES**   BAKE **8 MINUTES PER BATCH**   OVEN **350°F**

1½   cups all-purpose flour
¾   cup unsweetened Dutch-process cocoa powder
½   cup shortening
¼   cup butter, softened
1   cup packed brown sugar
½   teaspoon baking powder
¼   teaspoon salt
1   egg
1   teaspoon vanilla
1   cup miniature semisweet chocolate pieces
¾   cup finely chopped almonds (optional)
1   recipe Raspberry Ganache

1 Preheat oven to 350°F. In a small bowl stir together the flour and cocoa powder. In a large mixing bowl beat shortening and butter with an electric mixer on medium to high speed for 30 seconds. Add brown sugar, baking powder, and salt. Beat until combined, scraping sides of bowl occasionally. Beat in the egg and vanilla until combined. Beat in as much of the flour mixture as you can with the mixer. Using a wooden spoon, stir in any remaining flour mixture and the chocolate pieces.

2 Shape dough into 1-inch balls. If desired, roll balls in chopped almonds to coat. Place balls 1½ inches apart on an ungreased cookie sheet. Press your thumb into the center of each ball.

3 Bake for 8 to 10 minutes or until edges are set. If cookie centers puff during baking, re-press with the back of a small spoon. Transfer cookies to a wire rack and let cool. Spoon Raspberry Ganache evenly into the indentations in each each cookie. Let stand or chill until ganache is set. **MAKES ABOUT 56 COOKIES**

Raspberry Ganache: In a small microwave-safe bowl combine 6 ounces chopped (70 percent-cocao) dark chocolate, ⅓ cup whipping cream, and 1 tablespoon seedless raspberry jam. Microwave, uncovered, on 100 percent power (high) for 1 minute. Stir until smooth. If desired, stir in 1 tablespoon raspberry liqueur. Let stand about 15 minutes or until slightly thickened.

TO MAKE AHEAD AND STORE: Place cookies in a single layer in an airtight container; cover. Store in the refrigerator for up to 2 days. Or layer unfilled cookies between sheets of waxed paper in an airtight container; cover. Store at room temperature for up to 3 days or freeze for up to 3 months. Thaw cookies, if frozen. Fill cookies with Raspberry Ganache as directed.

In a *twinkling*

Make these cookies even more indulgent by adding a whole fresh raspberry to the center before the ganache sets.

Chocolate-Cherry-Walnut Thumbprints

PREP **40 MINUTES**   BAKE **8 MINUTES PER BATCH**   OVEN **350°F**

½ **cup semisweet chocolate pieces**

1 **tablespoon shortening**

2 **cups all-purpose flour**

1 **tablespoon unsweetened cocoa powder**

2 **teaspoons baking powder**

½ **teaspoon salt**

½ **cup butter, softened**

¾ **cup sugar**

1 **egg**

1 **tablespoon milk**

1 **teaspoon vanilla**

½ **cup finely chopped toasted walnuts**

¾ **cup cherry pie filling (with 36 to 40 cherries)**

¾ **cup semisweet chocolate pieces**

1 **tablespoon shortening**

1 Preheat oven to 350°F. Line a cookie sheet with parchment paper; set aside. In a small saucepan cook and stir the ½ cup chocolate pieces and 1 tablespoon shortening over low heat until chocolate melts. Cool.

2 In a medium bowl stir together the flour, cocoa powder, baking powder, and salt; set aside. In a large mixing bowl beat butter and sugar with an electric mixer on medium speed until fluffy. Add the cooled chocolate mixture. Beat until combined, scraping sides of bowl occasionally. Beat in the egg, milk, and vanilla until combined. Beat in as much of the flour mixture as you can with the mixer. Using a wooden spoon, stir in any remaining flour mixture.

3 Shape dough into 1-inch balls. Roll the balls in chopped walnuts to coat. Place balls 1 inch apart on the prepared cookie sheet. Press your thumb into the center of each ball. Bake for 8 to 10 minutes or until edges are firm. Transfer cookies to a wire rack and let cool.

4 Spoon a cherry with some of the sauce into the indentation in each cookie. In the same small saucepan cook and stir the ¾ cup chocolate pieces and 1 tablespoon shortening over low heat until chocolate melts. Drizzle chocolate over cookies. Let stand until chocolate is set. **MAKES 36 TO 40 COOKIES**

TO MAKE AHEAD AND STORE: Layer unfilled cookies between sheets of waxed paper in an airtight container; cover. Store at room temperature for up to 3 days or freeze for up to 3 months. Thaw cookies, if frozen. Fill and drizzle cookies as directed.

Storing Chocolate

Keep chocolate in a tightly covered container or sealed plastic bag in a cool, dry place. If stored at higher than 70°F, chocolate may "bloom" or develop a harmless gray film (you can still use the chocolate for baking if this occurs). Keep cocoa powder in a tightly covered container in that same cool, dry place. Bars and cacoa powder keep for up to 1 year.

Chocolate Bonbon Pops

PREP **20 MINUTES**   FREEZE **30 MINUTES**   CHILL **1 HOUR**

18 chocolate sandwich cookies with creme filling

¾ cup pecans, toasted

3 tablespoons orange juice

2 tablespoons unsweetened cocoa powder

2 tablespoons light corn syrup

20 lollipop sticks

1 cup milk chocolate pieces, white baking pieces, or semisweet chocolate pieces

1 teaspoon shortening

1 In a food processor combine cookies and pecans. Cover and process with on-off pulses until cookies are crushed. Add orange juice, cocoa powder, and corn syrup. Cover and process until combined.

2 Line a large cookie sheet with parchment paper. Shape cookie mixture into 1-inch balls. Place balls on the prepared cookie sheet; insert a lollipop stick into each ball. Freeze for 30 minutes.

3 In a small saucepan cook and stir chocolate pieces and shortening over low heat until chocolate melts. Spoon the melted chocolate over pops.

Loosely cover and chill about 1 hour or until chocolate is set. **MAKES ABOUT 20 POPS**

TO MAKE AHEAD AND STORE: Place pops in a single layer in an airtight container; cover. Store in the refrigerator for up to 7 days. Do not freeze.

In a *twinkling*

After spooning the melted chocolate over the cookie balls, sprinkle with a variety of ingredients, such as toasted coconut, nonpareils, decorative candy sprinkles, chopped nuts, chopped candy-coated chocolate pieces, crushed candy canes, crushed gingersnaps, or chopped chocolate-covered espresso beans. (Allow the chocolate coating to cool slightly—but not set up—before sprinkling with ingredients that can melt.)

Chocolate Crinkles

PREP **35 MINUTES**   COOL **15 MINUTES**   CHILL **2 HOURS**   BAKE **10 MINUTES PER BATCH**   OVEN **375°F**

- 4   ounces unsweetened chocolate, chopped
- ½   cup shortening
- 3   eggs, lightly beaten
- 2   cups granulated sugar
- 2   teaspoons baking powder
- 2   teaspoons vanilla
- ¼   teaspoon salt
- 2   cups all-purpose flour
- ⅔   cup powdered sugar

1 In a small saucepan cook and stir chocolate and shortening over low heat until chocolate melts. Cool for 15 minutes.

2 In a large bowl combine the eggs, sugar, baking powder, vanilla, and salt. Stir in chocolate mixture. Gradually stir in flour until thoroughly combined. Cover and chill dough about 2 hours or until easy to handle.

3 Preheat oven to 375°F. Lightly grease a cookie sheet. Shape dough into 1-inch balls. Roll balls in powdered sugar to generously coat. Place balls 2 inches apart on the prepared cookie sheet. Bake about 10 minutes or until edges are just set. Transfer cookies to a wire rack and let cool. **MAKES 60 COOKIES**

TO MAKE AHEAD AND STORE: Layer cookies between sheets of waxed paper in an airtight container; cover. Store at room temperature for up to 3 days or freeze for up to 3 months.

gift It

Useful Utensil

A shiny metal colander, lined with waxed paper and tied with a satin ribbon, makes a sparkling vessel in which to present cookies. And what cook wouldn't appreciate an extra colander to have on hand?

Rocky Road Tassies

PREP **40 MINUTES**   CHILL **30 MINUTES**   BAKE **21 MINUTES**   COOL **5 MINUTES**   OVEN **325°F**

½ cup butter, softened
1 3-ounce package cream cheese, softened
1 cup all-purpose flour
½ cup miniature semisweet chocolate pieces
2 tablespoons butter
⅓ cup sugar
1 egg
1 teaspoon vanilla
¼ cup chopped pecans, toasted
2 tablespoons miniature semisweet chocolate pieces
24 tiny marshmallows

1 In a medium mixing bowl beat the ½ cup butter and the cream cheese with an electric mixer on medium speed until combined. Beat in flour on low speed just until combined. Cover and chill dough for 30 to 60 minutes or until easy to handle.

2 Preheat oven to 325°F. Shape dough into 24 balls. Press each ball into the bottoms and up the sides of 24 ungreased 1¾-inch muffin cups.

3 For filling, in a small saucepan cook and stir the ½ cup chocolate pieces and the 2 tablespoons butter over low heat until chocolate melts. Remove from heat. Whisk in the sugar, egg, and vanilla. Spoon filling evenly into the pastry-lined muffin cups.

4 Bake for 20 to 25 minutes or until pastry is golden brown and filling puffs. Immediately top tassies evenly with pecans, the 2 tablespoons chocolate pieces, and the marshmallows. Bake for 1 to 2 minutes more or until marshmallows are soft. Cool in pan on a wire rack for 5 minutes. Carefully transfer tassies to a wire rack and let cool. **MAKES 24 TASSIES**

TO MAKE AHEAD AND STORE: Place tassies in a single layer in an airtight container; cover. Store in the refrigerator for up to 3 days or freeze for up to 3 months.

Almond-Hazelnut-Chocolate Crescents

PREP **30 MINUTES**   CHILL **2 HOURS**   BAKE **15 MINUTES PER BATCH**   OVEN **350°F**

1¾   cups all-purpose flour
1¼   cups finely ground almonds
½   cup finely ground toasted hazelnuts (filberts)
½   cup unsweetened cocoa powder
1¼   cups butter, softened
1   cup powdered sugar
1   teaspoon vanilla
6   ounces semisweet chocolate, chopped

1 In a medium bowl stir together the flour, almonds, hazelnuts, and cocoa powder. In a large mixing bowl beat butter with an electric mixer on medium to high speed for 30 seconds. Add sugar and vanilla. Beat until combined, scraping sides of bowl occasionally. Add the flour mixture, beating on low speed just until combined. Cover and chill dough about 2 hours or until easy to handle.

2 Preheat oven to 350°F. Shape dough into 1-inch balls. Roll each ball into a short log with tapered ends; curve log slightly into a crescent shape. Place crescents 1 inch apart on an ungreased cookie sheet.

3 Bake for 15 to 17 minutes or until edges are set. Transfer cookies to a wire rack and let cool. In a small heavy saucepan cook and stir chocolate over low heat until chocolate melts. Drizzle chocolate over cooled cookies. Let stand until chocolate is set. **MAKES ABOUT 48 COOKIES**

TO MAKE AHEAD AND STORE: Layer cookies between sheets of waxed paper in an airtight container; cover. Store at room temperature for up to 3 days or freeze for up to 3 months.

Reindeer Cookies

PREP **40 MINUTES**   BAKE **8 MINUTES PER BATCH**   OVEN **350°F**

½ cup butter, softened
½ cup shortening
1 cup sugar
¼ cup unsweetened cocoa powder
1 teaspoon baking powder
¼ teaspoon salt
1 egg
1 teaspoon vanilla
2¼ cups all-purpose flour
Canned chocolate frosting
Miniature pretzel twists
Halved red candied cherries or red candy-coated chocolate-covered peanuts

1 In a medium mixing bowl beat butter and shortening with an electric mixer on medium to high speed for 30 seconds. Add sugar, cocoa powder, baking powder, and salt. Beat until combined, scraping sides of bowl occasionally. Beat in the egg and vanilla until combined. Beat in as much of the flour as you can with the mixer. Using a wooden spoon, stir in any remaining flour. Divide dough in half. If necessary, cover and chill dough about 1 hour or until easy to handle.

2 Preheat oven to 350°F. On a lightly floured surface roll each dough half to ¼-inch thickness. Using a 2-inch triangular cookie cutter, cut out dough. (Or roll each dough half into an 8-inch square. Cut each big square into sixteen 2-inch squares. Cut each 2-inch square in half diagonally to make 64 triangles total.) Place triangles 2 inches apart on an ungreased cookie sheet.

3 Bake for 8 to 10 minutes or until edges are light brown. Transfer cookies to a wire rack and let cool.

4 Spoon frosting into a pastry bag fitted with a small round tip. For each reindeer, pipe a little frosting on two pretzels; attach pretzels to two points on each cookie for antlers. Use frosting to attach a cherry half to the opposite point for a nose. Pipe two dots of frosting for the eyes. Let stand until frosting is set.

MAKES 64 COOKIES

TO MAKE AHEAD AND STORE: Layer plain cookies between sheets of waxed paper in an airtight container; cover. Store at room temperature for up to 3 days or freeze for up to 3 months. Thaw cookies, if frozen. Decorate cookies as directed.

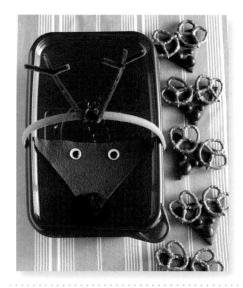

gift It

Jolly Reindeer Wrap

Kids can help make these cookies—as well as a cute way to present them. For the package, gather a red rectangular plastic storage container, a child's headband, some brown felt, craft eyeballs, a black pom-pom, and brown pipe cleaners. Fill the container with the cookies. Cut a piece of brown felt into a triangle the width of the lid; attach it to the lid of the container using fabric glue. Add two craft eyes and a black pom-pom for the nose to the felt using fabric glue. To create the antlers, twist a 3-inch piece of pipe cleaner around each end of one long pipe cleaner. Twist the long pipe cleaner around the headband and place the headband around the width of the container.

German Chocolate Wafer Cookies

START TO FINISH **30 MINUTES**

1   14-ounce package chocolate creme–filled sandwich cookies

1   16-ounce can chocolate frosting

1   15-ounce can coconut-pecan frosting (German chocolate cake frosting)

1 Place cookies on a wire rack set over waxed paper.

2 In a medium microwave-safe bowl microwave chocolate frosting, uncovered, on 100 percent power (high) for 30 seconds; stir. Microwave about 30 seconds more or until frosting is of drizzling consistency, stirring every 10 seconds.

3 Dip each cookie halfway into melted chocolate frosting, covering one large flat surface of cookie with chocolate. Gently shake off any excess chocolate. Place cookies on the wire rack. Let stand until frosting is set.

4 Top each cookie with 1 teaspoon of the coconut-pecan frosting. If desired, drizzle with some of the remaining melted chocolate frosting. **MAKES 40 COOKIES**

TO MAKE AHEAD AND STORE: Layer cookies between sheets of waxed paper in an airtight container; cover. Store in the refrigerator for up to 3 days or freeze for up to 3 months.

Chocolate Chip Cookie Dunkers

PREP **45 MINUTES**   BAKE **45 MINUTES**   COOL **1 HOUR**   OVEN **350°F/325°F**

¼ cup butter, softened
¼ cup shortening
½ cup packed brown sugar
¼ cup granulated sugar
¼ teaspoon baking soda
1 egg
1 teaspoon vanilla
1¼ cups all-purpose flour
½ cup miniature semisweet chocolate pieces
½ cup chopped walnuts, pecans, or hazelnuts (filberts) (optional)
6 ounces semisweet chocolate, chopped
1 tablespoon shortening

1 Preheat oven to 350°F. Line a 9x9x2-inch baking pan with foil, extending the foil over the sides of the pan.

2 In a medium mixing bowl beat butter and the ¼ cup shortening with an electric mixer on medium to high speed for 30 seconds. Add brown sugar, granulated sugar, and baking soda. Beat until combined, scraping sides of bowl occasionally. Beat in the egg and vanilla until combined. Beat in as much of the flour as you can with the mixer. Using a wooden spoon, stir in any remaining flour, the miniature semisweet chocolate pieces, and, if desired, nuts. Press dough evenly onto the bottom of the prepared baking pan.

3 Bake for 25 to 30 minutes or until golden brown and center is set. Cool in pan on a wire rack for 1 hour. Reduce oven temperature to 325°F.

4 Use the foil to lift the uncut cookies out of the pan. Place on a cutting board. Using a serrated knife, cut into 9x½-inch strips. Place strips, cut sides down, 1 inch apart on an ungreased cookie sheet. Bake for 10 minutes. Carefully turn strips over. Bake about 10 minutes more or until crisp. Cool completely on cookie sheet on a wire rack. If desired, trim ends.

5 In a small microwave-safe bowl combine the chopped chocolate and 1 tablespoon shortening. Microwave, uncovered, on 50 percent power (medium) for 2 to 3 minutes or until chocolate melts, stirring twice. Brush or spread melted chocolate on one end of each cookie, letting excess drip down sides of cookie. Let stand until chocolate is set.
MAKES 18 COOKIES

TO MAKE AHEAD AND STORE: Layer cookies between sheets of waxed paper in an airtight container; cover. Store at room temperature for up to 3 days or freeze for up to 3 months.

Chocolate-Hazelnut "Mousse" Cookies

PREP **40 MINUTES** FREEZE **30 MINUTES** BAKE **6 MINUTES PER BATCH** COOL **2 MINUTES PER BATCH**
OVEN **375°F**

2	ounces (60% cocao) dark chocolate
¾	cup all-purpose flour
¼	teaspoon baking soda
⅛	teaspoon salt
¼	cup butter, softened
½	cup packed brown sugar
2	teaspoons vanilla
1	recipe Chocolate-Hazelnut "Mousse"
72	toasted hazelnuts (filberts)

1 In a small saucepan cook and stir the dark chocolate over low heat until chocolate melts; let cool. In a small bowl stir together the flour, baking soda, and salt; set aside.

2 In a large mixing bowl beat butter with an electric mixer on medium to high speed for 30 seconds. Add brown sugar Beat until combined, scraping sides of bowl occasionally. Beat in the vanilla and cooled chocolate until combined. Beat in as much of the flour mixture as you can with the mixer. Using a wooden spoon, stir in any remaining flour mixture.

3 Shape dough into two 9-inch logs. Wrap each log in plastic wrap or waxed paper; freeze about 30 minutes or until firm.

4 Preheat oven to 375°F. Line a large cookie sheet with parchment paper. Cut logs crosswise into ¼-inch-thick slices. Place slices 1 inch apart on the prepared cookie sheet. Bake about 6 minutes or until edges are set. Cool on cookie sheet for 2 minutes. Transfer cookies to a wire rack and let cool.

5 Spoon Chocolate-Hazelnut "Mousse" into a pastry bag fitted with a star tip. Pipe "Mousse" onto each cookie. Top each with a toasted hazelnut.
MAKES ABOUT 72 COOKIES

Chocolate-Hazelnut "Mousse":
In a medium mixing bowl beat 3 tablespoons softened butter and ⅓ cup chocolate hazelnut spread with an electric mixer on medium to high speed until combined. Gradually beat in 1 cup powdered sugar until smooth. Beat in 2 to 3 teaspoons milk to make a mixture of piping consistency.

TO MAKE AHEAD AND STORE: Layer plain cookies between sheets of waxed paper in an airtight container; cover. Store in the refrigerator for up to 3 days or freeze for up to 3 months. Thaw cookies, if frozen. Top cookies with "Mousse" and hazelnuts as directed.

How to Skin Hazelnuts

When baking with hazelnuts, your goodies will test better if you remove their bitter brown skin before adding them to recipes. To do this, start by spreading shelled hazelnuts on an ungreased baking sheet; toast in a 350°F oven for 5 to 10 minutes, or until the skins begin to flake, stirring once or twice. Check often to make sure they aren't getting overly brown. Remove the nuts from the oven and place a handful of nuts at a time in a clean, dry cotton kitchen towel. Rub vigorously until the skins come off. If you like, put the skinned nuts in a fine-mesh sieve to shake out the little pieces of skin that can look like dirt. Repeat with remaining nuts.

Triple-Decker Decadence

PREP **40 MINUTES** CHILL **1 HOUR 30 MINUTES** BAKE **8 MINUTES PER BATCH** COOL **1 MINUTE PER BATCH**
OVEN **350°F**

1⅓ cups all-purpose flour
½ cup unsweetened cocoa powder
½ cup butter, softened
¾ cup granulated sugar
¼ cup packed dark brown sugar
½ teaspoon baking soda
⅛ teaspoon salt
⅛ teaspoon ground black pepper
1 egg
2 teaspoons vanilla
1 recipe Chocolate Ganache

1 In a small bowl stir together the flour and cocoa powder. In a large mixing bowl beat butter with an electric mixer on medium to high speed for 30 seconds. Add sugars, baking soda, salt, and pepper. Beat until combined, scraping sides of bowl occasionally. Beat in the egg and vanilla until combined. Beat in as much of the flour mixture as you can with the mixer. Using a wooden spoon, stir in any remaining flour mixture.

2 Divide dough in half. Shape each portion of dough into an 8-inch log. Wrap each log in plastic wrap or waxed paper; chill about 1 hour or until firm.

3 Preheat oven to 350°F. Cut logs crosswise into ¼-inch-thick slices. Place slices 2 inches apart on an ungreased cookie sheet. Bake about 8 minutes or until edges are set. Cool on cookie sheet for 1 minute. Transfer cookies to a wire rack and let cool.

4 To assemble cookies, spread 1 teaspoon Chocolate Ganache evenly onto the bottom of one cookie; press the bottom of a second cookie against the ganache. Spread 1 teaspoon Chocolate Ganache onto the top of sandwiched cookies; press the bottom of a third cookie against the ganache. Repeat with the remaining cookies and the ganache. Spoon the remaining ganache into a heavy resealable plastic bag and snip a small hole in one corner of the bag. Pipe the ganache over the tops of the cookie stacks. Chill until ganache is set. **MAKES ABOUT 14 COOKIE STACKS**

Chocolate Ganache: In a small microwave-safe bowl combine 6 ounces chopped bittersweet chocolate and ⅓ cup whipping cream. Microwave, uncovered, on 100 percent power (high) about 1 minute or until chocolate melts, stirring every 30 seconds. Let ganache stand about 30 minutes or until spreading consistency.

TO MAKE AHEAD AND STORE: Place cookies in a single layer in an airtight container; cover. Store in the refrigerator for up to 2 days. Or layer unfilled cookies between sheets of waxed paper in an airtight container; cover. Store at room temperature for up to 3 days or freeze for up to 3 months. Thaw cookies, if frozen. Assemble cookies as directed.

Toffee-Topped Fudge Brownie Tarts

PREP **30 MINUTES**   BAKE **12 MINUTES**   COOL **5 MINUTES**   OVEN **350°F**

- 3 **ounces unsweetened chocolate, chopped**
- ⅓ **cup butter, cut up**
- 1 **cup sugar**
- 2 **eggs, lightly beaten**
- 1 **teaspoon vanilla**
- ½ **cup all-purpose flour**
- ¼ **cup whipping cream**
- ½ **cup semisweet chocolate pieces**
- 3 **1.4-ounce bars chocolate-covered English toffee, chopped**

1 Preheat oven to 350°F. Grease twenty-four 1¾-inch muffin cups. In a medium saucepan cook and stir the unsweetened chocolate and butter over low heat until chocolate melts. Remove from heat. Add sugar, eggs, and vanilla. Using a wooden spoon, beat lightly just until combined. Stir in the flour until combined. Spoon a generous 1 tablespoon batter into each prepared muffin cup.

2 Bake for 12 minutes. Cool tarts in pan on wire rack for 5 minutes. Transfer tarts to a wire rack and let cool.

3 In a small saucepan heat the whipping cream over low heat just until simmering; remove from heat. Add chocolate pieces; stir until chocolate melts. Place chopped toffee in a shallow dish. Dip top of each tart into chocolate mixture, then into toffee, to coat. Let stand until chocolate is set.

MAKES 24 TARTS

TO MAKE AHEAD AND STORE: Place tarts in a single layer in an airtight container; cover. Store in the refrigerator for up to 3 days. Do not freeze.

Top It

Rich, fudgy chocolate meshes well with many ingredients, so consider topping these brownie tarts with other touches. Instead of English toffee, try fruit such as raspberries, a fresh strawberry slice, or a stemmed maraschino cherry. For a sophisticated touch, top each brownie with chocolate-dipped hazelnuts, chopped crystallized ginger, chocolate-covered espresso beans, or sliced glacé apricots. For a more whimsical touch, consider using chopped candy canes, mini malted milk balls, or chopped candy-coated chocolate pieces.

Double-Chocolate Chip Cookies

PREP **30 MINUTES**   BAKE **9 MINUTES PER BATCH**   COOL **2 MINUTES PER BATCH**   OVEN **350°F**

 4   ounces semisweet
      chocolate, chopped
 ½   cup butter, softened
 ½   cup shortening
1½   cups packed brown sugar
 1   teaspoon baking soda
 ½   teaspoon salt
 ½   teaspoon ground cinnamon
 2   eggs
 2   teaspoons vanilla
2½   cups all-purpose flour
 6   ounces (70% cocao) dark
      chocolate, coarsely
      chopped
 6   ounces semisweet
      chocolate, coarsely
      chopped
 1   cup chopped pecans,
      toasted

1 Preheat oven to 350°F. In a small saucepan cook and stir the 4 ounces semisweet chocolate over medium-low heat until chocolate melts; let cool.

2 In a large mixing bowl beat butter and shortening with an electric mixer on medium to high speed for 30 seconds. Add brown sugar, baking soda, salt, and cinnamon. Beat until combined, scraping sides of bowl occasionally. Beat in the cooled chocolate, the eggs, and vanilla until combined. Beat in as much of the flour as you can with the mixer. Using a wooden spoon, stir in any remaining flour, the dark chocolate, 6 ounces semisweet chocolate, and the nuts.

3 Drop dough by heaping teaspoons 2 inches apart onto an ungreased cookie sheet. Bake for 9 to 11 minutes or just until edges are set. Cool on cookie sheet for 2 minutes. Transfer cookies to a wire rack and let cool. **MAKES ABOUT 72 COOKIES**

TO MAKE AHEAD AND STORE: Layer cookies between sheets of waxed paper in an airtight container; cover. Store at room temperature for up to 1 week or freeze for up to 3 months.

How to Drop Dough

When a cookie recipe calls for dropping dough from a teaspoon or tablespoon, it is referring to flatware spoons rather than measuring spoons. To drop cookies, fill a spoon with cookie dough and use another spoon to push the dough onto the cookie sheet. You can also use a small cookie scoop, available at kitchenware shops, to ensure a uniform size and shape for every cookie in the batch.

Devilish Delights

PREP **25 MINUTES**   BAKE **8 MINUTES PER BATCH**   COOL **3 MINUTES PER BATCH**   OVEN **350°F**

6   tablespoons all-purpose flour
½   teaspoon baking powder
⅛   teaspoon salt
2   eggs
½   cup sugar
1   to 2 tablespoons coffee liqueur or strong brewed espresso
2   teaspoons vanilla
10 ounces espresso-flavor chocolate or bittersweet (67% cacao) chocolate, chopped
2   tablespoons butter
12 ounces (70% cacao) dark chocolate, chopped

1 Preheat oven to 350°F. Lightly grease a cookie sheet or line cookie sheet with parchment paper; set aside. In a small bowl stir together the flour, baking powder, and salt. In a large mixing bowl beat eggs, sugar, coffee liqueur, and vanilla with an electric mixer on medium speed until combined.

2 In a medium saucepan cook and stir the chopped espresso chocolate and butter over low heat until chocolate melts. Beat melted chocolate mixture into egg mixture until combined. Using a wooden spoon, stir in flour mixture just until combined. Stir in chopped dark chocolate.

3 Drop dough by heaping teaspoons onto the prepared cookie sheet. Bake for 8 to 9 minutes or until tops appear dry and centers remain soft. Cool on cookie sheet for 3 minutes. Transfer cookies to a wire rack and let cool. **MAKES ABOUT 36 COOKIES**

TO MAKE AHEAD AND STORE: Layer cookies between sheets of waxed paper in an airtight container; cover. Store at room temperature for up to 3 days or freeze for up to 3 months.

Espresso Express

If you don't have an espresso machine, you can purchase a cup of espresso to go from a local coffeehouse. You can also buy instant espresso powder and make as much as you need for a recipe, keeping the rest of the powder on hand for future baking projects.

Raspberry French Silk Bars

PREP **40 MINUTES**   BAKE **10 MINUTES**   CHILL **2 HOURS**   OVEN **375°F**

1   recipe Chocolate Crumb Crust

1   cup whipping cream

3   ounces semisweet chocolate, chopped

3   ounces bittersweet chocolate, chopped

⅓   cup sugar

⅓   cup butter

2   egg yolks, beaten

3   tablespoons crème de cacao or whipping cream

½   cup raspberry preserves or seedless raspberry jam

1   recipe Raspberry Ganache

32   fresh raspberries (optional)

1 Preheat oven to 375°F. Line a 13x9x2-inch baking pan with foil, extending the foil over the edges of the pan. Press Chocolate Crumb Crust evenly onto the bottom and slightly up the sides of the prepared baking pan. Bake about 10 minutes or until crust is set. Cool completely in pan on a wire rack.

2 Meanwhile, for filling, in a medium saucepan combine the whipping cream, chocolates, sugar, and butter. Cook and stir over low heat about 10 minutes or until chocolates melt. Remove from heat. Gradually stir half of the chocolate mixture into the beaten egg yolks. Add egg yolk mixture to chocolate mixture in saucepan. Cook and stir over medium-low heat about 5 minutes or until slightly thickened and bubbly.

3 Remove saucepan from heat. (Mixture may appear slightly curdled.) Stir in the crème de cacao. Place the saucepan in a bowl of ice water. Let stand about 20 minutes or until the chocolate mixture stiffens and becomes hard to stir, stirring occasionally. Transfer the filling to a medium mixing bowl.

4 Spread raspberry preserves evenly over the cooled Chocolate Crumb Crust. Beat filling with an electric mixer on medium to high speed for 2 to 3 minutes or until light and fluffy. Spread filling evenly over preserves. Cover and chill for 1 to 2 hours or until firm.

5 Remove bars from refrigerator. Spoon Raspberry Ganache over bars, gently spreading evenly. Cover and chill for 1 to 2 hours more or until ganache is set. Use the foil to lift the uncut bars out of the pan. Place on a cutting board; cut into bars. If desired, garnish bars with fresh raspberries. **MAKES 32 BARS**

Chocolate Crumb Crust: In a medium bowl stir together 2 cups finely crushed chocolate wafers, chocolate graham crackers, or other crisp chocolate cookies (about 38 cookies); ¼ cup all-purpose flour; and 2 tablespoons granulated sugar. Add ½ cup melted butter; stir until combined.

Raspberry Ganache: In a microwave-safe bowl combine 1 cup chopped semisweet chocolate or chocolate pieces, ⅓ cup whipping cream, and 1 tablespoon seedless raspberry jam. Microwave, uncovered, on 100 percent power (high) about 1 minute or until chocolate melts, stirring every 30 seconds. Let stand about 1 hour or until slightly thickened.

TO MAKE AHEAD AND STORE: Place bars in a single layer in an airtight container; cover. Store in the refrigerator for up to 3 days. Do not freeze.

Malt-Fudge Brownies

PREP **30 MINUTES**   BAKE **35 MINUTES**   OVEN **325°F**

- 1½ **cups all-purpose flour**
- ⅓ **cup malted milk powder**
- ½ **teaspoon salt**
- 1 **cup butter, cut up**
- 4 **ounces unsweetened chocolate, chopped**
- 2 **cups sugar**
- 4 **eggs**
- 1 **teaspoon vanilla**
- 1 **cup chopped walnuts, toasted**
- 4 **ounces malted milk balls, coarsely crushed (about 1 cup)**
- **Canned chocolate frosting**

1 Preheat oven to 325°F. Line a 13x9x2-inch baking pan with foil, extending the foil over the edges of the pan. Lightly grease foil. In a medium bowl stir together the flour, malted milk powder, and salt.

2 In a medium saucepan cook and stir butter and chocolate over low heat until chocolate melts. Remove from heat. Stir in sugar. Using a wooden spoon, beat in eggs, one at a time. Stir in vanilla. Stir in the flour mixture, walnuts, and half of the crushed malted milk balls. Spoon batter into the prepared baking pan, spreading evenly.

3 Bake for 35 minutes. Cool in pan on a wire rack. Use the foil to lift the uncut brownies out of the pan. Place on a cutting board; cut into brownies. Use a small amount of frosting to "glue" the remaining malted milk ball pieces on top of brownies. **MAKES 30 BROWNIES**

TO MAKE AHEAD AND STORE: Layer brownies between sheets of waxed paper in an airtight container; cover. Store in the refrigerator for up to 3 days or freeze for up to 3 months.

gift It

Uncommon Canister

No one will guess that this sophisticated wrapping starts with an empty oatmeal container. Cut a piece of decorative paper to fit an 18-ounce container. Wrap the paper around the container, anchoring the paper with double-sided tape. Trim overhang edges as needed. Use crafts glue to affix ribbon along the top and bottom rims of the canister. Trace the lid onto a piece of cardstock. Cut out the traced circle and pop it onto the top of the lid to cover the logo. Fill the canister with brownies and tie a ribbon around the entire package.

Triple-Chocolate and Espresso Brownies

PREP **30 MINUTES**   BAKE **30 MINUTES**   OVEN **350°F**

½ **cup butter, cut up**

4 **ounces bittersweet chocolate, chopped**

3 **ounces unsweetened chocolate, chopped**

⅔ **cup all-purpose flour**

¼ **teaspoon baking soda**

⅛ **teaspoon salt**

1 **cup sugar**

2 **eggs**

1 **tablespoon instant espresso coffee powder**

1 **teaspoon vanilla**

1 **cup miniature semisweet chocolate pieces**

1 **recipe Chocolate–Cream Cheese Frosting**

   Chocolate-covered espresso beans, chopped (optional)

1 In a medium saucepan cook and stir the butter, bittersweet chocolate, and unsweetened chocolate over low heat until chocolates melt; let cool. Preheat oven to 350°F. Line an 8x8x2-inch baking pan with foil, extending the foil over the edges of the pan. Grease foil; set pan aside.

2 In a small bowl stir together the flour, baking soda, and salt. Stir the sugar into the cooled chocolate mixture. Add the eggs, one at a time, beating with a wooden spoon just until combined after each addition. Stir in espresso powder and vanilla. Add the flour mixture to the chocolate mixture; stir just until combined. Stir in chocolate pieces. Spoon the batter into the prepared pan; spreading evenly.

3 Bake for 30 minutes. Cool in pan on a wire rack. Spread Chocolate–Cream Cheese Frosting evenly over cooled brownies. Use the foil to lift the uncut brownies out of the pan. Place on a cutting board; cut into brownies. If desired, sprinkle with chocolate-covered espresso beans. **MAKES 20 BROWNIES**

Chocolate–Cream Cheese Frosting: In a small saucepan cook and stir ½ cup semisweet chocolate pieces over low heat until chocolate melts. Remove from heat; let cool. In a medium mixing bowl beat one 3-ounce package cream cheese, softened, and ¼ cup powdered sugar with an electric mixer on low speed until combined. Beat in cooled chocolate until smooth.

TO MAKE AHEAD AND STORE: Place brownies in a single layer in an airtight container; cover. Store in the refrigerator for up to 3 days or freeze for up to 3 months. Thaw bars, if frozen. Before serving, let bars stand at room temperature for 15 minutes.

COFFEE AND COOKIE BROWNIES, PAGE 141

coffee creations

If you like coffee in your cup,
you'll love it in your cookie! Whether
paired with chocolate, spice, or something else
that's nice, a little bit of the brew adds depth,
character, and an invigorating touch to brownies,
biscotti, drops, and more.

★

Espresso Balls

PREP **25 MINUTES**   BAKE **15 MINUTES PER BATCH**   COOL **3 MINUTES PER BATCH**   OVEN **325°F**

1   cup butter, softened
½   cup powdered sugar
¼   cup unsweetened cocoa
     powder
1   tablespoon coffee liqueur
1   teaspoon vanilla
1¾   cups all-purpose flour
1½   cups hazelnuts (filberts),
     toasted and ground
¼   cup chocolate-covered
     coffee beans, ground

1 Preheat oven to 325°F. In a
large mixing bowl beat butter
with an electric mixer on medium
to high speed for 30 seconds.
Add powdered sugar and cocoa
powder. Beat until combined,
scraping sides of bowl occasionally.
Beat in the coffee liqueur and
vanilla until combined. Beat in as
much of the flour as you can with
the mixer. Using a wooden spoon,
stir in any remaining flour, ½ cup
of the ground hazelnuts, and the
ground coffee beans.

2 Shape dough into 1-inch balls.
Roll balls in the remaining
ground hazelnuts to coat.
Place balls 2 inches apart on an
ungreased cookie sheet.

3 Bake about 15 minutes or until
bottoms are light brown. Cool
on cookie sheet for 3 minutes.
Transfer cookies to a wire rack
and let cool. **MAKES 54 COOKIES**

TO MAKE AHEAD AND STORE: Layer
cookies between sheets of waxed
paper in an airtight container;
cover. Store at room temperature
for up to 3 days or freeze for up to
3 months.

In a *twinkling*

Emphasize the espresso
factor in these cookies by
topping each one with a
chocolate-covered
bean. Use a dot of melted
chocolate to keep the bean in
place, affixing the bean before
the chocolate dries.

Grinding Chocolate-Covered Espresso Beans

To grind chocolate-covered
espresso beans, you can use
a coffee grinder or a food
processor. The trick is not
to overprocess the beans,
because the chocolate may
start to melt. Instead, grind
with short pulses until you
reach the desired consistency.

Italian Chocolate-Spice Cookies

PREP **40 MINUTES**   BAKE **8 MINUTES PER BATCH**   OVEN **375°F**

3   cups all-purpose flour
1   cup granulated sugar
2   teaspoons baking powder
¼   cup unsweetened cocoa powder
1   teaspoon ground cinnamon
1   teaspoon ground cloves
1   cup butter
2   eggs
½   cup strong brewed coffee, cooled
1   teaspoon vanilla
½   cup pine nuts or chopped walnuts
1   recipe Powdered Sugar Icing

1 If desired, line a cookie sheet with parchment paper; set aside. In a large bowl stir together the flour, granulated sugar, baking powder, cocoa powder, cinnamon, and cloves. Using a pastry blender, cut in butter until mixture resembles coarse crumbs. Make a well in the center of the flour mixture.

2 In a medium bowl whisk together the eggs, coffee, and vanilla. Pour egg mixture into flour mixture; stir to combine. Stir in nuts. If necessary, cover and chill dough for 1 to 2 hours or until easy to handle.

3 Preheat oven to 375°F. Shape dough into 1¼-inch balls. Place balls 2 inches apart on ungreased or prepared cookie sheet.

4 Bake for 8 to 10 minutes or until edges are firm. (Cookies may still appear soft. Do not overbake.) Transfer cookies to a wire rack and let cool. Drizzle cookies with Powdered Sugar Icing. Let stand until icing is set.
MAKES ABOUT 36 COOKIES

Powdered Sugar Icing: In a small bowl stir together 1 cup powdered sugar and enough milk (1 to 2 tablespoons) to make an icing of drizzling consistency.

TO MAKE AHEAD AND STORE: Layer cookies between sheets of waxed paper in an airtight container; cover. Store at room temperature for up to 3 days. Or freeze unfrosted cookies for up to 3 months. Thaw cookies; prepare icing and ice cookies as directed.

Cappuccino Love Bites

PREP **25 MINUTES**   CHILL **1 HOUR**   BAKE **10 MINUTES PER BATCH**   OVEN **350°F**

1	cup butter-flavor shortening
1	cup sugar
1	teaspoon baking powder
¼	teaspoon salt
1	egg
1	tablespoon coffee liqueur or milk
1	teaspoon vanilla
2¼	cups all-purpose flour
½	cup sugar
2	tablespoons instant coffee crystals
48	milk chocolate candy kisses with stripes or almonds, unwrapped

1 In a large mixing bowl beat shortening with an electric mixer on medium to high speed for 30 seconds. Add the 1 cup sugar, the baking powder, and salt. Beat until combined, scraping sides of bowl occasionally. Beat in the egg, liqueur, and vanilla until combined. Beat in as much of the flour as you can with the mixer. Using a wooden spoon, stir in any remaining flour. If necessary, cover and chill dough about 1 hour or until easy to handle.

2 Preheat oven to 350°F. Lightly grease a cookie sheet. In a small bowl combine the ½ cup sugar and the coffee crystals. Shape dough into 1-inch balls. Roll balls in sugar mixture to coat. Place balls 2 inches apart on the prepared cookie sheet.

3 Bake about 10 minutes or until tops are cracked and sides are set (do not let edges brown). Immediately press a milk chocolate candy into the center of each cookie. If desired, when chocolate warms and softens from the hot cookies, swirl it gently with a knife. Transfer cookies to a wire rack and let cool. **MAKES 48 COOKIES**

TO MAKE AHEAD AND STORE: Layer cookies between sheets of waxed paper in an airtight container; cover. Store at room temperature for up to 3 days or freeze for up to 3 months.

Cocoa-Coffee Crinkles

PREP **35 MINUTES**   CHILL **1 HOUR**   BAKE **8 MINUTES PER BATCH**   OVEN **350°F**

½   cup butter, softened
1   cup packed brown sugar
⅔   cup unsweetened cocoa powder
1   tablespoon instant coffee crystals
1   teaspoon baking soda
1   teaspoon ground cinnamon
2   egg whites
1½ cups all-purpose flour
⅓   cup granulated sugar
2   tablespoons unsweetened cocoa powder

1 In a large mixing bowl beat butter with an electric mixer on medium to high speed for 30 seconds. Add brown sugar, the ⅔ cup cocoa powder, the coffee crystals, baking soda, and cinnamon. Beat until combined, scraping sides of bowl occasionally. Beat in the egg whites until combined. Beat in as much of the flour as you can with the mixer. Using a wooden spoon, stir in any remaining flour. Cover and chill dough about 1 hour or until easy to handle.

2 Preheat oven to 350°F. In a small bowl combine the granulated sugar and the 2 table-spoons cocoa powder. Shape dough into 1-inch balls; shape balls into 1½-inch logs. Roll logs in sugar mixture to coat (reserve any remaining sugar mixture). Place logs 2 inches apart on an ungreased cookie sheet.

3 Bake for 8 to 10 minutes or until edges are firm. Transfer cookies to a wire rack and let cool. Sprinkle cookies with any remaining sugar mixture. **MAKES ABOUT 42 COOKIES**

TO MAKE AHEAD AND STORE: Layer cookies between sheets of waxed paper in an airtight container; cover. Store at room temperature for up to 3 days or freeze for up to 3 months.

One Size for All

To make each ball of cookie dough consistent in size, pat all the dough into a 1-inch-thick rectangle. Using a sharp knife, cut the dough into forty-eight 1-inch pieces. Roll each piece into a ball.

Chocolate, Coffee, and Almond Cookies

PREP **45 MINUTES**   BAKE **8 MINUTES PER BATCH**   COOL **1 MINUTE PER BATCH**   OVEN **350°F**

½	cup instant coffee crystals
2	tablespoons hot water
1	cup butter, softened
1¼	cups sugar
¾	teaspoon baking soda
½	teaspoon salt
2	eggs
1	teaspoon vanilla
2⅔	cups all-purpose flour
2	cups semisweet chocolate pieces
¾	cup slivered almonds, toasted

1 Preheat oven to 350°F. Grease cookie sheets; set aside. In a small bowl dissolve coffee crystals in the hot water; set aside. In a large bowl beat butter with an electric mixer on medium speed until combined. Add sugar, baking soda, and salt. Beat until combined, scraping side of bowl occasionally. Beat in coffee mixture, eggs, and vanilla until combined. Beat in as much of the flour as you can with the mixer. Using a wooden spoon, stir in any remaining flour, chocolate pieces, and almonds.

2 Drop dough by heaping teaspoons 2 inches apart onto prepared cookie sheets. Bake for 8 to 10 minutes or until edges are firm and light brown. Cool on cookie sheets for 1 minute. Transfer cookies to wire racks; cool. **MAKES ABOUT 40 COOKIES**

TO STORE: Layer cookies between sheets of waxed paper in an airtight container; cover. Store at room temperature for up to 3 days or freeze for up to 3 months.

Caffe Macchiato Cups

PREP **40 MINUTES**   CHILL **1 HOUR**   BAKE **8 MINUTES PER BATCH**   COOL **5 MINUTES PER BATCH**   OVEN **375°F**

- 1   tablespoon coffee liqueur
- 1   teaspoon vanilla
- 1   teaspoon instant espresso coffee powder
- 1   cup butter, softened
- ½   cup granulated sugar
- 1   egg
- 2   cups all-purpose flour
- ¼   cup butter, softened
- 4   cups powdered sugar
- ¼   cup milk
- 2   teaspoons coffee liqueur or 1 teaspoon vanilla
-     Instant espresso coffee powder or unsweetened cocoa powder

1 In a small bowl stir together the 1 tablespoon coffee liqueur, vanilla, and the 1 teaspoon espresso coffee powder until coffee powder dissolves.

2 In a large mixing bowl beat the 1 cup butter with an electric mixer on medium to high speed for 30 seconds. Add granulated sugar. Beat until combined, scraping sides of bowl occasionally. Beat in the egg and liqueur mixture until combined. Beat in as much of the flour as you can with the mixer. Using a wooden spoon, stir in any remaining flour. Divide dough in half. Cover and chill dough about 1 hour or until easy to handle.

3 Preheat oven to 375°F. Shape each portion of dough into 24 balls. Press balls evenly into the bottoms and up the sides of 48 ungreased 1¾-inch muffin cups.*

4 Bake for 8 to 10 minutes or until light brown. Lightly press the bowl of a measuring teaspoon into the center of each shell. Cool in pan on a wire rack for 5 minutes. Gently remove shells from cups; cool completely on wire rack.

5 Meanwhile, for filling, in a medium mixing bowl beat the ¼ cup butter with an electric mixer on medium to high speed for 30 seconds. Add powdered sugar, milk, and the 2 teaspoons coffee liqueur. Beat until smooth, scraping sides of bowl occasionally. Pipe or spoon the filling into cooled shells. Sprinkle lightly with additional espresso coffee powder. **MAKES 48 CUPS**

*note If you don't have forty-eight 1¾-inch muffin cups, keep a portion of the dough chilled while you bake the first batch of cookies.

TO MAKE AHEAD AND STORE: Place filled cups in a single layer in an airtight container; cover. Store in the refrigerator for up to 3 days or freeze for up to 3 months.

Mocha Wands

PREP **50 MINUTES** BAKE **8 MINUTES PER BATCH** OVEN **375°F**

1 cup butter, softened
¾ cup sugar
4 teaspoons instant espresso coffee powder
½ teaspoon salt
¼ teaspoon baking powder
1 egg
1 teaspoon vanilla
2⅓ cups all-purpose flour
8 ounces semisweet chocolate, chopped
1 cup finely chopped pecans, toasted if desired

1 Preheat oven to 375°F. In a large mixing bowl beat butter with an electric mixer on medium to high speed for 30 seconds. Add sugar, espresso coffee powder, salt, and baking powder. Beat until combined, scraping sides of bowl occasionally. Beat in the egg and vanilla until combined. Beat in as much of the flour as you can with the mixer. Using a wooden spoon, stir in any remaining flour.

2 Pack unchilled dough into a cookie press fitted with a star plate. Force dough through the cookie press into 3-inch-long strips onto an ungreased cookie sheet. Use a small knife or metal spatula to cut dough from press; space strips about 1 inch apart.

3 Bake for 8 to 10 minutes or until edges of cookies are firm. Transfer cookies to a wire rack and let cool.

4 In a small saucepan cook and stir chocolate over low heat until chocolate melts. Carefully dip ends of cookies into melted chocolate. Sprinkle both sides evenly with pecans. Transfer to a baking sheet lined with waxed paper. Let stand until chocolate is firm. **MAKES ABOUT 72 COOKIES**

TO MAKE AHEAD AND STORE: Layer cookies between sheets of waxed paper in an airtight container; cover. Store at room temperature for up to 3 days. Or freeze undipped cookies for up to 3 months. Thaw cookies; dip in melted chocolate and sprinkle with pecans as directed.

gift It

Another Cup of Joe

An oversize coffee cup hints at the flavor of these cookies. Tie it with a colorful Christmas ribbon. If you like, offer a package of gourmet coffee to add to the theme.

Chunky Chocolate and Chai Biscotti

PREP **45 MINUTES**   BAKE **41 MINUTES**   COOL **15 MINUTES**   OVEN **325°F**

- 2¾ cups all-purpose flour
- ½ cup sugar
- ¼ cup instant chai latte mix
- 1½ teaspoons baking powder
- 1 teaspoon instant espresso coffee powder or instant coffee crystals
- ¼ teaspoon salt
- 3 eggs
- 6 tablespoons butter, melted
- 1 teaspoon vanilla
- 1 cup chopped coffee-flavor chocolate bar (about 5.25 ounces)

1 Preheat oven to 325°F. Lightly grease a large cookie sheet. In a large bowl stir together the flour, sugar, latte mix, baking powder, espresso coffee powder, and salt. In a medium bowl whisk together the eggs, butter, and vanilla. Add the egg mixture to the flour mixture; stir until well combined. Stir in the chopped chocolate.

2 Divide dough in half. Shape each portion into a 12-inch log. Place logs about 4 inches apart on the prepared cookie sheet; flatten logs slightly until about 1½ inches wide.

3 Bake for 25 to 30 minutes or until tops are light brown and cracked. Cool on cookie sheet on a wire rack for 15 minutes.

4 Transfer logs to a cutting board. Using a serrated knife, cut logs diagonally into ½-inch-thick slices. Place slices, cut sides down, on cookie sheet. Bake for 8 minutes. Turn slices over and bake for 8 to 10 minutes more or until

crisp and light brown. Transfer cookies to a wire rack and let cool. **MAKES ABOUT 30 BISCOTTI**

TO MAKE AHEAD AND STORE: Layer biscotti between sheets of waxed paper in an airtight container; cover. Store at room temperature for up to 2 days or freeze for up to 3 months.

Sugar-and-Spice Coffee Slices

PREP **25 MINUTES**   CHILL **2 HOURS**   BAKE **9 MINUTES PER BATCH**   COOL **1 MINUTE PER BATCH**   OVEN **375°F**

- 2 **tablespoons instant espresso coffee powder**
- 1 **tablespoon hot water**
- ½ **cup butter, softened**
- ¼ **cup shortening**
- 1 **cup granulated sugar**
- ½ **cup packed brown sugar**
- 1 **teaspoon baking powder**
- 1 **teaspoon ground cinnamon**
- ¼ **teaspoon salt**
- 1 **egg**
- 2 **cups all-purpose flour**
- 1 **recipe Coffee Topping Coffee beans (optional)**

1 In a small bowl stir together the espresso powder and hot water until espresso coffee powder dissolves. In a large mixing bowl beat butter and shortening with an electric mixer on medium to high speed for 30 seconds. Add granulated sugar, brown sugar, baking powder, cinnamon, and salt. Beat until combined, scraping sides of bowl occasionally. Beat in the espresso and egg until combined. Beat in as much of the flour as you can with the mixer. Using a wooden spoon, stir in any remaining flour.

2 Divide dough into thirds. Shape each portion into a 7x2x1-inch loaf. Wrap each loaf in plastic wrap; chill about 2 hours or until firm.*

3 Preheat oven to 375°F. Cut loaves crosswise into ⅜-inch-thick slices. Place slices 2 inches apart on an ungreased cookie sheet. Sprinkle slices evenly with Coffee Topping. If desired, gently press a few coffee beans onto each slice.

4 Bake for 9 to 10 minutes or until edges are light brown. Cool on cookie sheet for 1 minute. Transfer cookies to a wire rack and let cool. **MAKES ABOUT 48 COOKIES**

Coffee Topping: In a small bowl stir together ¼ cup granulated sugar and 1 teaspoon instant espresso coffee powder.

*note *You can chill the dough loaves for up to 3 days in the refrigerator or freeze them for up to 1 week before slicing and baking.*

TO MAKE AHEAD AND STORE: Layer cookies between sheets of waxed paper in an airtight container; cover. Store at room temperature for up to 1 week or freeze for up to 3 months.

Little Dippers

PREP **45 MINUTES**   BAKE **10 MINUTES PER BATCH**   STAND **1 HOUR**   OVEN **350°F**

2¼ **cups all-purpose flour**
¼ **cup unsweetened cocoa powder**
¼ **teaspoon salt**
¾ **cup butter, softened**
1 **cup sugar**
1 **egg**
1 **tablespoon instant espresso coffee powder**
8 **ounces sweet baking chocolate, chopped**
2 **teaspoons shortening**

1 Preheat oven to 350°F. In a medium bowl combine flour, cocoa powder, and salt. In a large mixing bowl beat butter with an electric mixer on medium to high speed for 30 seconds. Add sugar. Beat about 2 minutes or until fluffy, scraping sides of bowl occasionally. Beat in the egg and espresso coffee powder until combined. Beat in as much of the flour mixture as you can with the mixer. Using a wooden spoon, stir in any remaining flour mixture (dough will be crumbly). If necessary, gently knead dough until it clings together. Divide dough in half.

2 On a lightly floured surface roll each dough half to ¼-inch thickness. Using a 2½-inch star-shaped cookie cutter, cut out dough. Place cutouts 1 inch apart on an ungreased cookie sheet. Bake for 10 to 12 minutes or until edges are firm. Transfer cookies to a wire rack and let cool.

3 In a small microwave-safe bowl combine chopped chocolate and shortening. Microwave, uncovered, on 50 percent power (medium) about 2 minutes or until chocolate melts, stirring every 30 seconds. Dip one-third of each cooled cookie into melted chocolate; let excess drip back into bowl. Place cookies on waxed paper; let stand about 1 hour or until chocolate is set. **MAKES 48 COOKIES**

TO MAKE AHEAD AND STORE: Layer cookies between sheets of waxed paper in an airtight container; cover. Store at room temperature for up to 3 days or freeze for up to 3 months.

In a *twinkling*

Make your cookies truly sparkle this season with a touch of edible gold luster dust. Dip the cookies in the chocolate coating, as directed. Let stand about 1 hour until set. Following package directions, brush the luster dust on the chocolate.

Espresso-Nut Drop Cookies

PREP **30 MINUTES**   BAKE **13 MINUTES PER BATCH**   COOL **2 MINUTES PER BATCH**   OVEN **350°F**

- 1 **tablespoon instant espresso coffee powder**
- 1 **tablespoon water**
- 1½ **cups chunky peanut butter**
- ½ **cup butter, softened**
- 1½ **cups packed brown sugar**
- 1½ **teaspoons baking soda**
- ¼ **teaspoon salt**
- 2 **eggs**
- 1 **teaspoon vanilla**
- 1½ **cups regular rolled oats**
- ½ **cup whole wheat flour**
- 1 **cup dark chocolate pieces**
- 1 **cup hazelnuts (filberts), toasted and chopped**

1 Preheat oven to 350°F. In a small bowl stir together the espresso coffee powder and the water until coffee powder dissolves.

2 In a large mixing bowl beat peanut butter and butter with an electric mixer on medium to high speed for 30 seconds. Add brown sugar, baking soda, and salt. Beat until combined, scraping sides of bowl occasionally. Beat in the eggs, vanilla, and espresso mixture until combined. Beat in oats. Beat in as much of the flour as you can with the mixer. Using a wooden spoon, stir in any remaining flour, the chocolate pieces, and hazelnuts.

3 Using a ¼-cup measure, drop mounds of dough 3 inches apart onto an ungreased cookie sheet. Flatten dough mounds slightly. Bake for 13 to 15 minutes or until edges are light brown. Cool on cookie sheet for 2 minutes. Transfer cookies to a wire rack and let cool. **MAKES ABOUT 24 COOKIES**

TO MAKE AHEAD AND STORE: Layer cookies between sheets of waxed paper in an airtight container; cover. Store at room temperature for up to 3 days or freeze for up to 3 months.

Mocha Munchies

PREP **25 MINUTES** CHILL **30 MINUTES** BAKE **8 MINUTES PER BATCH** COOL **2 MINUTES PER BATCH**
OVEN **350°F**

10	ounces bittersweet chocolate, chopped
3	tablespoons butter
2	eggs
¾	cup packed brown sugar
1	tablespoon coffee liqueur
2	teaspoons vanilla
¼	teaspoon baking powder
¼	teaspoon salt
½	cup all-purpose flour
1	cup dark chocolate chunks
1	cup chocolate-covered espresso coffee beans, coarsely chopped
1	cup chopped pecans, toasted

1 In a large microwave-safe bowl combine bittersweet chocolate and butter. Microwave, uncovered, on 50 percent power (medium) for 2 to 3 minutes or until chocolate melts, stirring every 30 seconds.

2 Add eggs, brown sugar, coffee liqueur, vanilla, baking powder, and salt to melted chocolate. Beat with a wooden spoon until combined. Beat in flour until combined. Stir in dark chocolate chunks, espresso coffee beans, and pecans. Cover and chill dough for 30 minutes.

3 Preheat oven to 350°F. Lightly grease a large cookie sheet. Drop dough by rounded teaspoons 2 inches apart onto the prepared cookie sheet. Bake for 8 to 10 minutes or until edges are firm and tops are dull and crackled. Cool on cookie sheet for 2 minutes. Transfer cookies to a wire rack and let cool. **MAKES ABOUT 48 COOKIES**

TO MAKE AHEAD AND STORE: Layer cookies between sheets of waxed paper in an airtight container; cover. Store at room temperature for up to 3 days or freeze for up to 3 months.

Toffee-Coffee Brownies

PREP **25 MINUTES**   BAKE **35 MINUTES**   OVEN **350°F**

1	**19.5-ounce package brownie mix**
½	**cup toffee pieces**
2	**to 3 tablespoons instant espresso coffee powder or instant coffee crystals**
¾	**cup canned vanilla frosting**
1	**tablespoon Irish cream liqueur or coffee liqueur**
¼	**cup toffee pieces**

1 Preheat oven to 350°F. Line a 9x9x2-inch baking pan with foil, extending the foil over the edges of the pan. Grease foil.

2 Prepare brownie mix according to package directions, except stir the ½ cup toffee pieces and the espresso coffee powder into the batter. Spoon batter into the prepared pan, spreading evenly. Bake for 35 minutes. Cool in pan on a wire rack.

3 Use the foil to lift the uncut bars out of the pan. Place on a cutting board. In a small bowl stir together the vanilla frosting and liqueur. Spread frosting mixture evenly over cooled brownies. Sprinkle with the ¼ cup toffee pieces. Cut into bars. **MAKES 20 BROWNIES**

TO MAKE AHEAD AND STORE: Place bars in a single layer in an airtight container; cover. Store in the refrigerator for up to 3 days. Do not freeze.

Cappuccino-Caramel Oat Bars

PREP **30 MINUTES**   BAKE **20 MINUTES**   OVEN **350°F**

3	cups rolled oats
2⅓	cups all-purpose flour
1	cup chopped pecans
1	teaspoon baking soda
¼	teaspoon salt
1	cup butter, softened
2	cups packed brown sugar
2	eggs
1	tablespoon instant coffee crystals or instant espresso coffee powder
2	teaspoons vanilla
¾	cup caramel ice cream topping
½	cup chopped pecans
1	recipe Coffee Glaze (optional)

1 Preheat oven to 350°F. Lightly grease a 15x10x1-inch baking pan; set aside.

2 In a large bowl stir together the oats, flour, the 1 cup pecans, the baking soda, and salt. In a large mixing bowl beat butter with an electric mixer on medium to high speed for 30 seconds. Add brown sugar. Beat until combined, scraping sides of bowl occasionally. Beat in the eggs, the 1 tablespoon coffee crystals, and the vanilla until combined. Beat in as much of the oats mixture as you can with the mixer. Using a wooden spoon, stir in any remaining oats mixture.

3 Remove 2 cups of the dough; set aside. Press the remaining dough evenly onto the bottom of the prepared baking pan. Spread the caramel topping evenly over dough to within ¼ inch of the edges. Drop spoonfuls of the remaining dough over caramel topping. Sprinkle with the ½ cup pecans.

4 Bake for 20 to 25 minutes or until edges are set (do not overbake). Cool in pan on a wire rack. If desired, drizzle with Coffee Glaze. Let stand until glaze is set. Cut into bars. **MAKES 48 BARS**

Coffee Glaze: In a small bowl stir together 2 tablespoons very hot milk and 1 teaspoon instant coffee crystals until crystals dissolve. Stir in 1 cup powdered sugar until smooth.

TO MAKE AHEAD AND STORE: Place bars in a single layer in an airtight container; cover. Store at room temperature for up to 3 days or freeze for up to 1 month.

Coffee and Cookie Brownies

PREP **15 MINUTES**　BAKE **40 MINUTES**　OVEN **350°F**

1　**16.5-ounce roll refrigerated sugar cookie dough**

2　**eggs, lightly beaten**

1　**19.5-ounce package milk chocolate brownie mix**

½　**cup vegetable oil**

⅓　**cup coffee liqueur or cooled strong brewed coffee**

1　**cup semisweet or bittersweet chocolate pieces**

1 Preheat oven to 350°F. Line a 13x9x2-inch baking pan with foil, extending the foil over the edges of the pan. Press sugar cookie dough evenly onto the bottom of the prepared baking pan; set aside.

2 In a large bowl stir together the eggs, brownie mix, oil, and liqueur just until combined. Spoon over sugar cookie dough, spreading evenly. Sprinkle with chocolate pieces.

3 Bake about 40 minutes or until edges are set. Cool in pan on a wire rack. Use the foil to lift the uncut bars out of the pan. Place on a cutting board; cut into brownies. **MAKES 24 BROWNIES**

TO MAKE AHEAD AND STORE: Place brownies in a single layer in an airtight container; cover. Store in the refrigerator for up to 3 days or freeze for up to 3 months.

In a *twinkling*

Top these brownies, as shown, with a chocolate-covered espresso bean held in place with a dab of melted chocolate. Or use a mini malted milk ball in place of the bean.

CARAMEL SANDWICH COOKIES, PAGE 145

ooey, gooey
caramel

When it comes to confections, buttery-luscious caramel is in a class by itself. With a drizzle here and a slather there, these delectable drops, heavenly bars, and other divine caramel-enhanced creations will bring sweet decadence to any cookie tray.

★

Dulce de Leche Chocolate Cookies

PREP **45 MINUTES**   CHILL **5 HOURS**   BAKE **12 MINUTES PER BATCH**   COOL **2 MINUTES PER BATCH**
OVEN **325°F**

¾ cup butter, softened
1 cup sugar
¾ cup unsweetened Dutch-
   process cocoa powder
½ teaspoon ground
   cinnamon
¼ teaspoon salt
¼ teaspoon cayenne pepper
1 egg
1½ teaspoons vanilla
1¼ cups all-purpose flour
½ cup jarred or canned dulce
   de leche

1 In a large mixing bowl beat butter with an electric mixer on medium to high speed for 30 seconds. Add sugar, cocoa powder, cinnamon, salt, and cayenne pepper. Beat until combined, scraping sides of bowl occasionally. Beat in the egg and vanilla until combined. Beat in as much of the flour as you can with the mixer. Using a wooden spoon, stir in any remaining flour. Divide dough in half. Cover and chill dough about 1 hour or until easy to handle.

2 Shape each portion of dough into a 6-inch log. Wrap and chill logs about 4 hours or until firm.

3 Preheat oven to 325°F. Line a cookie sheet with parchment paper. Cut logs into ¼-inch-thick slices. Place slices 1 inch apart on the prepared cookie sheet. Bake for 12 to 14 minutes or until edges are firm. Cool on cookie sheet for 2 minutes. Transfer cookies to a wire rack and let cool.

4 To assemble, spread a rounded tablespoon of dulce de leche onto the bottom of one cookie; lightly press the bottom of a second cookie against the dulce de leche. Repeat with the remaining cookies and dulce de leche. **MAKES 24 SANDWICH COOKIES**

TO MAKE AHEAD AND STORE: Layer filled cookies between sheets of waxed paper in an airtight container; cover. Store in the refrigerator for up to 3 days. Or freeze unfilled cookies for up to 3 months. Thaw cookies. Assemble cookies as directed.

Dulce de Leche Defined

Popular in Latin America, *dulce de leche* (roughly translated as "candy of milk") is a confection that's traditionally made by cooking sugar and milk slowly over low heat until they reach a thick, spreadable consistency, golden color, and caramely flavor.

There's no substitute for dulce de leche—most caramel sauces won't be thick enough to spread between these cookies. Fortunately, dulce de leche is now widely available; look for it in the Mexican or Latin aisles of supermarkets or in Latin grocery stores.

Caramel Sandwich Cookies

PREP **45 MINUTES**   CHILL **2 HOURS**   BAKE **10 MINUTES PER BATCH**   COOL **1 MINUTE PER BATCH**
OVEN **350°F**

½   **cup sugar**

¼   **teaspoon fine sea salt**

⅔   **cup pecan pieces**

1   **cup unsalted butter, slightly softened and cut up**

2   **teaspoons vanilla**

2   **cups all-purpose flour**

1   **recipe Shortcut Caramel Filling**

6   **ounces white baking chocolate, chopped, or white baking pieces**

1   In a food processor combine sugar and salt. Cover and process with on-off pulses until fine and powdery. Add pecans; cover and process with on-off pulses until finely ground. Add butter and vanilla; cover and process with on-off pulses until the butter is smooth. Add the flour; cover and process with on-off pulses just until soft dough begins to form around the blade. Remove dough from processor and knead briefly to mix evenly.

2   Shape dough into a rectangular log about 12x2½ inches wide. Wrap and chill log about 2 hours or until firm.

3   Preheat to 350°F. Cut log into ¼-inch-thick slices. Place slices 1 inch apart on an ungreased cookie sheet. Bake for 10 to 12 minutes or until edges are golden brown, rotating pan from front to back about halfway through baking. Cool on cookie sheet for 1 minute. Transfer cookies to a wire rack and let cool.

4   To assemble, spread a little Shortcut Caramel Filling onto the bottom of one cookie; press the bottom of a second cookie against the filling. Repeat with the remaining cookies and filling.

5   Place chocolate in a medium microwave-safe bowl. Microwave, uncovered, on 100 percent power (high) for 1 to 1½ minutes or until chocolate melts, stirring every 30 seconds. Dip ends of sandwich cookies into melted chocolate. Place cookies on waxed paper. Let stand until chocolate is set. **MAKES 25 SANDWICH COOKIES**

Shortcut Caramel Filling:

In a small saucepan combine 24 unwrapped vanilla caramels and ¼ cup whipping cream. Cook and stir over medium-low heat until melted and smooth.

TO MAKE AHEAD AND STORE: Layer unfilled cookies between sheets of waxed paper in an airtight container; cover. Store at room temperature for up to 3 days or freeze for up to 3 months. Thaw cookies, if frozen. Assemble as directed.

In a *twinkling*

Instead of dipping the cookies in the melted white chocolate, drizzle it over the cookies in a fanciful design.

Caramel-Brittle Shortbread Thumbprints

PREP **30 MINUTES**   BAKE **10 MINUTES PER BATCH**   OVEN **375°F**

22   vanilla caramels, unwrapped
3   tablespoons whipping cream
1   cup butter, softened
⅔   cup packed brown sugar
½   teaspoon vanilla
2¾   cups all-purpose flour
¼   cup whipping cream
⅔   cup crushed peanut brittle
½   cup semisweet chocolate pieces
2   teaspoons shortening

1 Preheat oven to 375°F. In a small saucepan cook and stir caramels and the 3 tablespoons whipping cream over medium-low heat until melted and smooth. Set aside.

2 In a large mixing bowl beat butter with an electric mixer on medium to high speed for 1 minute. Add brown sugar and vanilla. Beat until combined, scraping sides of bowl occasionally. Beat in half of the flour and the ¼ cup whipping cream. Beat in the remaining flour on low speed just until combined. Stir in ⅓ cup of the crushed peanut brittle.

3 Shape dough into 1¼-inch balls. Place balls 2 inches apart on an ungreased cookie sheet. Press your thumb into the center of each ball.

4 Bake about 10 minutes or until edges are set. If cookie centers puff during baking, re-press with the back of a small spoon. Spoon about 1 teaspoon melted caramel mixture into indentation in each cookie. Transfer cookies to a wire rack. Sprinkle cookies evenly with the remaining crushed peanut brittle. Let cool.

5 In another small saucepan cook and stir chocolate pieces and shortening over low heat until chocolate melts. Cool slightly. Drizzle chocolate mixture over cookies. Let stand until chocolate is set. **MAKES ABOUT 42 COOKIES**

TO MAKE AHEAD AND STORE: Place cookies in a single layer in an airtight container; cover. Store at room temperature for up to 3 days or freeze for up to 3 months.

Quicker Caramels

Vanilla caramel candies have long been a baker's secret ingredient for making a quick caramel topping for their creations. Now there's an even quicker shortcut: miniature round caramel bits, available in the candy aisle of the supermarket. These little bits are 100 percent recipe-ready—no unwrapping needed. To use in place of vanilla caramels, substitute 1 cup miniature round caramel bits for each 24 wrapped vanilla caramels specified in a recipe.

Chocolate-Caramel Thumbprints

PREP **40 MINUTES**   CHILL **2 HOURS**   BAKE **10 MINUTES PER BATCH**   OVEN **350°F**

1 cup all-purpose flour
⅓ cup unsweetened cocoa powder
¼ teaspoon salt
1 egg
½ cup butter, softened
⅔ cup sugar
2 tablespoons milk
1 teaspoon vanilla
16 vanilla caramels, unwrapped*
3 tablespoons whipping cream*
1¼ cups finely chopped pecans
½ cup semisweet chocolate pieces
1 teaspoon shortening

1 In a small bowl combine the flour, cocoa powder, and salt. Separate egg; place yolk and white into separate bowls. Cover and chill egg white until needed.

2 In a large mixing bowl beat butter with an electric mixer on medium to high speed for 30 seconds. Add sugar. Beat until combined, scraping sides of bowl occasionally. Beat in the egg yolk, milk, and vanilla until combined. Beat in the flour mixture. Cover and chill dough about 2 hours or until easy to handle.

3 Preheat oven to 350°F. Lightly grease a cookie sheet. In a small saucepan cook and stir caramels and whipping cream over medium-low heat until melted and smooth; set aside.

4 Lightly beat reserved egg white. Shape dough into 1-inch balls. Roll balls in egg white, then in pecans to coat. Place balls 1 inch apart on the prepared cookie sheet. Press your thumb into the center of each ball.

5 Bake for 10 minutes or until edges are firm. If cookie centers puff during baking, re-press with the back of a small spoon. Spoon melted caramel mixture into indentations in cookies. Transfer cookies to a wire rack and let cool. (If necessary, reheat caramel mixture to keep it a spooning consistency.)

6 In another small saucepan cook and stir chocolate pieces and shortening over low heat until chocolate melts. Cool slightly. Drizzle chocolate over cookies. Let stand until chocolate is set.
MAKES ABOUT 32 COOKIES

note You may substitute ½ cup purchased caramel apple dip for the caramels and whipping cream. Place dip in a small microwave-safe bowl and microwave, uncovered, on 100 percent power (high) for 20 seconds. Stir before using.

TO MAKE AHEAD AND STORE:
Layer cookies between sheets of waxed paper in an airtight container; cover. Store in the refrigerator for up to 3 days or freeze for up to 3 months.

Doable Drizzling

It's easier to get caramel mixtures to drizzle evenly from a bag than from a spoon. For the bag method, prepare the mixture as directed in recipes; cool slightly. Spoon the melted caramel mixture into a heavy resealable plastic bag. Snip off a bottom corner of the bag and squeeze the caramel mixture through the tip. Be sure to use a heavy plastic bag—lightweight sandwich bags may be weakened by the warm caramel and burst at the seams.

Caramel-Cashew Cookies

PREP **35 MINUTES**   BAKE **10 MINUTES PER BATCH**   COOL **10 MINUTES PER BATCH**   OVEN **350°F**

2¼   cups dry-roasted cashews
2   tablespoons vegetable oil
¾   cup packed brown sugar
½   cup butter, softened
⅓   cup granulated sugar
1   egg
1   teaspoon vanilla
1½   cups all-purpose flour
     Granulated sugar
24   vanilla caramels, unwrapped
¼   cup whipping cream
     About 36 dry-roasted cashew halves

1 Preheat oven to 350°F. Place 1½ cups of the cashews in a food processor; cover and process until finely chopped. Gradually add the oil, processing about 2 minutes or until mixture is as creamy as peanut butter. Coarsely chop the remaining ¾ cup cashews.

2 In a large mixing bowl combine the cashew butter, the brown sugar, butter, and the ⅓ cup granulated sugar. Beat with an electric mixer on medium to high speed until light and fluffy, scraping sides of bowl occasionally. Beat in the egg and vanilla until combined. Gradually beat in the flour on low speed until combined. Stir in the coarsely chopped cashews.

3 Shape dough into 1½-inch balls. Place balls 2 inches apart on an ungreased cookie sheet. Using the bottom of a wet glass dipped in additional granulated sugar, flatten each ball to about ⅜-inch thickness.

4 Bake for 10 to 12 minutes or until bottoms are light golden brown and edges are firm. Transfer cookies to a wire rack and let cool.

5 In a small saucepan cook and stir the caramels and whipping cream over low heat until melted and smooth. Cool slightly (10 to 15 minutes). Spoon a small amount of caramel mixture on top of each cookie; add a cashew half. Let stand until caramel mixture is set.
MAKES ABOUT 36 COOKIES

TO MAKE AHEAD AND STORE: Layer undecorated cookies between sheets of waxed paper in an airtight container; cover. Store at room temperature for up to 3 days or freeze for up to 3 months. Thaw cookies, if frozen. Prepare caramel mixture and decorate cookies as directed.

In a *twinkling*

Make these bites into substantial sandwich cookies. Chop the 36 cashew halves. Slather one side of a cookie with the caramel icing, then sprinkle with the chopped cashews and top with another cookie.

Caramel Corn Cookies

PREP **35 MINUTES**   BAKE **8 MINUTES PER BATCH**   COOL **2 MINUTES PER BATCH**   OVEN **350°F**

½ cup shortening
¼ cup butter, softened
½ cup granulated sugar
½ cup packed brown sugar
½ cup yellow cornmeal
1 teaspoon baking soda
½ teaspoon salt
1 egg
¼ cup honey
1 tablespoon vanilla
1¾ cups all-purpose flour
1 cup miniature round caramel bits or butterscotch-flavor pieces
½ cup chopped honey-roasted peanuts
   Coarse sugar or turbinado sugar

1 Preheat oven to 350°F. Line a cookie sheet with parchment paper or lightly greased cookie sheet; set aside.

2 In a large mixing bowl beat shortening and butter with an electric mixer on medium to high speed for 30 seconds. Add granulated sugar, brown sugar, cornmeal, baking soda, and salt. Beat until combined, scraping sides of bowl occasionally. Beat in the egg, honey, and vanilla until combined. Beat in as much of the flour as you can with the mixer. Using a wooden spoon, stir in any remaining flour, the caramel bits, and peanuts.

3 Place coarse sugar in a small bowl. Shape dough into 1¼-inch balls. Roll balls in coarse sugar to coat. Place balls 2 inches apart on the prepared cookie sheet.

4 Bake for 8 to 10 minutes or until tops are golden and edges are firm. Cool on cookie sheet for 2 minutes. Transfer cookies to a wire rack and let cool.
MAKES ABOUT 48 COOKIES

TO MAKE AHEAD AND STORE: Layer cookies between sheets of waxed paper in an airtight container; cover. Store at room temperature for up to 3 days or freeze for up to 3 months.

Chocolate-Caramel Cupcake Bites

PREP **20 MINUTES**   BAKE **12 MINUTES**   COOL **2 MINUTES**   OVEN **350°F**

1   **cup butter, softened**
1   **cup packed brown sugar**
½   **cup granulated sugar**
½   **teaspoon baking soda**
½   **teaspoon salt**
3   **eggs**
2   **teaspoons vanilla**
⅓   **cup unsweetened cocoa powder**
2¼ **cups all-purpose flour**
1   **12-ounce package chocolate-covered caramel candies, such as Rolo, unwrapped**
2   **tablespoons whipping cream or milk**

1 Preheat oven to 350°F. Line twenty 2½-inch muffin cups with paper bake cups; set aside.

2 In a large mixing bowl beat butter with an electric mixer on medium to high speed for 30 seconds. Add the brown sugar, granulated sugar, baking soda, and salt. Beat until combined, scraping sides of bowl occasionally. Beat in the eggs, one at a time, and the vanilla until combined. Beat in cocoa powder until combined. Beat in as much of the flour as you can with the mixer. Using a wooden spoon, stir in any remaining flour.

3 Spoon about 3 tablespoons of the batter into each prepared muffin cup. Gently press 1 chocolate-covered caramel candy into the center of each muffin cup until the top of the candy is just below the batter.

4 Bake for 12 to 15 minutes or until set. Cool in pan on a wire rack for 2 minutes. Transfer cupcake cookies to wire rack and let cool. (Centers will fall slightly as cookies cool.)

5 Meanwhile, in a small saucepan heat and stir the remaining chocolate-covered caramel candies and the whipping cream over low heat until melted and smooth. Drizzle the caramel mixture over the cooled cupcake cookies. **MAKES 20 COOKIES**

TO MAKE AHEAD AND STORE: Place cupcake cookies in a single layer in an airtight container; cover. Store in the refrigerator for up to 3 days.

Salted Peanut Bars

PREP **25 MINUTES**   BAKE **12 MINUTES**   OVEN **350°F**

1   **cup all-purpose flour**
½   **cup crushed pretzels**
½   **teaspoon baking powder**
¼   **teaspoon baking soda**
½   **cup butter, softened**
⅔   **cup packed brown sugar**
2   **egg yolks**
2   **teaspoons vanilla**
1   **7-ounce jar marshmallow creme**
½   **cup creamy peanut butter**
¼   **cup powdered sugar**
1   **cup salted cocktail peanuts**
1   **14-ounce package vanilla caramels, unwrapped**
3   **tablespoons milk**

1 Preheat oven to 350°F. Line a 13x9x2-inch baking pan with foil, extending the foil over the edges of the pan.

2 In a small bowl combine the flour, pretzels, baking powder, and baking soda. In a large mixing bowl beat butter with an electric mixer on medium to high speed for 30 seconds. Add brown sugar, egg yolks, and vanilla. Beat until combined, scraping sides of bowl occasionally. Beat in as much of the flour mixture as you can with the mixer. Using a wooden spoon, stir in any remaining flour mixture.

Press dough evenly onto the bottom of the prepared baking pan. Bake for 12 to 14 minutes or until light brown.

3 Meanwhile, in a medium microwave-safe bowl combine marshmallow creme and peanut butter. Microwave, uncovered, on 100 percent power (high) for 1 minute or until softened and slightly melted, stirring after 30 seconds. Stir in the powdered sugar. Spread marshmallow mixture over hot crust. Sprinkle evenly with peanuts.

4 In a large saucepan combine the caramels and milk. Cook and stir over medium-low heat until melted and smooth. Pour caramel mixture evenly over the peanuts. Cool in pan on a wire rack. Use the foil to lift the uncut bars out of the pan. Place on a cutting board; cut into bars.
MAKES 48 BARS

TO MAKE AHEAD AND STORE: Place bars in a single layer in an airtight container; cover. Store in the refrigerator for up to 1 week.

Caramel-Nut Revel Bars

PREP **30 MINUTES**   BAKE **30 MINUTES**   OVEN **350°F**

½ cup butter, softened
1 cup packed brown sugar
½ teaspoon baking soda
1 egg
1 teaspoon vanilla
1¼ cups all-purpose flour
1½ cups quick-cooking rolled oats
20 vanilla caramels, unwrapped
2 tablespoons milk
2 cups tiny marshmallows
1 cup dry-roasted peanuts
1½ cups semisweet chocolate pieces
1 14-ounce can sweetened condensed milk
2 tablespoons butter
2 teaspoons vanilla

1 Preheat oven to 350°F. Line a 13x9x2-inch baking pan with foil, extending the foil over the edges of the pan.

2 In a large mixing bowl beat the ½ cup butter with an electric mixer on medium to high speed for 30 seconds. Add brown sugar and baking soda. Beat until combined, scraping sides of bowl occasionally. Beat in the egg and 1 teaspoon vanilla. Beat in as much of the flour as you can with the mixer. Stir in any remaining flour and the oats. Reserve ⅔ cup of the oats mixture. With floured hands, press the remaining oats mixture evenly onto the bottom of the prepared baking pan.

3 In a small saucepan cook and stir caramels and milk over low heat just until melted and smooth. Drizzle caramel mixture evenly over the oats mixture in the pan. Sprinkle evenly with 1½ cups of the marshmallows and ⅔ cup of the peanuts.

4 In a medium saucepan combine the chocolate pieces, sweetened condensed milk, and the 2 tablespoons butter. Cook over low heat until chocolate melts, stirring occasionally. Remove from heat. Stir in the 2 teaspoons vanilla. Pour chocolate mixture evenly over the marshmallows and nuts in pan. Drop spoonfuls of the reserved oats mixture over the chocolate mixture. Sprinkle evenly with the remaining marshmallows and peanuts.

5 Bake about 30 minutes or until golden. Cool in pan on a wire rack. Use the foil to lift the uncut bars out of the pan. Place on a cutting board; cut into bars.
MAKES ABOUT 36 BARS

TO MAKE AHEAD AND STORE: Place bars in a single layer in an airtight container; cover. Store at room temperature for up to 3 days or freeze for up to 3 months.

Chewy Chocolate-Caramel Bars

PREP **25 MINUTES**   BAKE **25 MINUTES**   OVEN **350°F**

1   package 2-layer-size German chocolate cake mix
¾   cup butter, melted
1   5-ounce can (⅔ cup) evaporated milk
1   14-ounce package vanilla caramels, unwrapped
1   cup chopped walnuts
1   cup semisweet chocolate pieces

1   Preheat oven to 350°F. Grease a 13x9x2-inch baking pan.

2   In a large mixing bowl combine cake mix, melted butter, and ⅓ cup of the evaporated milk. Beat with an electric mixer on medium speed until smooth. Spoon half of the dough into the prepared baking pan, spreading evenly.

3   In a large saucepan combine the caramels and the remaining ⅓ cup evaporated milk. Cook and stir over low heat until melted and smooth. Pour evenly over dough in the baking pan.

Sprinkle evenly with nuts and chocolate pieces. Crumble the remaining dough evenly over the nuts and chocolate pieces.

4   Bake for 25 minutes. Cool in pan on a wire rack. Cut into bars. **MAKES 48 BARS**

TO MAKE AHEAD AND STORE: Layer bars between sheets of waxed paper in an airtight container; cover. Store at room temperature for up to 3 days or freeze for up to 3 months.

Oatmeal-Caramel Bars

PREP **25 MINUTES**   BAKE **22 MINUTES**   OVEN **350°F**

1   cup butter, softened
2   cups packed brown sugar
2   eggs
2   teaspoons vanilla
1   teaspoon baking soda
2½   cups all-purpose flour
3   cups quick-cooking rolled oats
1   cup miniature semisweet chocolate pieces
½   cup chopped walnuts or pecans
30   vanilla caramels, unwrapped
3   tablespoons milk

1   Preheat oven to 350°F. Line a 15x10x1-inch baking pan with foil, extending the foil over the edges of the pan; set pan aside.

2   In a large mixing bowl beat butter with an electric mixer on medium to high speed for 30 seconds. Add the brown sugar. Beat until combined, scraping sides of bowl occasionally. Beat in the eggs, vanilla, and baking soda until combined. Beat in as much of the flour as you can with the mixer. Using a wooden spoon, stir in any remaining flour and the oats.

3   Remove and reserve one-third of the oats mixture. Press the remaining oats mixture evenly onto the bottom of the prepared baking pan. Sprinkle with chocolate pieces and nuts. In a medium saucepan cook and stir the caramels and milk over medium-low heat until melted and smooth. Drizzle caramel mixture evenly over chocolate and nuts. Drop spoonfuls of the reserved oats mixture over the caramel.

4   Bake for 22 to 25 minutes or until top is light brown. Cool in pan on a wire rack. Use the foil to lift the uncut bars out of the pan. Place on cutting board; cut into bars. **MAKES 60 BARS**

TO MAKE AHEAD AND STORE: Layer bars between sheets of waxed paper in an airtight container; cover. Store at room temperature for up to 3 days or freeze for up to 3 months.

CHEWY CHOCOLATE-CARAMEL BARS

Caramel-Apple Bars

PREP **20 MINUTES**   COOL **1 HOUR**   CHILL **15 MINUTES**

Nonstick cooking spray

1   10.5-ounce package tiny marshmallows (about 6 cups)

3   tablespoons butter, cut up

6   cups apple-and-cinnamon-flavor round toasted oat cereal

1   cup snipped dried apples

24 vanilla caramels, unwrapped

1   tablespoon milk

1   tablespoon butter

1   cup coarsely chopped peanuts or cashews

1 Line a 13x9x2-inch baking pan with foil, extending the foil over the edges of the pan. Lightly coat foil with cooking spray; set pan aside.

2 In a large microwave-safe bowl combine marshmallows and the 3 tablespoons butter. Microwave, uncovered, on 100 percent power (high) for 1 to 2 minutes or until marshmallows melt, stirring twice. Stir until smooth. Stir in cereal and dried apples.

3 Using the back of a buttered spoon, press cereal mixture evenly onto the bottom of the prepared baking pan. Let cool for 1 hour. Use the foil to lift the uncut bars out of the pan.

Place on a cutting board; cut into 2x1½-inch bars.

4 In a medium microwave-safe bowl combine caramels, milk, and the 1 tablespoon butter. Microwave, uncovered, on 100 percent power (high) for 45 to 60 seconds or until melted and smooth, stirring twice.

5 Line a cookie sheet with foil. Place chopped peanuts in a small bowl. Drizzle caramel mixture over one-third of each bar; dip the caramel-coated portions of the bars in the peanuts to coat. Place the bars on the prepared cookie sheet. Chill bars about 15 minutes or until caramel is set. **MAKES 32 BARS**

TO MAKE AHEAD AND STORE: Layer bars between sheets of waxed paper in an airtight container; cover. Store at room temperature for up to 3 days or freeze for up to 3 months.

Santa's Treats to Go

Sure, Santa's touched when you leave him cookies and a glass of milk, but with all the deliveries he has to make on Christmas Eve, does he really have time to sit down and enjoy them? Encourage the kids to help the jolly old soul stay on schedule by leaving him a to-go package. Start with a small gift bag and decorate it with color markers, stickers, glitter, ribbon, and rubber stamps. Fill it with cookies and a small carton of milk. This way, maybe his reindeers might get a few nibbles of your sweet treats too.

Caramel Swirl Brownies

PREP **25 MINUTES**   BAKE **25 MINUTES**   OVEN **350°F**

¾ **cup butter, cut up**

3 **ounces unsweetened chocolate, chopped**

1½ **cups sugar**

3 **eggs, lightly beaten**

1½ **teaspoons vanilla**

1 **cup all-purpose flour**

1 **recipe Caramel Swirl**

1 Preheat oven to 350°F. Line a 9x9x2-inch baking pan with foil, extending the foil over the edges of the pan. Grease foil.

2 In a medium saucepan cook and stir butter and chocolate over medium-low heat until chocolate melts. Remove from heat. Stir in the sugar, eggs, and vanilla. Stir in flour just until combined. Spoon the batter into the prepared baking pan, spreading evenly. Drop spoonfuls of Caramel Swirl over brownie batter. Using a thin metal spatula, swirl caramel mixture into the batter.

3 Bake for 25 to 30 minutes or until top springs back when lightly touched and the edges start to pull away from the sides of the pan. Cool in pan on a wire rack. Use the foil to lift the uncut brownies out of the pan. Place on a cutting board; cut into brownies.

MAKES 16 BROWNIES

Caramel Swirl: In a small saucepan combine 12 unwrapped vanilla caramels, one 3-ounce package cream cheese, 1 tablespoon sugar, and 1 tablespoon milk. Cook and stir over medium-low heat just until melted and smooth. In a small bowl beat 1 egg yolk; gradually stir into the caramel mixture.

TO MAKE AHEAD AND STORE: Place brownies in a single layer in an airtight container; cover. Store in the refrigerator for up to 3 days or freeze for up to 3 months.

What About Glass?

In a really tight pinch, you could substitute a 3-quart rectangular glass baking dish for a metal 13x9x2 baking pan; however, it's not ideal. Metal pans are better for getting evenly browned baked goods. But if glass is your only option, be sure to reduce the baking temperature by 25°F.

CHEWY GRANOLA BALLS, PAGE 163

fantastically fruity

Apples, cherries, cranberries,
and apricots add brightness, color,
and flavor to your cookie collection. Enjoy all
kinds of fruits layered into bars, swirled into
strudel cookies, nestled into mini tarts, and
served up in other irresistible ways.

★

Cran-Crazy Cookies

PREP **30 MINUTES**   BAKE **10 MINUTES PER BATCH**   COOL **2 MINUTES PER BATCH**   OVEN **350°F**

- ¾ cup butter, softened
- 1½ cups packed brown sugar
- 2 teaspoons finely shredded lemon peel
- ½ teaspoon baking soda
- ½ teaspoon baking powder
- ¼ teaspoon salt
- 2 eggs
- 2 teaspoons vanilla
- 2⅓ cups whole wheat flour
- 1½ cups chopped toasted walnuts
- 1½ cups dried cranberries

1 Preheat oven to 350°F. In a large mixing bowl beat butter with an electric mixer on medium to high speed for 30 seconds. Add brown sugar, lemon peel, baking soda, baking powder, and salt. Beat until combined, scraping sides of bowl occasionally. Beat in the eggs and vanilla until combined. Beat in as much of the flour as you can with the mixer. Using a wooden spoon, stir in any remaining flour, the walnuts, and cranberries.

2 Drop dough by rounded teaspoons 2 inches apart onto an ungreased cookie sheet. Bake for 10 to 12 minutes or until edges are light brown. Cool on cookie sheet for 2 minutes. Transfer cookies to a wire rack and let cool. **MAKES 60 COOKIES**

TO MAKE AHEAD AND STORE: Layer cookies between sheets of waxed paper in an airtight container; cover. Store at room temperature for up to 3 days or freeze for up to 3 months.

Fruit Forward

Dried fruit keeps much longer than fresh, making it easy to get a taste of fruity sweetness any time of year.

Store dried fruit in airtight containers at room temperature away from direct sunlight and heat sources. Stored properly, dried fruit should keep for 1 year (except figs, which keep for about 6 months).

Cherry Thumbprints

PREP 30 MINUTES   **CHILL 1 HOUR**   **BAKE 8 MINUTES PER BATCH**   **STAND 2 HOURS**   **OVEN 375°F**

- ⅔ **cup butter, softened**
- ½ **cup sugar**
- ⅛ **teaspoon salt**
- 1 **egg**
- 1 **teaspoon vanilla**
- 1⅔ **cups all-purpose flour**
- 2 **teaspoon finely shredded orange peel**
- ⅔ **cup finely chopped candied red and/or green cherries**

1. In a large mixing bowl beat butter with an electric mixer on medium to high speed for 30 seconds. Add sugar and salt. Beat until combined, scraping sides of bowl occasionally. Beat in the egg and vanilla until combined. Beat in as much of the flour as you can with the mixer. Using a wooden spoon, stir in any remaining flour and the orange peel. Cover and chill dough about 1 hour or until easy to handle.

2. Preheat oven to 375°F. Lightly grease a cookie sheet. Shape dough into 1-inch balls. Place balls 1 inch apart on the prepared cookie sheet. Press your thumb into the center of each ball.

3. Bake for 8 to 10 minutes or until edges are light brown. If cookie centers puff during baking, re-press with the back of a small spoon. Transfer cookies to a wire rack and let cool.

4. Spoon cherries into the indentations in the cookies. Let stand at least 2 hours for cherries to adhere to cookies. **MAKES ABOUT 40 COOKIES**

TO MAKE AHEAD AND STORE: Layer cookies between sheets of waxed paper in an airtight container; cover. Store at room temperature for up to 3 days or freeze for up to 3 months.

In a *twinkling*

Rather than using red or green candied cherries, use both in the same cookie. Drizzle tops with a powdered sugar glaze for extra embellishment.

Cherry-Walnut Balls

PREP **40 MINUTES**   BAKE **18 MINUTES PER BATCH**   COOL **5 MINUTES PER BATCH**   OVEN **325°F**

¼ cup coarsely chopped maraschino cherries
1 cup butter, softened
½ cup powdered sugar
½ teaspoon almond extract
½ teaspoon vanilla
2 cups all-purpose flour
¾ cup chopped walnuts, toasted
   Powdered sugar

1 Preheat oven to 325°F. Drain maraschino cherries on paper towels; pat dry to remove any excess liquid.

2 In a large mixing bowl beat butter with an electric mixer on medium to high speed for 30 seconds. Add the ½ cup powdered sugar, the almond extract, and vanilla. Beat until combined, scraping sides of bowl occasionally. Beat in as much of the flour as you can with the mixer. Using a wooden spoon, stir in any remaining flour, the nuts, and cherries.

3 Shape dough into 1-inch balls. Place balls 2 inches apart on an ungreased cookie sheet.

Bake for 18 to 20 minutes or until bottoms are light brown. Cool on cookie sheet for 5 minutes. Roll warm cookies in powdered sugar to coat. Transfer cookies to a wire rack and let cool. If desired, roll cooled cookies in additional powdered sugar before serving. **MAKES ABOUT 48 COOKIES**

TO MAKE AHEAD AND STORE: Layer cookies between sheets of waxed paper in an airtight container; cover. Store at room temperature for up to 3 days or freeze for up to 3 months.

In a *twinkling*

If you like, add a drop or two of red liquid food coloring to the dough for an extra touch of pink.

Chewy Granola Balls

PREP **40 MINUTES**   STAND **1 HOUR**

2½ cups wheat and rice cereal flakes with honey-nut pieces

2 cups regular rolled oats

1 cup mixed dried fruit bits

½ cup chopped almonds, toasted

½ cup packed brown sugar

½ cup light corn syrup

½ cup crunchy peanut butter

½ teaspoon almond extract

1 Line a large cookie sheet with waxed paper; set aside. In a large bowl stir together the cereal, oats, dried fruit, and almonds.

2 In a small saucepan combine the brown sugar and corn syrup. Bring to boiling, stirring constantly. Remove from heat; stir in peanut butter and almond extract until combined. Pour peanut butter mixture over cereal mixture; toss to coat.

3 Shape cereal mixture into 1¼-inch balls (you may need to work the mixture slightly with your hands until it clings together). Place balls on the prepared cookie sheet. Let stand at room temperature about 1 hour or until firm. **MAKES ABOUT 42 COOKIES**

TO MAKE AHEAD AND STORE: Layer cookies between sheets of waxed paper in an airtight container; cover. Store at room temperature for up to 2 days or freeze for up to 1 month.

Christmas Sandies

PREP **30 MINUTES**   BAKE **15 MINUTES PER BATCH**   OVEN **350°F**

1   cup butter, softened
½   cup powdered sugar
1   teaspoon vanilla
2   cups all-purpose flour
1   cup finely chopped dried cranberries*
2   teaspoons finely shredded lemon peel
    White, red, and green nonpareils

1 Preheat oven to 350°F. Line a cookie sheet with parchment paper. In a large mixing bowl beat butter with an electric mixer on medium to high speed for 30 seconds. Add powdered sugar. Beat until combined, scraping sides of bowl occasionally. Beat in the vanilla. Beat in as much of the flour as you can with the mixer. Using a wooden spoon, stir in any remaining flour, the cranberries, and lemon peel. (Use your hands to work in flour if mixture seems crumbly.)

2 Shape mixture into 1-inch balls. Roll balls in nonpareils to coat. Place balls 1 inch apart on the prepared cookie sheet.

3 Bake about 15 minutes or until bottoms of cookies are light brown. Transfer cookies to a wire rack and let cool. **MAKES 36 COOKIES**

*note To chop dried cranberries, place them in a food processor; cover and process until finely chopped. Or, finely chop them by hand.

TO MAKE AHEAD AND STORE: Layer cookies between sheets of waxed paper in an airtight container; cover. Store at room temperature for up to 3 days or freeze for up to 3 months.

gift It

Recycled Receptacle

Here's how to transform an aluminum foil box into a sensational way to present your Christmas Sandies:

Carefully disassemble and flatten the box; remove the cutting strip from the box. Lay two pieces of 12x12-inch decorative scrapbook paper side by side. Place unfolded box in the center of the two pieces of paper. Trace the outline of the box onto the paper; cut out traced shape. Glue paper to box. Re-form and glue box back together. Glue tinsel trim to box edges. To tie down the lid, glue ribbons to the box's lid and bottom. Line the box with parchment paper. Pack the cookies in paper candy cups to help keep them in place.

Blackberry Strudel Spirals

PREP **35 MINUTES**   CHILL **2 HOURS**   BAKE **12 MINUTES PER BATCH**   OVEN **400°F**

½   **cup butter, softened**
¾   **cup packed brown sugar**
¼   **teaspoon salt**
3   **cups all-purpose flour**
1   **8-ounce carton sour cream**
⅓   **cup seedless blackberry jam**
1   **cup flaked coconut**
¾   **cup chopped walnuts, toasted**
½   **cup dried currants or dried blueberries**
     Powdered sugar

1 In a large mixing bowl beat butter with an electric mixer on medium to high speed for 30 seconds. Add brown sugar and salt. Beat until combined, scraping sides of bowl occasionally. Beat in flour until mixture resembles coarse cornmeal. Beat in the sour cream until mixture is moistened and starts to cling. Gather dough into a ball. Divide dough into thirds.

2 On a lightly powdered-sugared surface roll out one dough portion into a 9-inch square. Spread about 2 tablespoons of the jam over the square; sprinkle with one-third each of the coconut, walnuts, and currants. Roll up dough into a spiral; pinch edges to seal. Wrap roll in plastic wrap or waxed paper. Repeat with the remaining dough, jam, coconut, walnuts, and currants. Chill rolls for 2 to 3 hours or until firm.

3 Preheat oven to 400°F. Line a large cookie sheet with parchment paper. Using a serrated knife, cut rolls crosswise into ½-inch-thick slices. Place slices 1 inch apart on the prepared cookie sheet.

4 Bake about 12 minutes or until tops are light brown.

Transfer cookies to a wire rack. While warm, sprinkle cookies lightly with powdered sugar. Cool completely on wire rack. **MAKES ABOUT 48 COOKIES**

TO MAKE AHEAD AND STORE: Layer cookies between sheets of waxed paper in an airtight container; cover. Store in the refrigerator for up to 3 days or freeze for up to 1 month.

Banana-Nut Shortbread

PREP **25 MINUTES**   CHILL **1 HOUR**   BAKE **30 MINUTES PER BATCH**   OVEN **300°F**

1   cup butter, softened
¼   cup mashed ripe banana
      (½ of a medium)
1   teaspoon vanilla
2¼ cups whole wheat flour
¾   cup packed brown sugar
1   teaspoon ground
      cinnamon
½   teaspoon ground nutmeg
⅔   cup finely chopped
      toasted walnuts
1   recipe Maple Icing

1 In a medium mixing bowl beat butter, banana, and vanilla with an electric mixer on medium speed until smooth. Cover and chill for 1 to 2 hours or freeze about 20 minutes or until firm.

2 Preheat oven to 300°F. In a large bowl stir together the flour, brown sugar, cinnamon, and nutmeg. Using a pastry blender, cut in butter mixture until mixture resembles fine crumbs and starts to cling together. Stir in chopped nuts. Knead dough until smooth; form into a ball. Divide dough in half.

3 On a lightly floured surface roll each dough half into an 8x6-inch rectangle. Cut each rectangle into sixteen 2x1½-inch rectangles. Place rectangles 1 inch apart on an ungreased cookie sheet.

4 Bake about 30 minutes or just until bottoms begin to brown.

Transfer cookies to a wire rack and let cool. Drizzle Maple Icing over cookies. Let stand until icing is set. **MAKES 32 COOKIES**

Maple Icing: In a medium bowl stir together 1½ cups powdered sugar, 1 to 2 tablespoons milk, and ¼ teaspoon maple flavoring to make an icing of drizzling consistency.

TO MAKE AHEAD AND STORE: Layer unfrosted cookies between sheets of waxed paper in an airtight container; cover. Store at room temperature for up to 3 days or freeze for up to 3 months. Thaw cookies, if frozen. Frost cookies as directed.

In a *twinkling*

After drizzling with the maple icing, top each rectangle with a dried banana chip or a large walnut half.

Apple-Toffee Tartlets

PREP **25 MINUTES**   BAKE **18 MINUTES**   OVEN **375°F**

1   15-ounce package rolled refrigerated unbaked piecrusts (2 crusts)
2   medium baking apples, cored and finely chopped
½   cup toffee pieces
¼   cup packed brown sugar
2   tablespoons butter, melted
⅛   teaspoon salt
    Powdered sugar (optional)

1 Preheat oven to 375°F. Let piecrusts stand according to package directions. In a medium bowl stir together apples, toffee pieces, brown sugar, melted butter, and salt.

2 On a lightly floured surface unroll piecrusts. Using a 3-inch round cookie cutter, cut out dough. Reroll scraps once to cut enough additional rounds to make 24 total. Press dough rounds into the bottoms and up the sides of 24 ungreased 1¾-inch muffin cups. Spoon about 1 tablespoon apple mixture into each cup.

3 Bake about 18 minutes or until crust is golden brown and filling is bubbly. Carefully transfer tartlets to a wire rack and let cool. If desired, sprinkle tartlets with powdered sugar before serving.
MAKES 24 TARTLETS

TO MAKE AHEAD AND STORE: Layer tartlets between sheets of waxed paper in an airtight container; cover. Store in the refrigerator for up to 3 days or freeze for up to 3 months.

Baking with Kids

Getting kids in on the holiday baking action is a great way to help them learn their way around the kitchen. These tips can make it more enjoyable for everyone:

◆ Let kids choose how much they want to help, and don't be surprised if their attention wanders before the job is done.

◆ Clear some space and don some aprons—little hands can make big messes, because kids simply aren't as coordinated as adults. Keep paper towels on hand to wipe up spills promptly.

◆ Keep safety in mind: Teach children to wash their hands often. Keep young children away from the hot stoves and baking sheets, powerful appliances, electrical outlets, and sharp knives. And remind them that no matter how good it looks, they shouldn't eat uncooked dough because of the raw egg it contains.

◆ Sneak in a lesson or two by telling kids how each ingredient works and what it adds to a recipe.

◆ While doable tasks for kids include pouring, stirring, sifting, and measuring, they'll especially enjoy shaping and decorating the cookies. Consider getting the dough ready for them in advance so they won't lose interest before these steps.

◆ Start developing good kitchen habits early—this is a good time to learn that cleanup is part of the project.

Cranberry-Fig Tassies

PREP **30 MINUTES**   CHILL **1 HOUR**   BAKE **30 MINUTES**   COOL **5 MINUTES**   OVEN **325°F**

½ cup butter, softened

1 3-ounce package cream cheese, softened

1 cup all-purpose flour

¼ cup finely chopped pecans

½ cup orange juice

⅓ cup finely chopped dried Calimyrna (light) figs

1 egg

1 teaspoon finely shredded orange peel

¾ cup packed brown sugar

½ teaspoon vanilla
   Dash salt

¼ cup finely chopped cranberries

1 recipe Sweetened Whipped Cream or powdered sugar (optional)

1 In a large mixing bowl beat butter and cream cheese with an electric mixer on medium to high speed for 30 seconds. Using a wooden spoon, stir in the flour and pecans. Cover and chill dough about 1 hour or until easy to handle.

2 Preheat oven to 325°F. Shape dough into 24 balls. Press each ball into the bottoms and up the sides of 24 ungreased 1¾-inch muffin cups. Set aside.

3 In a small saucepan combine orange juice and figs. Bring just to boiling; remove from heat. Let stand for 10 minutes to soften figs. Drain well.

4 In a medium bowl beat the egg with a fork. Stir in the orange peel, brown sugar, vanilla, and salt. Stir in the drained figs and the cranberries. Spoon about 2 teaspoons of the fig mixture into each dough-lined muffin cup. Do not overfill.

5 Bake for 30 to 35 minutes or until edges are golden.

Cool in pan on a wire rack for 5 minutes. Carefully transfer tassies to a wire rack and let cool. If desired, garnish cooled tassies with Sweetened Whipped Cream or sprinkle with powdered sugar before serving. MAKES 24 TASSIES

Sweetened Whipped Cream: In a medium mixing bowl beat ½ cup whipping cream, 1 tablespoon sugar, and ¼ teaspoon vanilla with an electric mixer on medium speed just until soft peaks form (tips curl).

TO MAKE AHEAD AND STORE: Place tassies in single layer in an airtight container. Store at room temperature for up to 24 hours or refrigerate for up to 3 days. Do not freeze. Before serving, let tassies stand at room temperature for 15 minutes.

Your Own Kind of Biscotti

Use the Christmas Biscotti recipe [opposite] as a template to stylize your own fruit-and-nut dunkers. Swap out the cranberries, apricots, and pistachios in the recipe, using equal amounts of your favorite dried fruits and nuts. Consider cherries, golden raisins, figs, and dates as well as chopped almonds, walnuts, macadamia nuts, and hazelnuts.

Christmas Biscotti

PREP **40 MINUTES**   BAKE **36 MINUTES**   COOL **30 MINUTES**   OVEN **375°F/325°F**

⅓ cup butter, softened

⅔ cup sugar

2 teaspoons baking powder

½ teaspoon ground nutmeg

¼ teaspoon salt

¼ teaspoon ground cinnamon

2 eggs

1 teaspoon vanilla

½ teaspoon rum extract

2 cups all-purpose flour

2 teaspoons finely shredded orange peel

½ cup pistachios, chopped

½ cup dried cranberries, chopped

½ cup dried apricots, chopped

1 recipe Powdered Sugar Icing

1 Preheat oven to 375°F. Line a large cookie sheet with parchment paper; set aside.

2 In a large mixing bowl beat butter with an electric mixer on medium to high speed for 30 seconds. Add sugar, baking powder, nutmeg, salt, and cinnamon. Beat until combined, scraping sides of bowl occasionally. Beat in the eggs, vanilla, and rum flavoring until combined. Beat in as much of the flour as you can with the mixer. Using a wooden spoon, stir in any remaining flour, the orange peel, pistachios, cranberries, and apricots. Divide dough into thirds.

3 On a lightly floured surface shape each dough portion into an 8-inch loaf. Place loaves 4 inches apart on the prepared cookie sheet; flatten loaves slightly until about 2 inches wide.

4 Bake for 20 to 25 minutes or until golden and tops are cracked. Cool on cookie sheet on a wire rack for 30 minutes.

5 Reduce oven temperature to 325°F. Transfer loaves to a cutting board. Using a serrated knife, cut loaves diagonally into ½-inch-thick slices. Place slices, cut sides down, on an ungreased cookie sheet.

6 Bake for 8 minutes. Turn slices over; bake for 8 to 10 minutes more or until dry and crisp. Transfer cookies to a wire rack and let cool. Drizzle Powdered Sugar Icing over cookies. Let stand until icing is set. **MAKES ABOUT 36 BISCOTTI**

Powdered Sugar Icing: In a small bowl stir together 1 cup powdered sugar and enough milk (1 to 2 tablespoons) to make an icing of drizzling consistency.

TO MAKE AHEAD AND STORE: Layer biscotti between sheets of waxed paper in an airtight container; cover. Store at room temperature for up to 3 days or freeze for up to 3 months.

White Chocolate and Cranberry Bars

PREP **25 MINUTES**   BAKE **40 MINUTES**   OVEN **350°F**

2   cups all-purpose flour
2   teaspoons freshly grated nutmeg or 1 teaspoon ground nutmeg
1   teaspoon baking powder
¼   teaspoon baking soda
2   cups packed brown sugar
⅔   cup butter
2   eggs
2   teaspoons vanilla
¾   cup dried cranberries
1½ cups fresh or frozen cranberries, thawed
3   ounces white baking chocolate, coarsely chopped

1   Preheat oven to 350°F. Line a 13x9x2-inch baking pan with foil, extending the foil over the edges of the pan. Grease foil. In a medium bowl stir together the flour, nutmeg, baking powder, and baking soda.

2   In a medium saucepan cook and stir the brown sugar and butter over medium heat until melted and smooth. Cool slightly. Add eggs, one at a time, beating well after each addition. Stir in vanilla. Add the flour mixture; stir just until combined. Stir in dried cranberries. Spoon batter into the prepared baking pan, spreading evenly. Sprinkle fresh cranberries evenly over batter.

3   Bake about 40 minutes or until a wooden toothpick inserted near the center comes out clean. Sprinkle white chocolate evenly over bars. Cool in pan on a wire rack. Use the foil to lift the uncut bars out of the pan. Place on a cutting board; cut into bars.
MAKES 12 BARS

TO MAKE AHEAD AND STORE: Layer bars between sheets of waxed paper in an airtight container; cover. Store at room temperature for up to 3 days or freeze for up to 3 months.

gift It

Good Things in Small Packages

Inexpensive waxed paper bags turn into nifty little packages when tied with colorful printed ribbons. Simply slide a cookie bar into a bag; then tie a ribbon around the square into a bow to make it look like a small package. Look for waxed paper bags near the paper lunch sacks in your supermarket or at crafts stores.

Cherry Crumble Pie Bars

PREP **25 MINUTES**   BAKE **55 MINUTES**   OVEN **350°F**

- 2 cups all-purpose flour
- 1¼ cups finely ground almonds
- ¾ cup packed brown sugar
- 1 cup butter, cut up
- ¾ cup granulated sugar
- 1 tablespoon cornstarch
- ½ teaspoon finely shredded lemon peel
- 4 cups frozen unsweetened pitted tart red cherries, thawed and drained
- ½ teaspoon almond extract

1 Preheat oven to 350°F. Line a 13x9x2-inch baking pan with foil, extending the foil over the edges of the pan.

2 For crust, in a large bowl stir together the flour, almonds, and brown sugar. Using a pastry blender, cut in the butter until mixture resembles fine crumbs. Remove and reserve 1½ cups of the crumb mixture. Press the remaining crumb mixture evenly onto the bottom of the prepared baking pan. Bake for 15 minutes.

3 Meanwhile, for filling, in another large bowl stir together the granulated sugar, cornstarch, and lemon peel. Add cherries and almond extract; toss gently to combine. Spoon filling over the hot baked crust, spreading evenly. Sprinkle evenly with the reserved crumb mixture.

4 Bake about 40 minutes more or until filling is bubbly and topping is light brown. Cool in pan on a wire rack. Use the foil to lift the uncut bars out of the pan. Place on a cutting board; cut into bars. **MAKES 32 BARS**

TO MAKE AHEAD AND STORE: Layer bars between sheets of waxed paper in an airtight container; cover. Store in the refrigerator for up to 2 days or freeze for up to 3 months.

Frosted Apple Pie Bars

PREP **40 MINUTES**   BAKE **45 MINUTES**   OVEN **350°F**

- 3 cups all-purpose flour
- 2 tablespoons granulated sugar
- ½ teaspoon salt
- ½ cup shortening
- ½ cup butter, cut up
- 2 egg yolks, beaten
- ⅓ cup milk
- 1 to 2 tablespoons water
- 6 cups peeled, cored, and thinly sliced cooking apples (2¼ pounds)
- 1 cup granulated sugar
- 1 cup crushed cornflakes
- ½ teaspoon ground cinnamon
- ½ teaspoon freshly grated nutmeg or ¼ teaspoon ground nutmeg
- 1 egg white, beaten
- 1 recipe Powdered Sugar Icing
   Freshly grated nutmeg or ground nutmeg (optional)

1 For pastry, in a large bowl stir together flour, the 2 table-spoons granulated sugar, and the salt. Using a pastry blender, cut in the shortening and butter until pieces are pea size.

2 In a small bowl whisk together the egg yolks and milk. Gradually stir egg yolk mixture into flour mixture, tossing with a fork to moisten. Sprinkle the water over the flour mixture, gently tossing until all of the mixture is moistened. Using your fingers, gently knead the pastry just until a ball forms. Divide dough into two portions, making one portion slightly larger than the other. Wrap and chill dough until needed.

3 For filling, in an extra-large bowl stir together apples, the 1 cup granulated sugar, the cornflakes, cinnamon, and the ½ teaspoon nutmeg.

4 Preheat oven to 350°F. Press the larger portion of dough evenly onto the bottom of an ungreased 15x10x1-inch baking pan. Spoon the filling over the dough, spreading evenly.

5 Roll the remaining dough portion between two pieces of waxed paper to a 15x10-inch rectangle. Carefully peel off the top sheet of waxed paper. Invert dough over the filling in the pan; carefully peel off waxed paper. Using wet fingers, crimp the edges of the dough to seal. Using a sharp knife, cut a few slits in the top pastry; brush top lightly with egg white.

6 Bake for 45 to 50 minutes or until pastry is golden, fruit is tender, and filling is bubbly. Cool completely in pan on a wire rack. Cut into bars.

7 Drizzle Powdered Sugar Icing over bars and, if desired, sprinkle with additional nutmeg. Let stand until icing is set. **MAKES 32 BARS**

Powdered Sugar Icing: In a medium bowl stir together 1½ cups powdered sugar, ¼ teaspoon vanilla, and enough milk (1 to 2 tablespoons) to make an icing of drizzling consistency.

TO MAKE AHEAD AND STORE: Layer bars between sheets of waxed paper in an airtight container; cover. Store in the refrigerator for up to 3 days or freeze for up to 3 months.

A Doable Drizzle

It's amazing what a simple drizzle of powdered sugar can do to a cookie or a bar. The only trick to this three-ingredient topping is to get it to drizzling consistency. Start with the minimum amount of milk given in the range. At this stage, the icing will likely drop in clumps as you try to pour it from a spoon. Add an additional teaspoon of milk, stirring it thoroughly into the mixture. Test to see if it will drizzle from the spoon. If not, continue adding additional milk by the teaspoon (or half-teaspoon if you're making a small amount) until the icing flows in a drizzle. Always make sure the milk is fully incorporated before adding additional milk— it doesn't take much for the icing to go from too stiff to perfect.

Cranberry-Pear Bars

PREP **25 MINUTES** BAKE **20 MINUTES** OVEN **350°F**

1 package 2-layer-size white or yellow cake mix

2 eggs

½ cup butter, melted

1 tablespoon finely shredded orange peel

1 firm pear, peeled, cored, and chopped

1 cup fresh or frozen cranberries, thawed

½ cup chopped pecans

1 recipe Easy Orange Frosting

1 Preheat oven to 350°F. Grease a 15x10x1-inch baking pan.

2 In a large mixing bowl combine the cake mix, eggs, melted butter, and orange peel. Beat with an electric mixer on medium speed until combined. Fold in the chopped pear, cranberries, and pecans. Pour batter into the prepared baking pan, spreading evenly.

3 Bake for 20 to 25 minutes or until a wooden toothpick inserted in the center comes out clean. Cool in pan on a wire rack. Spread Easy Orange Frosting evenly over bars. Cut into bars.
MAKES 48 BARS

Easy Orange Frosting: In a medium bowl stir together one 16-ounce can vanilla frosting, ½ teaspoon finely shredded orange peel, and ¼ teaspoon ground cinnamon.

TO MAKE AHEAD AND STORE: Place bars in a single layer in an airtight container; cover. Store at room temperature for up to 3 days. Or freeze unfrosted bars for up to 3 months. Thaw bars; frost as directed.

In a *twinkling*

Add a subtle dusting of color by sprinkling the tops of the bars with ground cinnamon just before serving.

Blueberry Swirl Cheesecake Bars

PREP **25 MINUTES** BAKE **40 MINUTES** COOL **1 HOUR** CHILL **1 HOUR** OVEN **350°F**

2 **tablespoons granulated sugar**
2 **teaspoons cornstarch**
1 **cup fresh or frozen blueberries**
¼ **cup orange juice**
2 **cups all-purpose flour**
½ **cup powdered sugar**
1 **cup butter, cut up**
1 **8-ounce package cream cheese, softened**
½ **cup granulated sugar**
1 **tablespoon all-purpose flour**
2 **eggs, lightly beaten**
1 **teaspoon vanilla**
   Powdered sugar (optional)

1 Preheat oven to 350°F. Line a 13x9x2-inch baking pan with foil, extending the foil over the edges of the pan. Set pan aside.

2 In a small saucepan stir together the 2 tablespoons granulated sugar and the cornstarch. Stir in blueberries and orange juice. Cook and stir over medium heat until thickened and bubbly. Remove from heat; set aside.*

3 For crust, in a large mixing bowl stir together 2 cups flour and the powdered sugar. Cut in butter until mixture resembles fine crumbs and starts to cling together (mixture will still be crumbly). Press crumb mixture evenly onto the bottom of the prepared baking pan. Bake for 20 minutes.

4 Meanwhile, in a medium mixing bowl beat cream cheese, ½ cup sugar, and 1 tablespoon flour with an electric mixer on medium speed until smooth. Beat in the eggs and vanilla until combined. Pour over hot baked crust, spreading evenly.

Spoon blueberry mixture in small mounds over the cheese layer. Using a thin metal spatula or table knife, marble the layers together.

5 Bake for 20 minutes more or until center is set. Cool in pan on a wire rack for 1 hour. Cover and chill at least 1 hour. Use the foil to lift the uncut bars out of the pan. Place on a cutting board; cut into bars. If desired, sprinkle with powdered sugar before serving.

MAKES 36 BARS

note For easier preparation, omit Step 2 and substitute ¾ cup canned blueberry pie filling for the 2 tablespoons sugar, cornstarch, blueberries, and orange juice.

TO MAKE AHEAD AND STORE: Place bars in a single layer in an airtight container; cover. Store in the refrigerator for up to 2 days. Do not freeze.

LIME ZINGERS, PAGE 197

citrusy
sensations

Here's something every
cookie collection needs: a tart and
tingly squeeze of citrus. These recipes call
on lemon, lime, orange, and tangerine for an
irresistibly zesty contrast to the sweet, rich
goodies on the tray.

✶

Lemon Tarts

PREP **40 MINUTES**   BAKE **10 MINUTES**   COOL **10 MINUTES**   CHILL **1 HOUR**   OVEN **375°F**

1¼   cups all-purpose flour
⅓   cup sugar
2   teaspoons finely shredded lemon peel
½   cup butter, cut up
1   egg yolk, lightly beaten
2   tablespoons cold water
⅔   cup sugar
1   tablespoon cornstarch
2   teaspoons finely shredded lemon peel
½   cup lemon juice
¼   cup water
2   tablespoons butter
3   egg yolks, lightly beaten
    Lemon peel strips (optional)

1 In a medium bowl stir together flour, the ⅓ cup sugar, and 2 teaspoons lemon peel. Using a pastry blender, cut in the ½ cup butter until mixture resembles coarse crumbs. In a small bowl stir together the 1 egg yolk and the 2 tablespoons cold water. Gradually stir egg yolk mixture into flour mixture. Gently knead to form a ball. If necessary, cover and chill dough for 30 to 60 minutes or until easy to handle.

2 Preheat oven to 375°F. For filling, in a medium saucepan stir together the ⅔ cup sugar and the cornstarch. Stir in 2 teaspoons lemon peel, the lemon juice, the ¼ cup water, and the 2 tablespoons butter. Cook and stir over medium heat until thick and bubbly.

3 Gradually stir about half of the hot lemon mixture into the 3 egg yolks. Return egg yolk mixture to saucepan. Bring to a gentle boil over medium heat; reduce heat. Cook and stir for 2 minutes. Transfer filling to a small bowl; cover surface with plastic wrap. Chill filling until needed.

4 Shape dough into 36 balls. Press each ball into the bottoms and up the sides of thirty-six 1¾-inch muffin cups. Bake about 10 minutes or until golden. Cool in pan on a wire rack for 10 minutes. Carefully transfer crusts to a wire rack and let cool.

5 Spoon 1 rounded teaspoon filling into each crust. Cover and chill for 1 to 2 hours before serving. If desired, garnish tarts with lemon peel strips. **MAKES 36 TARTS**

TO MAKE AHEAD AND STORE:
Prepare dough as directed in Step 1; wrap the dough in plastic wrap and freeze for up to 1 month. Thaw frozen dough in the refrigerator overnight. Or place unfilled baked crusts in a single layer in an airtight container; cover and store at room temperature for up to 24 hours before filling. Lemon filling may also be chilled for up to 24 hours.

In a *twinkling*

Top each tart with a fresh blueberry or raspberry—two fruits that go beautifully with lemon.

Tropical Dream Tassies

PREP **55 MINUTES**   BAKE **30 MINUTES**   COOL **10 MINUTES**   CHILL **2 HOURS**   OVEN **325°F**

½   cup butter, softened
1   3-ounce package cream cheese, softened
1   cup all-purpose flour
¼   cup finely chopped macadamia nuts
2   egg yolks
½   of a 14-ounce can sweetened condensed milk (⅔ cup)
½   teaspoon finely shredded lime peel
¼   cup lime juice
1   to 2 drops green liquid food coloring (optional)
1   recipe Sweetened Whipped Cream
     Toasted coconut (optional)

1 In a medium bowl beat butter and cream cheese with an electric mixer on medium to high speed until combined. Add the flour and macadamia nuts. Beat on low speed just until combined. Cover and chill dough for 30 to 60 minutes or until easy to handle.

2 Preheat oven to 325°F. Shape dough into 24 balls. Press each ball into the bottoms and up the sides of 24 ungreased 1¾-inch muffin cups. Bake for 20 to 25 minutes or until edges are golden brown.

3 Meanwhile, for filling, in a medium bowl beat egg yolks with a whisk. Gradually whisk in sweetened condensed milk. Add lime peel, lime juice, and, if desired, green food coloring. Stir just until combined (mixture will thicken slightly). Spoon about 1 tablespoon filling into each pastry-lined muffin cup.

4 Bake about 10 minutes or until filling is set in center. Cool in pan on a wire rack for 10 minutes. Carefully transfer tassies to a wire rack and let cool. Chill about 2 hours or until completely chilled. Just before serving, top tassies with Sweetened Whipped Cream and, if desired, toasted coconut.
MAKES 24 TASSIES

Sweetened Whipped Cream:
In a medium mixing bowl beat ½ cup whipping cream, 1 tablespoon sugar, and ¼ teaspoon vanilla with an electric mixer on medium speed just until soft peaks form (tips curl).

TO MAKE AHEAD AND STORE:
Prepare dough as directed in Step 1; wrap the dough in plastic wrap and freeze for up to 1 month. Thaw frozen dough in the refrigerator overnight. Or place tassies in a single layer in an airtight container; cover. Store in the refrigerator for up to 2 days.

Saving Sweetened Condensed Milk

When a recipe calls only for a portion of a can of sweetened condensed milk, save the rest for another baking project. Transfer the extra milk into a clean jar or a container and store it in the refrigerator for up to 3 weeks.

Little Lemon Snow Bites

PREP **25 MINUTES**   BAKE **7 MINUTES PER BATCH**   COOL **1 MINUTE PER BATCH**   OVEN **375°F**

1   **17.5-ounce package sugar cookie mix**
¼   **cup crushed lemon drops**
⅔   **cup lemon curd**
⅔   **cup frozen whipped dessert topping, thawed**
2   **tablespoons powdered sugar**

1 Preheat oven to 375°F. Line a cookie sheet with parchment paper or foil. Prepare cookie mix according to package directions. Stir in the crushed lemon drops. If necessary, cover and chill dough about 1 hour or until easy to handle.

2 Shape dough into 1-inch balls. Place balls 2 inches apart on the prepared cookie sheet. Bake for 7 to 9 minutes or until edges are firm and bottoms are light brown. Cool on cookie sheet for 1 minute. Transfer cookies to a wire rack and let cool.

3 For filling, in a small bowl stir together the lemon curd and whipped topping. To assemble cookies, spread 1 rounded teaspoon filling onto the bottom of one cookie; lightly press the bottom of a second cookie against the filling. Repeat with the remaining cookies and filling. Before serving, sprinkle sandwich cookies with powdered sugar.

MAKES ABOUT 24 SANDWICH COOKIES

TO MAKE AHEAD AND STORE: Place sandwich cookies in a single layer in an airtight container; cover. Store in the refrigerator for up to 3 days or freeze for up to 1 month.

The Magical Two-Ingredient Filling

The filling for Little Lemon Snow Bites is a simple combination of lemon curd and whipped dessert topping, a perfect combination of sweetness and zip. Use the formula (1 part whipped topping to 1 part lemon curd) in other desserts. Try it layered in parfaits and trifles, spooned into meringue shells or baked tartlet shells, or dolloped on top of angel food cake.

Orange–Poppy Seed Turnover Cookies

PREP **30 MINUTES**   CHILL **1 HOUR**   BAKE **8 MINUTES PER BATCH**   OVEN **375°F**

1   recipe Cutout Dough
1   tablespoon finely
      shredded orange peel
1   teaspoon orange juice
½   cup finely chopped
      toasted almonds
1   tablespoon poppy seeds
1   recipe Orange Glaze
      (optional)

1 Prepare dough as directed. Divide dough in half. Stir orange peel, orange juice, and almonds into one dough half. Stir poppy seeds into the remaining dough half. Cover and chill dough for 1 to 2 hours or until easy to handle.

2 Preheat oven to 375°F. Divide each portion of dough in half. On a lightly floured surface carefully roll one portion of the poppy seed dough to ⅛-inch thickness. Using a 2-inch round cookie cutter, cut out dough. Place cutouts 1 inch apart on an ungreased cookie sheet.

3 Shape one portion of the orange dough into ¾-inch balls. Form each ball into a small crescent shape that fits on half of a poppy seed circle. Place a crescent on one half of a poppy seed circle, leaving a ⅛-inch edge. Carefully fold poppy seed circles over orange crescents (you may need to slightly stretch the circles). Use the tines of a fork to seal edges. Repeat with the remaining poppy seed and orange dough portions.

4 Bake for 8 to 10 minutes or until edges are firm and bottoms are light brown. Transfer cookies to a wire rack and let cool. If desired, drizzle Orange Glaze evenly over cookies. Let stand until glaze is set. **MAKES 36 COOKIES**

Cutout Dough: In a large mixing bowl beat ½ cup butter, softened, and one 3-ounce package cream cheese, softened, with an electric mixer on medium to high speed for 30 seconds. Add 1½ cups powdered sugar, 1 teaspoon baking powder, and ¼ teaspoon salt. Beat until combined, scraping sides of bowl occasionally. Beat in 1 egg and 1 teaspoon vanilla until combined. Gradually add 2 cups all-purpose flour, beating in as much of the flour as you can with the mixer. Using a wooden spoon, stir in any remaining flour.

Orange Glaze: In a small bowl stir together 1 cup powdered sugar, 1 to 2 tablespoons orange juice, and ⅛ teaspoon almond extract to make a glaze of drizzling consistency.

TO MAKE AHEAD AND STORE: Layer cookies between sheets of waxed paper in an airtight container; cover. Store in the refrigerator for up to 3 days or freeze for up to 3 months.

In a *twinkling*

If you like, skip the Orange Glaze and sprinkle cookies with orange-colored sugar before baking. Or glaze the baked and cooled cookies as directed and sprinkle with orange-colored sugar before the glaze sets.

Pistachio-Lime Balls

PREP **25 MINUTES**   BAKE **15 MINUTES PER BATCH**   COOL **5 MINUTES PER BATCH**   OVEN **325°F**

- 1   **cup butter, softened**
- ½   **cup powdered sugar**
- 2   **cups all-purpose flour**
- 1   **cup coarsely ground dry-roasted pistachios**
- 1   **tablespoon finely shredded lime peel**
-      **Green coarse sugar or granulated sugar**
-      **Powdered sugar**

1 Preheat oven to 325°F. In a large mixing bowl beat butter with an electric mixer on medium to high speed for 30 seconds. Add the ½ cup powdered sugar. Beat until combined, scraping sides of bowl occasionally. Beat in as much of the flour as you can with the mixer. Using a wooden spoon, stir in any remaining flour, the pistachios, and lime peel.

2 Shape dough into 1-inch balls. Roll each ball in green sugar to coat. Place balls 2 inches apart on an ungreased cookie sheet.

3 Bake about 15 minutes or until bottoms are light brown. Cool on cookie sheet for 5 minutes. Roll warm cookies in powdered sugar to coat. Transfer cookies to a wire rack and let cool. If desired, roll cooled cookies in additional powdered sugar before serving. **MAKES ABOUT 48 COOKIES**

TO MAKE AHEAD AND STORE: Layer cookies between sheets of waxed paper in an airtight container; cover. Store at room temperature for up to 3 days or freeze for up to 3 months.

Lemon Dreams

START TO FINISH **25 MINUTES**

- 1   **10-ounce jar lemon curd, stirred to loosen**
- 2   **8.25-ounce packages soft sugar cookies or gingerbread cookies (24 cookies)**
- 1   **16-ounce can vanilla frosting**

1 Spoon 2 to 3 teaspoons lemon curd onto the center of the top of each cookie. Spread lemon curd almost to the edge of each cookie.

2 In a medium bowl stir together the frosting and the remaining lemon curd. Spoon frosting mixture into a pastry bag fitted with a medium star tip. Pipe stars or rosettes around the edge of each cookie. **MAKES 24 COOKIES**

TO MAKE AHEAD AND STORE: Place cookies in a single layer in an airtight container; cover. Store in the refrigerator for up to 2 days. Do not freeze.

Tangerine Butter Cookies

PREP **45 MINUTES**   BAKE **9 MINUTES PER BATCH**   OVEN **350°F**

¾	cup butter, softened
1½	cups sugar
1½	teaspoons baking soda
1½	teaspoons cream of tartar
1	teaspoon salt
2	eggs
2	teaspoons finely shredded tangerine peel or orange peel
1	teaspoon vanilla
1	teaspoon orange extract
¾	cup olive oil
½	cup white cornmeal
4	cups all-purpose flour
½	cup sugar

1 In a very large mixing bowl beat butter with an electric mixer on medium to high speed for 30 seconds. Add the 1½ cups sugar, the baking soda, cream of tartar, and salt. Beat until light and fluffy, scraping sides of bowl occasionally. Beat in the eggs, tangerine peel, vanilla, and orange extract until combined. Gradually beat in the olive oil until smooth. Beat in cornmeal until combined. Beat in as much of the flour as you can with the mixer. Using a wooden spoon, stir in any remaining flour. If necessary, cover and chill dough for 30 to 60 minutes or until easy to handle.

2 Preheat oven to 350°F. Place the ½ cup sugar in a small bowl. Shape dough into 1-inch balls. Roll balls in sugar to coat. Place balls 2 inches apart on an ungreased cookie sheet. Using a wooden skewer or toothpick, press an "X" into each ball.

3 Bake for 9 to 11 minutes or until tops are very light brown. Lightly press cookies again with wooden skewer to make deeper "X" indentations. Transfer cookies to a wire rack and let cool. **MAKES ABOUT 84 COOKIES**

TO MAKE AHEAD AND STORE: Layer cookies between sheets of waxed paper in an airtight container; cover. Store at room temperature for up to 3 days or freeze for up to 3 months.

The Best Zester

The handiest gadget for shredding citrus peel is the Microplane, a long, thin, rasp-style grater. This lightweight tool will produce the finest pieces of peel. Simply rub the clean, dry citrus fruit across its surface. You can also use a box grater, which has fine and coarse holes, letting you choose whichever size of shreds you wish.

For thin strips of citrus peel (versus superfine shreds), use a citrus zester. This tool is comprised of a handle and a curved metal end that has a row of round, sharp-rimmed holes.

No matter which tool you use, make sure you remove just the colored part of the peel (the zest). Do not use the white part of the peel (the pith), because it is bitter.

Lemon Drop Sandwiches

PREP **45 MINUTES**   BAKE **1 HOUR 30 MINUTES**   OVEN **200°F**

- 3 **egg whites**
- ½ **teaspoon vanilla**
- ¼ **teaspoon cream of tartar**
- ⅛ **teaspoon salt**
- ¾ **cup sugar**
- 1 **teaspoon finely shredded lemon peel**
- 1 **recipe Lemon Frosting**

1 Preheat oven to 200°F. Line a cookie sheet with parchment paper; set aside. In a large mixing bowl beat egg whites, vanilla, cream of tartar, and salt with an electric mixer on medium speed until soft peaks form (tips curl). Gradually add sugar, 1 tablespoon at a time, beating on high speed until stiff peaks form (tips stand straight). Gently stir in lemon peel.

2 Spoon egg white mixture into a pastry bag fitted with a ½-inch round tip. Pipe 1½-inch rounds 1 inch apart onto the prepared cookie sheet.

3 Bake for 1½ to 1¾ hours or until cookies appear dry and are firm when lightly touched. Transfer cookies to a wire rack and let cool.

4 To assemble cookies, spread about 1 teaspoon Lemon Frosting onto the bottom of one cookie; press the bottom of a second cookie against the frosting. Repeat with the remaining cookies and frosting. Serve immediately or let cookies stand at room temperature for up to 2 hours before serving. **MAKES ABOUT 36 SANDWICH COOKIES**

Lemon Frosting: In a medium mixing bowl beat ⅓ cup softened butter and 2 teaspoons finely shredded lemon peel with an electric mixer on medium to high speed until fluffy. Gradually beat in 2 cups powdered sugar. Beat in lemon juice, 1 teaspoon at a time, to make a frosting of spreading consistency.

TO MAKE AHEAD AND STORE: Layer unfilled cookies between sheets of waxed paper in an airtight container; cover. Store at room temperature for up to 2 days or freeze for up to 1 month. Thaw cookies, if frozen. Assemble as directed.

Lemony Spritz

PREP **50 MINUTES**   BAKE **8 MINUTES**   OVEN **375°F**

1½	cups butter, softened
1	cup granulated sugar
1	teaspoon baking powder
1	egg
1	teaspoon vanilla
½	teaspoon lemon extract
3½	cups all-purpose flour
1	recipe Lemon Glaze
	Colored sugar (optional)

1 Preheat oven to 375°F. In a large mixing bowl beat butter with an electric mixer on medium speed for 30 seconds. Add granulated sugar and baking powder. Beat until combined, scraping sides of bowl occasionally. Beat in the egg, vanilla, and lemon extract until combined. Beat in as much of the flour as you can with the mixer. Using a wooden spoon, stir in any remaining flour.

2 Pack unchilled dough into a cookie press. Force dough through the cookie press 2 inches apart onto an ungreased cookie sheet.

3 Bake for 8 to 10 minutes or until edges of cookies are firm but not brown. Transfer cookies to a wire rack and let cool. Drizzle or brush Lemon Glaze onto cookies; if desired, sprinkle with colored sugar. Let stand until glaze is set.
MAKES ABOUT 70 COOKIES

Lemon Glaze: In a small bowl stir together 1½ cups powdered sugar, 2 teaspoons finely shredded lemon peel, and 1½ teaspoons lemon juice. Stir in milk, 1 teaspoon at a time, to make an icing of drizzling consistency.

TO MAKE AHEAD AND STORE: Layer unglazed cookies between sheets of waxed paper in an airtight container; cover. Store at room temperature for up to 3 days or freeze for up to 1 month. Thaw cookies, if frozen. Glaze cookies as directed.

Parchment Paper

One way to make sure cookies never stick to the baking sheet is to line the pan with parchment paper. A few tips:

+ Parchment is somewhat pricey, so reserve its use for especially delicate cookies, such as macarons, meringues, and thin cutout cookies—its perfect nonstick surface helps eliminate breakage.

+ When lining baking sheets with parchment paper, avoid letting the parchment hang over the edges of the sheet. Cut to fit, if necessary.

+ If you're using only a portion of the baking sheet, trim the excess parchment paper—use only enough to accommodate the cookies you're baking.

+ Do not allow the parchment sheet to touch the oven rack or the oven wall.

+ You need not grease parchment paper when baking cookies.

+ Cleanup is easy—simply throw the parchment away.

Lemon Cream Icebox Cookie Sandwiches

PREP **30 MINUTES**   CHILL **1 HOUR**   BAKE **8 MINUTES PER BATCH**   COOL **1 MINUTE PER BATCH**   OVEN **375°F**

1   cup butter-flavor
      shortening
1   cup granulated sugar
1   teaspoon baking powder
¼   teaspoon salt
1   egg
1   teaspoon vanilla
2¼ cups all-purpose flour
2   teaspoons finely shredded
      lemon peel
1   recipe Lemon Cream
      Frosting or 1¼ cups
      lemon curd
      Yellow gumdrops
      (optional)
      Powdered sugar

1 In a large mixing bowl beat shortening with an electric mixer on medium to high speed for 30 seconds. Add granulated sugar, baking powder, and salt. Beat until combined, scraping sides of bowl occasionally. Beat in the egg and vanilla until combined. Beat in as much of the flour as you can with the mixer. Using a wooden spoon, stir in any remaining flour and the lemon peel.

2 Divide dough in half. Roll each portion into a 10-inch log. Wrap each log in plastic wrap or waxed paper; chill for 1 to 3 hours or until firm.

3 Preheat oven to 375°F. Cut logs crosswise into ¼-inch-thick slices. Place slices 2 inches apart on an ungreased cookie sheet. Bake for 8 to 10 minutes or until set. Cool on cookie sheet for 1 minute. Transfer cookies to a wire rack and let cool.

4 To assemble cookies, spread about 1 tablespoon Lemon Cream Frosting or 1½ teaspoons lemon curd onto the bottom of one cookie; press the bottom of a second cookie against the frosting. Repeat with the remaining cookies and frosting.

5 If desired, cut gumdrops into slivers. Spread a little frosting on top of each sandwich cookie; arrange gumdrops slivers on frosting to form a flower. Before serving, sprinkle cookies with powdered sugar. **MAKES ABOUT 36 SANDWICH COOKIES**

Lemon Cream Frosting: In a large mixing bowl beat one 8-ounce package cream cheese, softened, and ⅔ cup butter, softened, with an electric mixer on medium speed until smooth. Gradually beat in 3⅓ cups powdered sugar until combined. Stir in 1 tablespoon finely shredded lemon peel.

TO MAKE AHEAD AND STORE: Place sandwich cookies in a single layer in an airtight container; cover. Store at room temperature for up to 3 days or freeze for up to 3 months. Thaw cookies, if frozen. Before serving, sprinkle cookies with powdered sugar.

Citrus by the Numbers

If you're wondering how many lemons, limes, or oranges to buy for a recipe, use this as a guide:

+ 1 medium lemon yields 2 teaspoons shredded peel and 3 tablespoons juice.

+ 1 medium lime yields 1½ teaspoons shredded peel and 2 tablespoons juice.

+ 1 medium orange yields 1 tablespoon shredded peel and ⅓ cup juice.

Lemon-Blueberry Fans

PREP **1 HOUR**   CHILL **1 HOUR**   BAKE **8 MINUTES PER BATCH**   COOL **1 MINUTE PER BATCH**   OVEN **375°F**

1   **cup butter, softened**
1   **3-ounce package cream cheese, softened**
1   **cup sugar**
¼   **teaspoon salt**
1   **teaspoon finely shredded lemon peel**
1   **teaspoon vanilla**
½   **teaspoon lemon extract**
2   **tablespoons cornstarch**
2½ **cups all-purpose flour**
⅔   **cup blueberry or raspberry jam or preserves**

1 In a very large mixing bowl beat butter and cream cheese with an electric mixer on medium to high speed for 30 seconds. Add sugar and salt. Beat until light and fluffy, scraping sides of bowl occasionally. Beat in the 1 teaspoon lemon peel, the vanilla, and lemon extract until combined. Beat in cornstarch. Beat in as much of the flour as you can with the mixer. Using a wooden spoon, stir in any remaining flour. Divide dough in half. Cover and chill dough for 1 to 2 hours or until easy to handle.

2 Preheat oven to 375°F. On a lightly floured surface roll each dough half to ⅛-inch thickness. Using a 2½-inch round cookie cutter, cut out dough. Place cutouts 1 inch apart on an ungreased cookie sheet.

3 Spoon ½ teaspoon of the jam onto the center of each round. To shape fans, bring opposite sides of each dough round up over the jam and pinch them together where they meet, forming a point at one end.

4 Bake for 8 to 10 minutes or until edges are light brown. Cool on cookie sheet for 1 minute. Transfer cookies to a wire rack and let cool. **MAKES ABOUT 54 COOKIES**

TO MAKE AHEAD AND STORE: Layer cookies between sheets of waxed paper in an airtight container; cover. Store in the refrigerator for up to 3 days or freeze for up to 1 month.

In a *twinkling*

Sprinkle with powdered sugar and/or finely shredded lemon peel just before serving.

Lime Shortbread Trees

PREP **1 HOUR 15 MINUTES**   BAKE **15 MINUTES PER BATCH**   COOL **10 MINUTES PER BATCH**   OVEN **325°F**

 1   cup butter, softened
 ½   cup powdered sugar
 2   teaspoons finely shredded lime peel
 ¼   teaspoon salt
2¼   cups all-purpose flour
 1   cup powdered sugar
     Milk
     Green food coloring (optional)
     Small decorative candies

1 In a large mixing bowl beat butter with an electric mixer on medium to high speed for 30 seconds. Add the ½ cup powdered sugar, the lime peel, and salt. Beat until combined, scraping sides of bowl occasionally. Beat in flour until dough just comes together. Divide dough in half. If necessary, cover and chill dough for 30 minutes or until it is easy to handle.

2 Preheat oven to 325°F. On a large ungreased cookie sheet roll half of the dough into a 13x4-inch rectangle. Score one long side at 1½-inch intervals.

Starting ¾ inch from the corner of the opposite long side, score at 1½-inch intervals. Using a long sharp knife, cut across the dough, connecting the scored marks to make 15 triangles (trees); do not separate. Remove dough scraps from edges. Shape 15 small rectangles from the dough scraps; place them at the bottom of the trees as trunks. Repeat with remaining dough half.

3 Bake about 15 minutes or until edges just begin to brown. While still hot, re-cut trees with the long sharp knife. Cool on cookie sheet for 10 minutes. Transfer cookies to a wire rack and let cool.

4 For icing, in a small bowl stir together the 1 cup powdered sugar and enough milk, 1 to 2 teaspoons at a time, to make an icing of spreading consistency. If desired, tint some of the icing with green food coloring. Spread icing on cookies; decorate with small candies. **MAKES 30 COOKIES**

TO MAKE AHEAD AND STORE: Layer unfrosted cookies between sheets of waxed paper in an airtight container; cover. Store at room temperature for up to 3 days or freeze for up to 3 months. Thaw cookies, if frozen. Ice cookies as directed.

Roll On!

It may seem strange to roll the cookie dough directly on the sheet, but in this case, doing so helps you create extra-tender cookies. Plus, you won't need a cookie cutter—you simply cut the dough into triangles and remove the scraps to perfectly shape the cookies (and perfectly space them on the sheet).

Orange-Kissed Chocolate Brownies

PREP **40 MINUTES** BAKE **25 MINUTES** CHILL **30 MINUTES** COOL **15 MINUTES** OVEN **350°F**

4	eggs
2	cups granulated sugar
1¼	cups all-purpose flour
1	cup unsweetened Dutch-process cocoa powder
1	cup butter, melted
¼	cup butter, softened
1	teaspoon finely shredded orange peel
3½	cups powdered sugar
2	to 3 tablespoons orange juice
4	ounces semisweet chocolate
½	cup butter
2	tablespoons light corn syrup

1 Preheat oven to 350°F. Line a 13x9x2-inch baking pan with foil, extending the foil over the edges of the pan. Lightly grease foil. In a large mixing bowl beat eggs and granulated sugar with an electric mixer on medium speed for 3 to 5 minutes or until pale yellow and thickened. In a small bowl stir together the flour and cocoa powder. Add flour mixture to egg mixture. Beat just until smooth, scraping sides of bowl occasionally. Using a wooden spoon, stir in the melted butter until combined. Pour batter into the prepared baking pan, spreading evenly.

2 Bake for 25 to 30 minutes or until a wooden toothpick inserted near the center comes out clean. Cool in pan on a wire rack.

3 For frosting, in a large mixing bowl beat the ¼ cup butter and the orange peel on medium speed until smooth. Add 1 cup of the powdered sugar and 1 tablespoon of the orange juice; beat until combined. Beat in the remaining 2½ cups powdered sugar and enough of the remaining 1 to 2 tablespoons orange juice to make a frosting of spreading consistency. Spread frosting evenly over cooled brownies. Cover and chill for 30 minutes.

4 Meanwhile, in a medium saucepan cook and stir semisweet chocolate and the ½ cup butter over low heat until chocolate melts. Remove from heat; stir in corn syrup. Cool for 15 minutes.

5 Slowly pour melted chocolate mixture over the frosted brownies. Tilt pan gently to spread chocolate over the entire top. Chill brownies until chocolate is set. Use the foil to lift the uncut brownies out of the pan. Place on a cutting board; cut into brownies.

MAKES 32 BROWNIES

TO MAKE AHEAD AND STORE: Place brownies in a single layer in an airtight container; cover. Store in the refrigerator for up to 5 days or freeze for up to 3 months. Thaw brownies if frozen. Before serving, let brownies stand at room temperature for 15 minutes.

Lemony Glazed Shortbread Bars

PREP **40 MINUTES**   BAKE **40 MINUTES**   OVEN **300°F**

- 3 cups all-purpose flour
- ⅓ cup cornstarch
- 1¼ cups powdered sugar
- ¼ cup finely shredded lemon peel
- 1½ cups butter, softened
- 1 tablespoon lemon juice
- ½ teaspoon salt
- ½ teaspoon vanilla
- 1 recipe Lemony Glaze

1 Preheat oven to 300°F. Line a 13x9x2-inch baking pan with foil, extending the foil over the edges of the pan. Lightly grease foil; set pan aside.

2 In a medium bowl stir together the flour and cornstarch. In a small bowl stir together the powdered sugar and lemon peel. Using a wooden spoon, work the lemon peel into the powdered sugar until sugar is yellow and very fragrant.*

3 In a large mixing bowl beat butter, lemon juice, salt, and vanilla with an electric mixer on medium speed until combined. Gradually beat in the powdered sugar mixture. Using a wooden spoon, stir in the flour mixture. Press dough evenly onto the bottom of the prepared baking pan.

4 Bake about 40 minutes or until pale golden in color and edges begin to brown. Immediately spoon Lemony Glaze over bars, gently spreading evenly. Cool completely in pan on a wire rack. Use the foil to lift the uncut bars out of the pan. Place on a cutting board; cut into bars. **MAKES 32 BARS**

Lemony Glaze: In a medium bowl whisk together 2½ cups powdered sugar, 2 teaspoons finely shredded lemon peel, 3 tablespoons lemon juice, 1 tablespoon light corn syrup, and ½ teaspoon vanilla.

note Rubbing the lemon peel with the sugar helps release the lemon oils. Use the back of the wooden spoon to press the mixture into the sides of the bowl and release the oils.

TO MAKE AHEAD AND STORE: Layer bars between sheets of waxed paper in an airtight container; cover. Store in the refrigerator for up to 3 days or freeze for up to 1 month.

gift It

Jolly Jar

Start with a wide-mouth glass jar or canister with a lid. Once the glaze on the bars has dried, place them in the jar. Thread a wide ribbon through the front of a small picture frame with the glass removed. Affix the ribbon to the jar with crafts glue. Tie a gift tag to the top of the lid with colored string or twine.

Lemon-Lime Bars

PREP **20 MINUTES**   BAKE **40 MINUTES**   CHILL **2 HOURS**   OVEN **350°F**

- ⅔ cup butter, softened
- ½ cup packed brown sugar
- 2 cups all-purpose flour
- 2 teaspoons finely shredded lemon peel
- 6 eggs
- 2¼ cups granulated sugar
- ½ cup all-purpose flour
- ½ cup lemon juice
- ¾ teaspoon baking powder
- ⅛ teaspoon ground nutmeg
- 2 teaspoons finely shredded lemon peel
- 1 teaspoon finely shredded lime peel
  Powdered sugar
- 1 recipe Candied Citrus Slices or Candied Citrus Strips

1 Preheat oven to 350°F. Line a 13x9x2-inch baking pan with foil, extending the foil over the edges of the pan.

2 For crust, in a large mixing bowl beat butter with an electric mixer on medium to high speed for 30 seconds. Add brown sugar. Beat until combined, scraping sides of bowl occasionally. Beat in the 2 cups flour until mixture is crumbly. Stir in 2 teaspoons lemon peel. Press crust mixture evenly onto bottom of the prepared baking pan. Bake for 20 minutes.

3 Meanwhile, for filling, in a medium mixing bowl combine eggs, granulated sugar, the ½ cup flour, lemon juice, baking powder, and nutmeg. Beat with an electric mixer on medium speed for 2 minutes. Stir in 2 teaspoons lemon peel and the lime peel. Pour filling over hot crust, spreading evenly.

4 Bake about 20 minutes more or until edges are brown and center appears set. Cool in pan on a wire rack. Cover and chill bars for 2 hours. Use the foil to lift the uncut bars out of the pan. Place on a cutting board; cut into bars. Sprinkle bars with powdered sugar. Top with Candied Citrus Slices or Candied Citrus Strips.
MAKES 16 TO 20 BARS

Candied Citrus Slices: Thinly slice 2 lemons or 10 Key limes.

In a large skillet combine ¾ cup granulated sugar and ¼ cup water. Bring to boiling. Add citrus slices; reduce heat. Simmer gently, uncovered, for 1 to 2 minutes or just until softened. Transfer slices to a wire rack and let cool.

Candied Citrus Strips: Remove peel from 2 lemons or 2 limes; scrape away the white pith. Cut peel into thin strips. Cook as directed for Candied Citrus Slices.

TO MAKE AHEAD AND STORE: Place bars in a single layer in an airtight container; cover. Store in the refrigerator for up to 3 days. Do not freeze.

Lime Zingers

PREP **40 MINUTES**   BAKE **8 MINUTES PER BATCH**   OVEN **350°F**

1   cup butter, softened
½   cup sugar
2   teaspoons finely shredded
      lime peel
¼   cup lime juice
1   teaspoon vanilla
2¼ cups all-purpose flour
¾   cup finely chopped
      Brazil nuts or hazelnuts
      (filberts)
1   recipe Lime–Cream Cheese
      Frosting

1 Preheat oven to 350°F. In a large mixing bowl beat butter with an electric mixer on medium to high speed for 30 seconds. Add sugar. Beat until combined, scraping sides of bowl occasionally. Beat in the lime peel, lime juice, and vanilla until combined. Beat in as much of the flour as you can with the mixer. Using a wooden spoon, stir in any remaining flour and the nuts.

2 Divide dough in half. On a lightly floured surface roll each dough half to ¼-inch thickness. Using 1- to 2-inch cookie cutters, cut out dough. Place cutouts 1 inch apart on an ungreased cookie sheet.

3 Bake for 8 to 10 minutes or until edges are light brown. Transfer cookies to a wire rack and let cool. Spread Lime–Cream Cheese Frosting on cookies. **MAKES ABOUT 72 COOKIES**

Lime–Cream Cheese Frosting:
In a medium mixing bowl combine 4 ounces cream cheese, softened; 1 cup powdered sugar; 1 tablespoon lime juice; 1 teaspoon vanilla; and ½ teaspoon finely shredded lime peel. Beat with an electric mixer on medium speed until smooth.

TO MAKE AHEAD AND STORE:
Layer cookies between sheets of waxed paper in an airtight container; cover. Store at room temperature for up to 3 days. Or freeze unfrosted cookies for up to 3 months. Thaw cookies; frost as directed.

Brazil Nuts

As their name suggests, Brazil nuts hail from South America; they're actually the seeds of a tree that grows in the Amazon Rainforest. Find these rich, flavorful nuts in the baking aisle of well-stocked supermarkets. Because they're rich in selenium, an antioxidant, you can also find them in health foods stores.

MINI RASPBERRY AND WHITE CHOCOLATE
WHOOPIE PIES, PAGE 201

spoonfuls
of jelly

Jams and jellies pack
summer's fruits into a rich and thick,
satisfyingly winter-perfect treat. Here, their
jeweled colors shimmer in a showcase of thumbprints,
bars, mini tarts, and more, adding sparkle
to the season's lineup
of sweets.

✦

White Chocolate and Raspberry Cookies

PREP **35 MINUTES**   BAKE **7 MINUTES PER BATCH**   COOL **1 MINUTE PER BATCH**   OVEN **375°F**

- 11 ounces white baking chocolate, chopped
- ½ cup butter, softened
- 1 cup sugar
- 1 teaspoon baking soda
- ¼ teaspoon salt
- 2 eggs
- 2¾ cups all-purpose flour
- ½ cup seedless raspberry jam
- ½ teaspoon shortening

1 Preheat oven to 375°F. Lightly grease a cookie sheet; set aside. In a small saucepan cook and stir 4 ounces of the white chocolate over low heat until melted. Cool slightly.

2 In a large mixing bowl beat butter with an electric mixer on medium to high speed for 30 seconds. Add sugar, baking soda, and salt. Beat until combined, scraping sides of bowl occasionally. Beat in the eggs and melted white chocolate until combined. Beat in as much of the flour as you can with the mixer. Using a wooden spoon, stir in any remaining flour and 4 ounces of the chopped white chocolate.

3 Drop dough by rounded teaspoons 2 inches apart onto the prepared cookie sheet.

Bake for 7 to 9 minutes or until edges are light brown. Cool on cookie sheet for 1 minute. Transfer cookies to a wire rack and let cool.

4 Before serving, in a small saucepan cook and stir raspberry jam over low heat until melted. Spoon about ½ teaspoon jam on top of each cookie. In a small saucepan combine the remaining 3 ounces white chocolate and shortening. Cook and stir over low heat until

chocolate melts; drizzle over cookies. Let stand until chocolate is set. **MAKES ABOUT 48 COOKIES**

TO MAKE AHEAD AND STORE: Layer undecorated cookies between sheets of waxed paper in an airtight container; cover. Store at room temperature for up to 3 days or freeze for up to 3 months. Thaw cookies, if frozen. Decorate with jam and melted chocolate as directed.

Mini Raspberry and White Chocolate Whoopie Pies

PREP **1 HOUR**   BAKE **7 MINUTES PER BATCH**   CHILL **30 MINUTES**   OVEN **375°F**

½   cup butter, softened
1   cup sugar
½   teaspoon baking soda
¼   teaspoon salt
1   egg
1   teaspoon vanilla
2   cups all-purpose flour
½   cup buttermilk
1   recipe White Chocolate
    and Mascarpone Filling
½   cup seedless raspberry
    jam

1 Preheat oven to 375°F. Line a cookie sheet with parchment paper; set aside.

2 In a large mixing bowl beat butter with an electric mixer on medium to high speed for 30 seconds. Add sugar, baking soda, and salt. Beat until combined, scraping sides of bowl occasionally. Beat in the egg and vanilla until

combined. Alternately add the flour and buttermilk, beating on low speed after each addition just until combined.

3 Drop dough by rounded teaspoons 1 inch apart onto the prepared cookie sheet. Bake for 7 to 8 minutes or until tops are set. Cool completely on cookie sheet on a wire rack. Peel cooled cookies off the paper.

4 Spoon White Chocolate and Mascarpone Filling into a pastry bag fitted with a small star tip. To assemble, spread about ¼ teaspoon raspberry jam on the bottom of one cookie; pipe a small amount of filling on top. Press the bottom of a second cookie against the filling. Repeat with remaining cookies, jam, and filling. If desired, pipe additional filling on top of sandwich cookies. Chill for

30 minutes before serving. **MAKES ABOUT 72 SANDWICH COOKIES**

White Chocolate and Mascarpone Filling: In a small saucepan combine 3 ounces chopped white baking chocolate and ¼ cup whipping cream. Cook and stir over low heat until chocolate nearly melts. Remove from heat; stir until smooth. Cool for 15 minutes. Meanwhile, in a large mixing bowl beat ½ cup mascarpone cheese and ¼ cup softened butter with an electric mixer on medium to high speed until smooth. Beat in ½ teaspoon vanilla. Gradually add 4 cups powdered sugar, beating until smooth. Beat in the cooled white chocolate mixture. Chill about 30 minutes or until firm enough to pipe.

TO MAKE AHEAD AND STORE: Place cookies in a single layer in an airtight container; cover. Store in the refrigerator for up to 3 days or freeze for up to 3 months. If frozen, thaw for at least 1 hour in the refrigerator before serving.

In a *twinkling*

A simple sprinkling of colored sugar adds extra holiday appeal. Before baking, pat the dough mounds down slightly and sprinkle the tops with red- or green-colored sugar. Continue as directed.

Cranberry-Eggnog Twirls

PREP **25 MINUTES**   CHILL **5 HOURS**   BAKE **10 MINUTES PER BATCH**   COOL **1 MINUTE PER BATCH**   OVEN **375°F**

1	cup butter, softened
1½	cups sugar
½	teaspoon baking powder
½	teaspoon salt
½	teaspoon ground nutmeg
2	eggs
1	teaspoon rum extract
3¼	cups all-purpose flour
½	cup cranberry preserves or jam
1½	teaspoons cornstarch
½	cup finely chopped pecans, toasted

1 In a large mixing bowl beat butter with an electric mixer on medium to high speed for 30 seconds. Add sugar, baking powder, salt, and nutmeg. Beat until combined, scraping sides of bowl occasionally. Beat in the eggs and rum extract until combined. Beat in as much of the flour as you can with the mixer. Using a wooden spoon, stir in any remaining flour. Divide dough in half. Cover and chill dough about 1 hour or until easy to handle.

2 Meanwhile, for filling, in a small saucepan combine preserves and cornstarch. Cook and stir until thickened and bubbly. Remove from heat. Stir in pecans. Cover and let cool.

3 Roll half of the dough between two sheets of waxed paper into a 10-inch square. Spread half of the filling over the dough square to within ½ inch of edges; roll up dough tightly. Moisten edges with water and pinch to seal. Wrap in waxed paper or plastic wrap. Repeat with remaining dough and filling. Chill rolls for 4 to 24 hours.

4 Preheat oven to 375°F. Line a large cookie sheet with parchment paper. Cut rolls crosswise into ¼-inch-thick slices.

Place slices 2 inches apart on the prepared cookie sheet. Bake for 10 to 12 minutes or until edges are firm and bottoms are light brown. Cool on cookie sheet for 1 minute. Transfer cookies to a wire rack and let cool. **MAKES ABOUT 60 COOKIES**

TO MAKE AHEAD AND STORE: Layer cookies between sheets of waxed paper in an airtight container; cover. Store at room temperature for up to 3 days or freeze for up to 3 months.

Stay in Shape

Follow these tips to help your pinwheels keep their pretty round shapes:

+ Once you've shaped the dough into the cylinder, slide the dough into a tall, straight-sided drinking glass before you place it in the refrigerator; this will help prevent the dough from developing a flat side while it chills.

+ Don't shorten the chilling time; you'll get cleaner slices—with clearer demarcations between the layers—with firm dough.

+ While you're slicing one cylinder, keep the other cylinder(s) chilled.

+ Use a sharp, thin-blade knife to cut across the dough into ¼-inch slices.

+ As you slice each cylinder, rotate the roll frequently to avoid flattening one side.

Marmalade Mingles

PREP **45 MINUTES**   CHILL **2 HOURS**   BAKE **8 MINUTES PER BATCH**   OVEN **375°F**

½ cup butter, softened
½ cup packed brown sugar
1 egg yolk
1 tablespoon milk
½ teaspoon ground ginger
¼ teaspoon baking soda
¼ teaspoon ground cinnamon
⅛ teaspoon salt
⅛ teaspoon ground cloves
1½ cups all-purpose flour
¼ cup orange marmalade, fruit pieces snipped
2 ounces white baking chocolate, chopped
½ teaspoon shortening

1 In a large mixing bowl beat butter with an electric mixer on medium to high speed for 30 seconds. Add brown sugar. Beat until combined, scraping sides of bowl occasionally. Beat in the egg yolk, milk, ginger, baking soda, cinnamon, salt, and cloves until combined. Beat in as much of the flour as you can with the mixer. Using a wooden spoon, stir in any remaining flour.

2 Divide dough in half. Shape each half into a 9-inch log. Wrap each log in plastic wrap or waxed paper; chill about 2 hours or until firm.

3 Preheat oven to 375°F. Cut logs crosswise into ¼-inch-thick slices. Place slices 1 inch apart on an ungreased cookie sheet. Bake for 8 to 10 minutes or until bottoms are light brown. Transfer cookies to a wire rack and let cool.

4 To assemble, spread ¼ teaspoon of the marmalade on the bottom of one cookie; press the bottom of a second cookie against the marmalade. Repeat with the remaining cookies and marmalade. In a small saucepan combine white chocolate and shortening. Cook and stir over low heat until chocolate melts. Spoon chocolate into a heavy resealable plastic bag. Seal bag and snip a small hole in one corner. Drizzle chocolate over cookies. Let stand until chocolate is set. **MAKES 36 SANDWICH COOKIES**

TO MAKE AHEAD AND STORE: Layer unfilled cookies between sheets of waxed paper in an airtight container; cover. Store at room temperature for up to 3 days or freeze for up to 3 months. Thaw cookies, if frozen. Assemble and decorate as directed.

Blackberry-Sage Thumbprints

PREP **35 MINUTES**   BAKE **10 MINUTES PER BATCH**   COOL **1 MINUTE PER BATCH**   OVEN **350°F**

    2   cups all-purpose flour
    ⅔   cup yellow cornmeal
   1½   teaspoons dried sage,
          crushed
    ¼   teaspoon baking powder
    1   cup butter, softened
    1   cup packed brown sugar
    2   egg yolks
    2   teaspoons finely shredded
          lemon peel
   1½   teaspoons vanilla
    ¾   cup blackberry preserves

1 Preheat oven to 350°F. In a medium bowl stir together flour, cornmeal, sage, and baking powder. In a large mixing bowl beat butter with an electric mixer on medium to high speed for 30 seconds. Add brown sugar. Beat until combined, scraping sides of bowl occasionally. Beat in the egg yolks, lemon peel, and vanilla until combined. Beat in as much of the flour mixture as you can with the mixer. Using a wooden spoon, stir in any remaining flour mixture.

2 Shape dough into ¾-inch balls. Place balls 1 inch apart on an ungreased cookie sheet. Press your thumb into the center of each ball. Spoon about ¼ teaspoon blackberry preserves into the indentation in each cookie.

3 Bake for 10 to 12 minutes or until bottoms are light brown. Cool on cookie sheet for 1 minute. Transfer cookies to a wire rack and let cool. **MAKES 60 COOKIES**

TO MAKE AHEAD AND STORE: Layer cookies between sheets of waxed paper in an airtight container; cover. Store at room temperature for up to 3 days or freeze for up to 3 months.

In a *twinkling*

Give a Christmassy hue— as well as a visual clue to the flavor of these cookies—by garnishing each with a small fresh sage leaf.

Red Currant–Poppy Seed Thumbprints

PREP **25 MINUTES**   BAKE **10 MINUTES PER BATCH**   OVEN **350°F**

- 2⅔ cups all-purpose flour
- 2 tablespoons poppy seeds
- 2 teaspoons finely shredded orange peel
- ½ teaspoon salt
- 1 cup butter, softened
- ½ cup sugar
- 2 egg yolks
- 1 tablespoon orange liqueur or orange juice
- ⅓ to ½ cup red currant jelly, melted and cooled

1 Preheat oven to 350°F. In a small bowl combine the flour, poppy seeds, orange peel, and salt. In a large mixing bowl beat butter and sugar with an electric mixer on medium speed until combined. Add the egg yolks and liqueur. Beat until combined, scraping sides of bowl occasionally. Beat in as much of the flour mixture as you can with the mixer. Using a wooden spoon, stir in any remaining flour mixture.

2 Shape dough into 1-inch balls. Place balls 1 inch apart on an ungreased cookie sheet. Press your thumb into the center of each ball.

3 Bake for 10 to 12 minutes or until edges are light brown. If cookie centers puff during baking, re-press with the back of a small spoon. Transfer cookies to a wire rack and let cool. Spoon about ½ teaspoon jelly into the indentation in each cooled cookie. **MAKES ABOUT 36 COOKIES**

TO MAKE AHEAD AND STORE:
Layer cookies between sheets of waxed paper in an airtight container; cover. Store in the refrigerator for up to 3 days or freeze for up to 1 month.

Getting Jelly from the Jar to the Cookie

You can fill the indentations of your thumbprint cookies by using a small teaspoon from your flatware set. However, an even easier way to do it is to fill a small, heavy resealable plastic bag with the jam or jelly (cooled if melted) and snip a small hole in a bottom corner of the bag. Then squeeze the jam or jelly into the indentation.

Raspberry-Almond Meringues

PREP **45 MINUTES**   BAKE **20 MINUTES**   STAND **1 HOUR**   OVEN **300°F**

- 3   egg whites
- ¾   cup blanched whole almonds
- 2   tablespoons granulated sugar
- ¼   teaspoon almond extract
- ⅛   teaspoon salt
- ⅓   cup granulated sugar
- ¼   to ⅓ cup red raspberry preserves or jam
         Powdered sugar

1 Let egg whites stand at room temperature for 30 minutes. Meanwhile, preheat oven to 300°F. Line two large cookie sheets with foil or parchment paper; set aside.

2 Place almonds and the 2 tablespoons granulated sugar in a food processor. Cover and process until almonds are finely ground.

3 For meringue, in a large mixing bowl combine egg whites, almond extract, and salt. Beat with an electric mixer on medium speed until soft peaks form (tips curl). Add the ⅓ cup granulated sugar, 1 tablespoon at a time, beating on high speed until stiff peaks form (tips stand straight). Fold in ground almond mixture.

4 Spoon meringue into a pastry bag fitted with a small open star tip or a large round tip. Pipe 1½-inch circles 1 inch apart onto the prepared cookie sheets, building up the sides to form shells. (If the tip gets clogged, use a toothpick to unclog it.) Place baking sheets on separate racks in the oven. Bake for 20 minutes. Turn off oven. Let cookies dry in oven with the door closed for 1 hour. Transfer cookies to a wire rack and let cool.

5 Before serving, spoon ¼ to ½ teaspoon preserves into the center of each cookie. Sprinkle lightly with powdered sugar.
MAKES ABOUT 48 COOKIES

TO MAKE AHEAD AND STORE: Layer unfilled cookies between sheets of waxed paper in an airtight container; cover. Store at room temperature for up to 3 days or freeze for up to 3 months. Thaw cookies, if frozen. Fill cookies as directed.

Grinding Nuts

When grinding nuts, be sure to add sugar to the food processor bowl, as directed in the recipe. The sugar will absorb some of the oil from the nuts, helping you avoid ending up with nut butter instead of ground nuts. Use quick on-off pulses for better control, and check the nuts often until you reach the desired finely ground stage.

Strawberry Cheesecake Tartlets

PREP **25 MINUTES**   BAKE **15 MINUTES**   CHILL **2 HOURS**   OVEN **350°F**

1   cup all-purpose flour
¼   cup sugar
¼   cup ground toasted almonds
¼   cup butter
1   egg yolk, lightly beaten
2   to 3 tablespoons water
1   4-serving-size package cheesecake instant pudding mix
1   cup evaporated milk
2   teaspoons vanilla
½   teaspoon almond extract
⅓   cup strawberry preserves
     Sliced strawberries and/or toasted sliced almonds

1 In a medium bowl stir together the flour, sugar, and ground almonds. Using a pastry blender, cut in butter until pieces are pea size. In a small bowl stir together the egg yolk and 2 tablespoons of the water. Gradually stir the egg mixture into the flour mixture until combined. If necessary, add enough of the additional water to make a dough that starts to cling. Gently knead dough just until smooth; form dough into a ball. If necessary, cover and chill dough about 1 hour or until easy to handle.

2 Preheat oven to 350°F. Shape dough into 24 balls. Press balls evenly into the bottoms and up the sides of 24 ungreased 1¾-inch muffin cups. Bake about 15 minutes or until light brown. Cool completely in pan on a wire rack. Remove cooled shells from pan.

3 For filling, in a medium mixing bowl combine pudding mix, evaporated milk, vanilla, and almond extract. Beat with an electric mixer on medium speed about 2 minutes or until smooth and fluffy. Spoon 2 teaspoons of the filling into each shell. Cover and chill for 2 to 24 hours.

4 Before serving, top each cookie with about ½ teaspoon of the preserves, a strawberry slice, and/or a few sliced almonds.
MAKES 24 TARTLETS

TO MAKE AHEAD AND STORE: Layer filled tartlets between sheets of waxed paper in an airtight container; cover. Store in the refrigerator for up to 3 days or freeze for up to 1 month. Thaw cookies, if frozen. Top with preserves and, if desired, garnish as directed.

Switching Up the Jam

In most cookies with jam or jelly as an ingredient, you can substitute one flavor of jam for another. For instance, in the Strawberry Cheesecake Tartlets, try raspberry preserves instead of strawberry, and use fresh raspberries instead of fresh strawberries. For the Raspberry-Almond Meringues, page 206, try any preserves that go well with almonds, such as cherry or apricot. After all, the best cookies are those made with the flavors you like best!

Mocha and Apricot Jam Bites

PREP **30 MINUTES**   BAKE **8 MINUTES PER BATCH**   OVEN **375°F**

1½   **cups butter, softened**

½   **of an 8-ounce package cream cheese, softened**

1   **cup granulated sugar**

¼   **cup unsweetened cocoa powder**

4   **teaspoons instant espresso coffee powder**

1   **teaspoon baking powder**

¼   **teaspoon salt**

1   **egg**

1   **teaspoon vanilla**

3½   **cups all-purpose flour**

½   **cup apricot jam or preserves** *

   Powdered sugar

1 Preheat oven to 375°F. In a large mixing bowl beat butter and cream cheese with an electric mixer on medium to high speed for 30 seconds. Add granulated sugar, cocoa powder, espresso powder, baking powder, and salt. Beat until combined, scraping sides of bowl occasionally. Beat in the egg and vanilla until combined. Beat in as much of the flour as you can with the mixer. Using a wooden spoon, stir in any remaining flour.

2 Pack unchilled dough into a cookie press fitted with a star or flower plate. Force dough through press onto an ungreased cookie sheet, spacing cookies 1 inch apart. Bake for 8 to 10 minutes or until edges are firm. Transfer cookies to a wire rack and let cool.

3 Just before serving, spoon about ¼ teaspoon apricot jam onto the center of each cookie. Sprinkle with powdered sugar.

MAKES ABOUT 84 COOKIES

note Use kitchen scissors to cut up any large pieces of fruit in the jam or preserves.

TO MAKE AHEAD AND STORE: Layer unfilled cookies between sheets of waxed paper in an airtight container; cover. Store at room temperature for up to 3 days or freeze for up to 3 months. Thaw cookies, if frozen. Fill cookies as directed.

Orange-Fig Pillows

PREP **40 MINUTES**   CHILL **1 HOUR**   BAKE **8 MINUTES PER BATCH**   OVEN **375°F**

⅔   **cup butter, softened**
½   **cup packed brown sugar**
½   **teaspoon baking powder**
½   **teaspoon ground cinnamon**
¼   **teaspoon baking soda**
¼   **teaspoon salt**
1   **egg**
1   **teaspoon vanilla**
2   **cups all-purpose flour**
¼   **cup fig preserves or jam**
½   **teaspoon finely shredded orange peel or lemon peel**
    Powdered sugar (optional)

1 In a large mixing bowl beat butter with an electric mixer on medium to high speed for 30 seconds. Add brown sugar, baking powder, cinnamon, baking soda, and salt. Beat until combined, scraping sides of bowl occasionally. Beat in the egg and vanilla until combined. Beat in as much of the flour as you can with the mixer. Using a wooden spoon, stir in any remaining flour. Divide dough in half. Cover and chill dough about 1 hour or until easy to handle.

2 Preheat oven to 375°F. Grease two large cookie sheets. For filling, in a small bowl stir together the fig preserves and orange peel.

3 On a lightly floured surface roll each dough half into a 12x8-inch rectangle. Using a fluted pastry wheel, cut around the edge of each rectangle. Using the pastry wheel, cut each rectangle into twenty-four 2-inch squares. Place half of the squares 1 inch apart on the prepared cookie sheets. Spoon ½ teaspoon of the preserves in the center of each square on the cookie sheets. Top each with a second dough square. Using the tines of a fork, gently press edges to seal.

4 Bake for 8 to 10 minutes or until edges are light brown. Transfer cookies to a wire rack and let cool. If desired, sprinkle cookies with powdered sugar just before serving. **MAKES 24 COOKIES**

TO MAKE AHEAD AND STORE: Layer cookies between sheets of waxed paper in an airtight container; cover. Store at room temperature for up to 3 days or freeze for up to 3 months. If using, sprinkle powdered sugar on cookies just before serving.

Not Your Ordinary Jam

While supermarket aisles brim with ever-popular varieties of fruit preserves, consider seeking out lesser-known options for your jam-filled cookies. Peruse gourmet shops and online sources for specialty jars—you'll find anything from pear-ginger preserves to fig jam, and a new find might just become an ongoing holiday tradition.

In a *twinkling*

Before baking, lightly brush the tops of the cookies with milk and sprinkle with coarse sugar. Use white coarse sugar in combination with red and/or green coarse sugar to create holiday sparkle.

Cranberry-Orange Gingerbread Squares

PREP **35 MINUTES**   BAKE **7 MINUTES PER BATCH**   COOL **1 MINUTE PER BATCH**   OVEN **375°F**

¼ **cup cranberry jam or preserves**

½ **teaspoon finely shredded orange peel**

1 **18- to 20-ounce roll refrigerated gingerbread cookie dough**

2 **tablespoons all-purpose flour**

1 **recipe Orange Icing**

1 Preheat oven to 375°F. Line two cookie sheets with foil. For filling, in a small bowl stir together jam and orange peel.

2 Place cookie dough in a large bowl; knead in the 2 tablespoons flour. Divide dough in half. On a lightly floured surface roll each dough half into a 10½x8½-inch rectangle. Using a fluted pastry wheel, cut around the edge of each rectangle. Using the pastry wheel, cut each rectangle into twenty 2-inch squares. Place half of the squares 1 inch apart on the prepared cookie sheets. Spoon ½ teaspoon of the filling onto the center of each square on the cookie sheets. Top each with a second dough square. Using the tines of a fork, gently press edges to seal.

3 Bake for 7 to 9 minutes or until edges are light brown. Cool on cookie sheet for 1 minute. Transfer cookies to a wire rack and let cool.

4 Drizzle Orange Icing over tops of cookies. Let stand until icing is set. **MAKES 20 COOKIES**

Orange Icing: In a small bowl stir together 1 cup powdered sugar, ½ teaspoon finely shredded orange peel, and enough orange juice (3 to 4 teaspoons) to make an icing of drizzling consistency.

TO MAKE AHEAD AND STORE: Layer cookies between sheets of waxed paper in an airtight container; cover. Store at room temperature for up to 3 days. Or freeze undecorated cookies for up to 3 months. Thaw cookies; drizzle with Orange Icing as directed.

A Once-a-Year Treat—All Year Long

In most markets, purchased gingerbread cookie dough is only available seasonally, so if your family loves gingerbread cookies— and you love the ease of using this convenient product—stock up during the holiday season. Keep the dough in your freezer; thaw as needed in the refrigerator.

Raspberry Cookie Sandwiches

PREP **40 MINUTES**   CHILL **1 HOUR**   BAKE **7 MINUTES PER BATCH**   OVEN **375°F**

⅓ cup butter, softened
⅓ cup shortening
¾ cup granulated sugar
1½ teaspoons baking powder
¼ teaspoon salt
¼ teaspoon ground cinnamon
⅛ teaspoon ground cloves
1 egg
1 tablespoon milk
½ teaspoon vanilla
½ teaspoon finely shredded
   lemon peel
2 cups all-purpose flour
   Powdered sugar
⅓ to ½ cup raspberry,
   apricot, or strawberry
   preserves or jam or
   orange marmalade

1 In a large mixing bowl beat butter and shortening with an electric mixer on medium to high speed for 30 seconds. Add granulated sugar, baking powder, salt, cinnamon, and cloves. Beat until combined, scraping sides of bowl occasionally. Beat in the egg, milk, vanilla, and lemon peel until combined. Beat in as much of the flour as you can with the mixer. Using a wooden spoon, stir in any remaining flour. Divide dough in half. Cover and chill dough about 1 hour or until easy to handle.

2 Preheat oven to 375°F. On a lightly floured surface roll each dough half to ⅛- to ¼-inch thickness. Using a 2½-inch cookie cutter, cut out dough into desired shape. Place cutouts 1 inch apart on an ungreased cookie sheet. Using a ¾-inch cookie cutter, cut desired shape from centers of half of the cookies. Bake for 7 to 10 minutes or until edges are light brown. Transfer cookies to a wire rack and let cool.

3 Sift powdered sugar onto the cookies with the centers cut out. To assemble cookies, spread a scant teaspoon of preserves over the bottom of one of the whole cookies; press the bottom of a cutout sugar cookie against the preserves. Repeat with the remaining cookies and preserves. Serve within 2 hours. **MAKES ABOUT 20 SANDWICH COOKIES**

TO MAKE AHEAD AND STORE: Layer the unfilled cookies between sheets of waxed paper in an airtight container; cover. Store at room temperature for up to 3 days or freeze for up to 3 months. Thaw cookies, if frozen. Assemble cookies as directed.

Almond-Apricot Windows

PREP **50 MINUTES**   CHILL **2 HOURS**   BAKE **10 MINUTES PER BATCH**   COOL **2 MINUTES PER BATCH**
OVEN **325°F**

1   cup blanched almonds, toasted and chopped
1   tablespoon sugar
1   cup butter, softened
⅔   cup sugar
1   egg
1   egg yolk
½   teaspoon salt
½   teaspoon vanilla
½   teaspoon almond extract
¼   teaspoon ground nutmeg
2⅔   cups all-purpose flour
¾   cup apricot jam

1 In a food processor combine almonds and the 1 tablespoon sugar. Cover and process until nuts are finely ground.

2 In a large mixing bowl beat butter with an electric mixer on medium to high speed for 30 seconds. Add the ⅔ cup sugar. Beat until combined, scraping sides of bowl occasionally. Beat in the ground almonds, the egg, egg yolk, salt, vanilla, almond extract, and nutmeg until combined. Beat in as much of the flour as you can with the mixer. Using a wooden spoon, stir in any remaining flour.

3 Divide dough into four portions. Cover and chill dough about 2 hours or until easy to handle.

4 Preheat oven to 325°F. On a lightly floured surface roll each dough portion to ¼-inch thickness. Using a fluted 2- to 3-inch cookie cutter, cut out dough. Place cutouts 1 inch apart on an ungreased cookie sheet. Using a fluted 1-inch cookie cutter, cut out centers of half of the cookies.

5 Bake for 10 to 12 minutes or until tops are a pale golden brown. Cool on cookie sheet for 2 minutes. Transfer cookies to a wire rack and let cool.

6 To assemble cookies, spread 1 slightly rounded teaspoon of the jam onto the bottom of one of the whole cookies; press the bottom of a cutout cookie against the jam. Repeat with the remaining cookies and jam. **MAKES ABOUT 30 SANDWICH COOKIES**

TO MAKE AHEAD AND STORE: Layer sandwich cookies between sheets of waxed paper in an airtight container; cover. Store in the refrigerator for up to 3 days or freeze for up to 1 month.

gift It

Sheer Delight

Wrapping these cookies in a see-through wine bag lets the cookies star as part of the pretty presentation. Place the cookies on a narrow rectangular platter. Carefully slide the platter into a sheer wine bag. Attach two jingle bells and a gift tag to the closure ties on the bag.

Chocolate-Cherry Pockets

PREP **45 MINUTES**   CHILL **2 HOURS**   BAKE **8 MINUTES PER BATCH**   OVEN **375°F**

½	cup butter, softened
1	3-ounce package cream cheese, softened
1½	cups powdered sugar
⅓	cup unsweetened cocoa powder
½	teaspoon baking powder
¼	teaspoon baking soda
¼	teaspoon salt
1	egg
½	teaspoon vanilla
1¾	cups all-purpose flour
½	cup cherry preserves
2	tablespoons snipped dried cherries
1	teaspoon brandy (optional)
4	ounces bittersweet or semisweet chocolate, chopped
2	teaspoons shortening
	Sliced almonds, toasted

1 In a large mixing bowl beat butter and cream cheese with an electric mixer on medium to high speed for 30 seconds. Add powdered sugar, cocoa powder, baking powder, baking soda, and salt. Beat until combined, scraping sides of bowl occasionally. Beat in the egg and vanilla until combined. Beat in as much of the flour as you can with the mixer. Using a wooden spoon, stir in any remaining flour. Divide dough in half. Cover and chill dough about 2 hours or until easy to handle.

2 For the cherry filling, in a small bowl stir together the cherry preserves, dried cherries, and brandy, if using.

3 Preheat oven to 375°F. Line two cookie sheets with foil. On a lightly floured surface roll each dough half to about ⅛-inch thickness. Using a 3-inch scalloped or plain round cookie cutter, cut out dough. Place cutouts ½ inch apart on the prepared cookie sheets.

4 Spoon a scant teaspoon of the cherry filling onto the center of each cutout. Brush edges of the cutouts lightly with water. Fold each cutout in half over filling; gently press edges to seal. Bake for 8 to 9 minutes or until edges are firm. Transfer cookies to a wire rack and let cool.

5 In a small saucepan combine chocolate and shortening. Cook and stir over low heat until chocolate melts. Spoon chocolate into a heavy resealable plastic bag. Seal bag and snip a small hole in one corner. Drizzle chocolate over cookies; sprinkle with almonds. If desired, drizzle cookies again with chocolate. Let stand until chocolate is set. **MAKES ABOUT 30 COOKIES**

TO MAKE AHEAD AND STORE:
Layer cookies between sheets of waxed paper in an airtight container; cover. Store at room temperature for up to 3 days. Or freeze undecorated cookies for up to 3 months. Thaw cookies; drizzle with chocolate and sprinkle with almonds as directed.

PB and J Bars

PREP **25 MINUTES**   BAKE **25 MINUTES**   OVEN **375°F**

- ¼ **cup butter, softened**
- ¼ **cup shortening**
- ¼ **cup creamy peanut butter**
- 1 **cup packed brown sugar**
- ½ **teaspoon baking powder**
- ½ **teaspoon salt**
- ½ **teaspoon ground cinnamon**
- ¼ **teaspoon ground nutmeg**
- 1 **egg**
- 2 **teaspoons vanilla**
- 2 **cups all-purpose flour**
- 1 **10-ounce jar strawberry preserves**
- 1 **cup regular rolled oats**
- ¼ **cup packed brown sugar**
- ¼ **teaspoon ground cinnamon**
- 2 **tablespoons butter**

1 Preheat oven to 375°F. Line a 13x9x2-inch baking pan with foil, extending the foil over the edges of the pan. In a large mixing bowl beat butter, shortening, and peanut butter with an electric mixer on medium to high speed for 30 seconds. Add the 1 cup brown sugar, the baking powder, salt, ½ teaspoon cinnamon, and the nutmeg. Beat until combined, scraping sides of bowl occasionally. Beat in the egg and vanilla until combined. Beat in as much of the flour as you can with the mixer. Using a wooden spoon, stir in any remaining flour.

2 Press 2 cups of the dough evenly onto the bottom of the prepared baking pan. Bake about 10 minutes or until set. Spread preserves evenly over hot crust.

3 Add oats, ¼ cup brown sugar, and ¼ teaspoon cinnamon to the remaining dough. Using a pastry blender, cut in the 2 tablespoons butter until combined (mixture will be crumbly). Sprinkle crumb mixture over preserves. Bake for 15 to 18 minutes more or until top is light brown. Cool in pan on a wire rack.

4 Use the foil to lift the uncut bars out of the pan. Place on a cutting board; cut into bars.
MAKES 24 BARS

TO MAKE AHEAD AND STORE: Place bars in a single layer in an airtight container; cover. Store in the refrigerator for up to 3 days or freeze for up to 3 months.

Ruby Linzer Bars

PREP **25 MINUTES**   BAKE **30 MINUTES**   COOL **5 MINUTES**   OVEN **300°F**

- 1 cup butter-flavor shortening
- 1 cup sugar
- 1 teaspoon baking powder
- ¼ teaspoon salt
- 1 egg
- 1 teaspoon vanilla
- ½ teaspoon almond extract
- 2¼ cups all-purpose flour
- 1 cup chopped toasted almonds
- ½ cup raspberry preserves
- 1 recipe Almond Glaze

1 Preheat oven to 300°F. In a large mixing bowl beat shortening with an electric mixer on medium to high speed for 30 seconds. Add sugar, baking powder, and salt. Beat until combined, scraping sides of bowl occasionally. Beat in the egg, vanilla, and almond extract until combined. Beat in as much flour as you can with the mixer. Using a wooden spoon, stir in any remaining flour.

2 Divide dough into thirds. Shape each portion into a 10-inch log. Roll logs in chopped almonds to coat. Place logs 3 to 4 inches apart on an ungreased large cookie sheet. Flatten each log to 1-inch thickness. Using your fingers or the back of a spoon, make a ½-inch-deep, 1-inch-wide indentation down the center of each log.

3 Bake about 30 minutes or until edges are firm and light brown. Cool on cookie sheet for 5 minutes. If indentations puff during baking, re-press with the back of a spoon. Transfer logs to a wire rack and cool completely.

4 Spoon the preserves evenly down the centers of the logs. Drizzle Almond Glaze over logs. Let stand until glaze is set. Using a serrated knife, cut logs diagonally into 1-inch-thick slices. **MAKES ABOUT 36 BARS**

Almond Glaze: In a small bowl stir together ½ cup powdered sugar, 1 teaspoon milk, and ¼ teaspoon almond extract. Stir in enough additional milk, ½ teaspoon at a time, to make a glaze of drizzling consistency.

TO MAKE AHEAD AND STORE: Place unfilled logs in a single layer in an airtight container; cover. Store at room temperature for up to 3 days or freeze for up to 3 months. Thaw logs, if frozen. Fill logs with preserves, drizzle with glaze, and slice as directed.

Cherry-Almond Bars

PREP **20 MINUTES**   BAKE **35 MINUTES**   OVEN **350°F**

- 1 cup butter, softened
- 2 cups packed brown sugar
- 2 teaspoons baking powder
- 1 egg
- 1 teaspoon almond extract
- 2 cups all-purpose flour
- 2 cups regular rolled oats
- ½ cup sliced almonds
- 1 12-ounce jar cherry preserves

1 Preheat oven to 350°F. Line a 13x9x2-inch baking pan with foil, extending the foil over the edges of the pan. Grease foil; set pan aside.

2 In a large mixing bowl beat butter with an electric mixer on medium to high speed for 30 seconds. Add brown sugar and baking powder. Beat until combined, scraping sides of bowl occasionally. Beat in the egg and almond extract until combined. Beat in as much of the flour as you can with the mixer. Using a wooden spoon, stir in any remaining flour, the oats, and almonds.

3 Remove and reserve ½ cup of the dough. Press the remaining dough evenly onto the bottom of the prepared baking pan. Spread the preserves evenly over dough. Crumble the reserved dough evenly over preserves.

4 Bake about 35 minutes or until light brown. Cool completely in pan on a wire rack. Use the foil to lift the uncut bars out of the pan. Place on a cutting board; cut into bars. **MAKES 36 BARS**

TO MAKE AHEAD AND STORE: Place bars in a single layer in an airtight container; cover. Store in the refrigerator for up to 3 days or freeze for up to 1 month.

RUBY LINZER BARS

PUMPKIN-SPICED WHOOPIE PIES, PAGE 220

pumpkin pleasures

Few ingredients add
warmth and seasonality to sweets
quite like pumpkin. The baker's favorite
gourd works its magic in all kinds of cookies,
paired with all kinds of ingredients—fruits,
nuts, toffee, white chocolate, and more.

★

Pumpkin-Spiced Whoopie Pies

PREP **45 MINUTES**   BAKE **9 MINUTES PER BATCH**   COOL **2 MINUTES PER BATCH**   CHILL **30 MINUTES**
OVEN **350°F**   *PICTURED ON PAGE 218*

½   cup shortening
½   cup granulated sugar
½   cup packed brown sugar
1   teaspoon baking soda
1   teaspoon pumpkin pie spice
⅛   teaspoon salt
1   egg
1   teaspoon vanilla
2⅓   cups all-purpose flour
1   cup milk
1   recipe Pumpkin-Ricotta Filling
1   recipe White Chocolate Glaze
    Dry-roasted pistachios, chopped

1 Preheat oven to 350°F. Line a large cookie sheet with parchment paper or foil. Lightly grease the foil, if using. Set cookie sheet aside.

2 In a large mixing bowl beat shortening with an electric mixer on medium to high speed for 30 seconds. Add granulated sugar, brown sugar, baking soda, pumpkin pie spice, and salt. Beat until combined, scraping sides of bowl occasionally. Beat in the egg and vanilla until combined.

Alternately add the flour and milk, beating on low speed after each addition just until combined.

3 Spoon batter in 2-inch-diameter rounds about ½ inch high onto the prepared cookie sheet; leave 2 inches between each dough round. Bake for 9 to 11 minutes or until tops are set. Cool on cookie sheet for 2 minutes. Transfer cookies to a wire rack and let cool.

4 To assemble, spread a rounded teaspoon of the Pumpkin-Ricotta Filling onto the bottom of one cookie; press the bottom of a second cookie against the filling. Repeat with the remaining cookies and filling. Drizzle or spread one side of sandwich cookies with White Chocolate Glaze. Sprinkle glaze with chopped pistachios. Chill about 30 minutes or until glaze is set. **MAKES ABOUT 20 SANDWICH COOKIES**

Pumpkin-Ricotta Filling: In a large bowl whisk together 1½ cups powdered sugar, ¾ cup canned pumpkin, ½ cup ricotta cheese, ½ cup mascarpone cheese, and 1 teaspoon pumpkin pie spice until smooth. Stir in ¼ cup chopped dry roasted pistachios. Cover and chill for 1 hour.

White Chocolate Glaze:
Place 3 tablespoons whipping cream in a small microwave-safe bowl. Microwave, uncovered, on 50 percent power (medium) for 30 to 40 seconds or until cream comes to boiling. Add 4 ounces chopped white baking chocolate (do not stir). Let stand for 5 minutes. Stir until smooth. Let stand for 5 to 15 minutes before using. The glaze firms up as it stands. If you want a glaze that runs down the sides of the cookies, let it stand for 5 minutes. If you want glaze that spreads like thin frosting, let it stand for 15 minutes.

TO MAKE AHEAD AND STORE:
Place filled and glazed whoopie pies in a single layer in an airtight container; cover. Store in the refrigerator for up to 1 day or freeze for up to 3 months. Thaw in the refrigerator, if frozen. Let stand at room temperature for 30 minutes before serving.

Nutmeg-Pumpkin Cookies

PREP 20 MINUTES   BAKE **11 MINUTES PER BATCH**   COOL **2 MINUTES PER BATCH**   OVEN **350°F**

- 1 cup butter, softened
- 1 cup packed brown sugar
- 2 teaspoons freshly grated nutmeg or 1 teaspoon ground nutmeg
- 1 teaspoon baking soda
- 1 cup canned pumpkin
- 1 egg
- 2 teaspoons vanilla
- 2 cups all-purpose flour
- 2 cups white baking pieces
  Pecan halves (optional)

1 Preheat oven to 350°F. In a large mixing bowl beat butter with an electric mixer on medium to high speed for 30 seconds. Add brown sugar, nutmeg, and baking soda. Beat until combined, scraping sides of bowl occasionally. Beat in the pumpkin, egg, and vanilla until combined. Beat in as much of the flour as you can with the mixer. Using a wooden spoon, stir in any remaining flour and the white baking pieces.

2 Drop dough by rounded teaspoons 2 inches apart onto an ungreased cookie sheet. If desired, press a pecan half gently onto each cookie.

3 Bake for 11 to 14 minutes or until edges are firm. Cool on cookie sheet for 2 minutes. Transfer cookies to a wire rack and let cool. **MAKES ABOUT 60 COOKIES**

TO MAKE AHEAD AND STORE: Layer cookies between sheets of waxed paper in an airtight container; cover. Store at room temperature for up to 3 days or freeze for up to 3 months.

gift It

Tall Beauty

With the right touches, a potato chip canister makes a dashing container for presenting round drop cookies. To pretty it up, line the inside of the can with parchment paper. Measure and cut a piece of wrapping paper to fit around the can. Tape the paper in place. Tape some tinsel just under the top of the can and decorate the lid with tinsel.

For another dressy presentation, fill the wrapped can with the cookies and place the lid on the container. Cut out two 6x8-inch pieces of decorative scrapbook paper with differing designs. Glue the paper around the ends of the can, allowing some of the paper to hang over the ends. Cut the excess paper at the ends into fringes and tie the fringes together.

Melt-in-Your-Mouth Pumpkin Cookies

PREP **30 MINUTES**   BAKE **10 MINUTES PER BATCH**   OVEN **350°F**

- 2   **cups butter, softened**
- 2   **cups granulated sugar**
- 2   **teaspoons baking powder**
- 2   **teaspoons baking soda**
- 1   **teaspoon salt**
- 1   **teaspoon ground cinnamon**
- 1   **teaspoon ground nutmeg**
- 2   **eggs**
- 2   **teaspoons vanilla**
- 1   **15-ounce can pumpkin**
- 4   **cups all-purpose flour**
- ½   **cup butter**
- ½   **cup packed brown sugar**
- ¼   **cup milk**
- 1   **teaspoon vanilla**
- 2¾   **cups powdered sugar**
       Ground cinnamon (optional)

1 Preheat oven to 350°F. In a large mixing bowl beat the 2 cups butter with an electric mixer on medium to high speed for 30 seconds. Add granulated sugar, baking powder, baking soda, salt, cinnamon, and nutmeg. Beat until combined, scraping sides of bowl occasionally. Beat in the eggs and the 2 teaspoons vanilla until combined. Beat in pumpkin. Beat in as much of the flour as you can with the mixer. Using a wooden spoon, stir in any remaining flour.

2 Drop dough by heaping teaspoons 2 inches apart on an ungreased cookie sheet. Bake for 10 to 12 minutes or until tops are set. Transfer cookies to a wire rack and let cool.

3 In a small saucepan heat the ½ cup butter and brown sugar until melted and smooth. Transfer to a medium bowl. Stir in the milk and the 1 teaspoon vanilla. Beat in powdered sugar until smooth. Spread frosting on tops of cooled cookies. If desired, sprinkle additional cinnamon on frosting. Let stand until frosting is set. **MAKES ABOUT 60 COOKIES**

TO MAKE AHEAD AND STORE: Layer unfrosted cookies between sheets of waxed paper in an airtight container; cover. Store at room temperature for up to 3 days or freeze for up to 3 months. Thaw cookies, if frozen. Prepare frosting and frost cookies as directed.

Pumpkin-Spiced Balls

PREP **30 MINUTES**   BAKE **16 MINUTES PER BATCH**   STAND **1 HOUR**   OVEN **325°F**

1 cup butter, softened
½ cup powdered sugar
1 teaspoon vanilla
½ teaspoon pumpkin pie spice
2 cups all-purpose flour
1 cup chopped pecans, toasted
1 recipe Pumpkin-Spiced Glaze

1 Preheat oven to 325°F. In a large mixing bowl beat butter with an electric mixer on medium to high speed for 30 seconds. Add powdered sugar and vanilla. Beat until combined, scraping sides of bowl occasionally. Beat in the pumpkin pie spice and as much of the flour as you can with the electric mixer. Using a wooden spoon, stir in any remaining flour and the pecans.

2 Shape dough into into 1-inch balls. Place balls 2 inches apart on an ungreased cookie sheet.

3 Bake for 16 to 18 minutes or until bottoms are light brown. Transfer cookies to a wire rack and let cool.

4 Dip the tops of the cooled cookies into Pumpkin-Spiced Glaze. Let stand about 1 hour or until glaze is set. **MAKES ABOUT 48 COOKIES**

Pumpkin-Spiced Glaze: In a small bowl combine ¾ cup powdered sugar and 1 teaspoon pumpkin pie spice. Whisk in enough half-and-half, light cream, or milk (3 to 4 teaspoons) to make glaze of desired consistency.

TO MAKE AHEAD AND STORE: Layer cookies between sheets of waxed paper in an airtight container; cover. Store at room temperature for up to 3 days or freeze for up to 3 months.

Making Your Own Pumpkin Pie Spice

If you don't have pumpkin pie spice in your cupboard, you can make your own with spices you're more likely to have on hand. For each teaspoon called for, combine ½ teaspoon ground cinnamon, ¼ teaspoon ground ginger, ¼ teaspoon ground allspice, and ⅛ teaspoon ground nutmeg.

Pumpkin Pie Drops

PREP **30 MINUTES**   BAKE **10 MINUTES PER BATCH**   OVEN **375°F**

1   cup butter, softened
½   cup granulated sugar
½   cup packed brown sugar
2   teaspoons pumpkin pie spice
1   teaspoon baking powder
½   teaspoon baking soda
¼   teaspoon salt
1   egg
1   cup canned pumpkin
1   to 2 tablespoons finely chopped crystallized ginger
2   cups all-purpose flour
½   cup chopped almonds, toasted (optional)
1   recipe Browned-Butter Icing

1 Preheat oven to 375°F. In a large mixing bowl beat butter with an electric mixer on medium to high speed for 30 seconds. Add granulated sugar, brown sugar, pumpkin pie spice, baking powder, baking soda, and salt. Beat until combined, scraping sides of bowl occasionally. Beat in the egg, pumpkin, and the crystallized ginger until combined. Gradually beat in flour until combined. If desired, stir in ½ cup almonds.

2 Drop dough by rounded teaspoons 2 inches apart onto an ungreased cookie sheet. Bake for 10 to 12 minutes or until bottoms are light brown. Transfer cookies to a wire rack and let cool.

3 Spoon Browned-Butter Icing into a heavy resealable plastic bag. Seal bag and snip a small hole in one corner. Drizzle icing over cookies. Let stand until icing is set. **MAKES ABOUT 48 COOKIES**

Browned-Butter Icing: In a medium saucepan heat ⅓ cup butter over low heat until butter melts. Continue heating butter until it turns a delicate brown. Remove pan from heat. Slowly whisk in 2½ cups powdered sugar, 1 teaspoon vanilla, and enough milk (2 to 3 tablespoons) to make an icing of drizzling consistency.

TO MAKE AHEAD AND STORE: Layer cookies between sheets of waxed paper in an airtight container; cover. Store at room temperature for up to 3 days. Or freeze unfrosted cookies for up to 3 months. Thaw cookies; prepare icing and ice cookies as directed.

Freezing Leftover Pumpkin

Some of these recipes call for less than a whole can of pumpkin. Fortunately, pumpkin freezes well, so you can store the extra to use the next time you bake. To freeze, transfer the pumpkin from the can to an airtight freezer container or resealable plastic freezer bag, allowing room for the pumpkin to expand while freezing. Label and freeze up to 3 months. Thaw in the refrigerator before using. Note that frozen pumpkin may take on an altered appearance after thawing, but this will not affect your recipe.

If you know you'll be baking again within the next few days, you can refrigerate your leftover pumpkin. Transfer the pumpkin to an airtight container or resealable plastic bag and refrigerate for up to 3 days.

In a *twinkling*

After drizzling the cookies with the luscious Browned-Butter Icing, top these gems off with a sprinkling of toasted chopped almonds and finely chopped crystallized ginger.

Pumpkin-Pecan Tassies

PREP **30 MINUTES**   BAKE **35 MINUTES**   OVEN **350°F**

1   **15-ounce package rolled refrigerated unbaked piecrusts (2 crusts)**

¾   **cup canned pumpkin**

¼   **cup granulated sugar**

1   **teaspoon pumpkin pie spice**

⅛   **teaspoon salt**

1   **egg, lightly beaten**

¼   **cup half-and-half, light cream, or milk**

⅓   **cup chopped pecans**

1   **tablespoon packed brown sugar**

1   **tablespoon butter, melted**
     Maple syrup (optional)

1   Let piecrusts stand according to package directions. Preheat oven to 350°F. Unroll piecrusts. Using a 2½-inch round cookie cutter, cut 12 rounds from each piecrust. Gently ease pastry rounds into the bottoms and up the sides of 24 ungreased 1¾-inch muffin cups; set aside.

2   For filling, in a large bowl stir together the pumpkin, granulated sugar, pumpkin pie spice, and salt. Add egg; stir until combined. Gradually stir in half-and-half just until combined.

3   For pecan topping, stir together pecans, brown sugar, and melted butter.

4   Spoon about 2 teaspoons filling into each pastry-lined cup. Top each with a scant 1 teaspoon pecan topping. Bake about 35 minutes or until filling is set and crust is golden brown. Carefully remove tassies from muffin cups. Transfer tassies to a wire rack and let cool. If desired, just before serving, drizzle tassies with maple syrup. **MAKES 24 TASSIES**

TO MAKE AHEAD AND STORE: Place tassies in a single layer in an airtight container; cover. Store in the refrigerator for up to 2 days or freeze for up to 3 months. Thaw about 1 hour at room temperature, if frozen.

Punkin' Dunkin' Sticks

PREP **35 MINUTES**   BAKE **5 MINUTES PER BATCH**   COOL **1 MINUTE PER BATCH**   STAND **2 HOURS**   OVEN **400°F**

1	cup butter, softened
½	cup sugar
1	teaspoon ground cinnamon
¾	teaspoon baking powder
½	teaspoon ground nutmeg
½	teaspoon ground ginger
¼	teaspoon salt
¼	teaspoon ground cloves
⅓	cup canned pumpkin
1	egg
1	teaspoon vanilla
2½	cups all-purpose flour
1	recipe Cream Cheese Glaze
	Freshly grated nutmeg (optional)

1 Preheat oven to 400°F. In a large mixing bowl beat butter with an electric mixer on medium to high speed for 30 seconds. Add sugar, cinnamon, baking powder, the ground nutmeg, the ginger, salt, and cloves. Beat until combined, scraping sides of bowl occasionally. Beat in the pumpkin, egg, and vanilla until combined. Beat in as much of the flour as you can with the mixer. Using a wooden spoon, stir in any remaining flour.

2 Place dough in a pastry bag fitted with a large open tip. Using a corkscrew motion, pipe dough onto an ungreased cookie sheet into 4-inch-long strips.

3 Bake for 5 to 7 minutes or just until firm to the touch but not brown. Cool on cookie sheet for 1 minute. Transfer cookies to a wire rack and let cool.

4 Drizzle Cream Cheese Glaze over half of each cookie. If desired, sprinkle glaze with freshly grated nutmeg. Let stand about 2 hours or until glaze is set. **MAKES ABOUT 30 COOKIES**

Cream Cheese Glaze: In a medium mixing bowl beat half of a 3-ounce package cream cheese, softened, and 1 tablespoon butter, softened, with an electric mixer on medium speed until smooth. Add ¼ teaspoon finely shredded lemon peel, 1 teaspoon lemon juice, and ¼ teaspoon finely shredded orange peel. Beat until combined. Beat in ¾ cup powdered sugar until combined. Beat in enough milk (2 to 3 teaspoons) to make a glaze of drizzling consistency.

TO MAKE AHEAD AND STORE: Layer cookies between sheets of waxed paper in an airtight container; cover. Store at room temperature for up to 3 days or freeze for up to 3 months.

Pipe Like a Pro

Here's how to handle a pastry bag to pipe perfect shapes every time:

✦ Place the empty bag, tip down, in a tall drinking glass. Fold the edges of the bag down over the glass.

✦ Scoop dough into the bag with a spatula until the bag is filled, doing your best to avoid creating air pockets. Remove the bag from the glass; twist the top of the bag between your thumb and forefinger to secure.

✦ To pipe, use one hand to squeeze the bag firmly from the top, retwisting the end of the bag as needed. Use your other hand to guide the tip.

Pumpkin Pockets

PREP **30 MINUTES**   COOL **1 HOUR**   CHILL **1 HOUR**   BAKE **8 MINUTES PER BATCH**   OVEN **375°F**

½   cup water
1   tablespoon granulated sugar
2   teaspoons cornstarch
½   cup pumpkin butter
½   cup snipped pitted whole dates
3   cups all-purpose flour
2   teaspoons ground ginger
1   teaspoon baking soda
1   teaspoon ground cinnamon
½   teaspoon salt
¼   teaspoon ground cloves
¾   cup butter, softened
¾   cup packed brown sugar
½   cup molasses
1   egg

1 In a small saucepan combine the water, granulated sugar, and the cornstarch. Stir in pumpkin butter* and dates. Bring to boiling, stirring to dissolve sugar; reduce heat. Simmer, uncovered, about 15 minutes or until thick, stirring frequently. Remove from heat; cool filling for at least 1 hour.

2 Meanwhile, in a medium bowl stir together the flour, ginger, baking soda, cinnamon, salt, and cloves. In a large mixing bowl beat butter with an electric mixer on medium to high speed for 30 seconds. Add brown sugar and molasses. Beat until combined, scraping sides of bowl occasionally. Beat in the egg until combined. Beat in as much of the flour mixture as you can with the mixer. Using a wooden spoon, stir in any remaining flour mixture. Divide dough into thirds. Cover and chill dough about 1 hour or until easy to handle.

3 Preheat oven to 375°F. Line a large cookie sheet with parchment paper. On a lightly floured surface roll one dough portion to ⅛-inch thickness. Using a floured 2-inch fluted round cookie cutter, cut out dough. Place half of the cutouts 2 inches apart on the prepared cookie sheet. Spread about ½ teaspoon of the filling over the center of each cutout on the cookie sheet.

4 Using a floured ½- to ¾-inch hors d'oeuvre cutter, cut out centers from the remaining cutouts. Place on top of cutouts with filling; press the edges together with floured fingers or the tines of a fork to seal.

5 Bake for 8 to 9 minutes or just until edges are firm. Transfer cookies to a wire rack and let cool. Repeat with the remaining dough portions and filling. **MAKES ABOUT 60 COOKIES**

note To spice up the filling, add ⅛ teaspoon cayenne pepper with the pumpkin butter.

TO MAKE AHEAD AND STORE: Layer cookies between sheets of waxed paper in an airtight container; cover. Store at room temperature for up to 3 days or freeze for up to 3 months.

Star Pumpkin Cookies

PREP **30 MINUTES**   BAKE **8 MINUTES PER BATCH**   COOL **1 MINUTE PER BATCH**   OVEN **375°F**

1   **17.5-ounce package sugar cookie mix**
⅓   **cup butter, melted**
1   **egg**
2   **teaspoons pumpkin pie spice**
½   **teaspoon ground nutmeg**
1   **recipe Browned-Butter Drizzle**

1 Preheat oven to 375°F. In a large bowl combine the cookie mix, melted butter, egg, pumpkin pie spice, and nutmeg. Using a wooden spoon, stir until a stiff dough forms. If necessary, gently knead dough until it clings together.

2 On a lightly floured surface roll dough to ¼-inch thickness. Using a 1½- to 2½-inch star-shape cookie cutter, cut out dough. Place cutouts 1 inch apart on an ungreased cookie sheet.

3 Bake about 8 minutes or until bottoms are light brown. Cool on cookie sheet for 1 minute. Transfer cookies to a wire rack and let cool. Drizzle with Browned-Butter Drizzle. Let stand until drizzle is set. **MAKES 36 LARGE STARS OR 72 SMALL STARS**

Browned-Butter Drizzle: In a small saucepan heat 2 tablespoons butter over low heat until butter melts. Continue heating butter until it turns a delicate brown. Remove pan from heat. Whisk in 2 cups powdered sugar, 2 tablespoons milk, and 1 teaspoon vanilla. Immediately drizzle over cooled cookies (icing will harden quickly).

TO MAKE AHEAD AND STORE: Layer cookies between sheets of waxed paper in an airtight container; cover. Store at room temperature for up to 3 days. Or freeze unfrosted cookies for up to 3 months. Thaw cookies; prepare drizzle and ice cookies as directed.

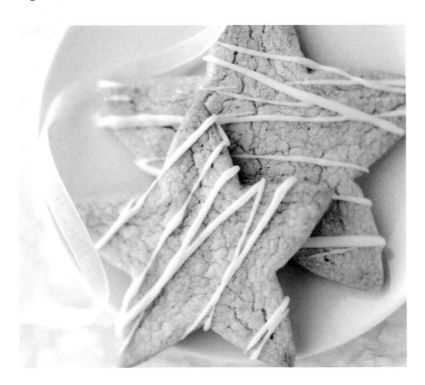

Pumpkin Cheesecake Bars with Chocolate Topping

PREP **35 MINUTES**   BAKE **40 MINUTES**   CHILL **2 HOURS**   OVEN **350°F**

1	17.5-ounce package oatmeal cookie mix
½	cup butter, cut up
2	8-ounce packages cream cheese, softened
1¾	cups sugar
3	eggs
1	15-ounce can pumpkin
1	teaspoon vanilla
½	teaspoon pumpkin pie spice
¼	teaspoon salt
1	cup semisweet chocolate pieces
¼	cup butter
48	pecan halves

1 Preheat oven to 350°F. Line a 15x10x1-inch baking pan with foil, extending the foil over the edges of the pan. Lightly grease foil. Place the cookie mix in a large bowl. Using a pastry blender, cut in the ½ cup butter until mixture resembles coarse crumbs. Press flour mixture evenly onto the bottom of the prepared baking pan. Bake about 10 minutes or until set.

2 In a large mixing bowl combine the cream cheese and sugar. Beat with an electric mixer on medium speed until combined. Add the eggs, one at a time, beating on low speed after each addition until just combined. Stir in pumpkin, vanilla, pumpkin pie spice, and salt. Pour pumpkin mixture over the hot crust. Bake for 30 to 35 minutes or until slightly puffed around edges and just set in center. Cool in pan on a wire rack.

3 In a small microwave-safe bowl combine the chocolate pieces and the ¼ cup butter. Microwave on 100 percent power (high) for 30 to 60 seconds or until softened; stir until smooth. Spoon the chocolate over the cooled bars, carefully spreading evenly. Gently press pecan halves evenly over the top of the bars. Cover and chill for 2 to 24 hours. Use the foil to lift the uncut bars out of the pan. Place on cutting board; cut into bars. **MAKES 48 BARS**

TO MAKE AHEAD AND STORE:
Place bars in a single layer in an airtight container; cover. Store in the refrigerator for up to 3 days. Do not freeze.

A Clean Cut

For smooth, smudge-free sides to your bars, hold a thin-blade knife under hot running water to warm it. Wipe the blade dry. Repeat as needed.

Toffee-Pumpkin Pie Bars

PREP **30 MINUTES**   BAKE **40 MINUTES**   OVEN **375°F**

1   recipe Ginger Crumb Crust
1   15-ounce can pumpkin
¾   cup packed brown sugar
1   teaspoon ground cinnamon
¾   teaspoon ground ginger
½   teaspoon salt
¼   teaspoon ground cloves
4   eggs, lightly beaten
1½   cups half-and-half or light cream
½   cup toffee pieces
½   cup chopped pecans, toasted

1 Preheat oven to 375°F. Line a 13x9x2-inch baking pan with foil, extending the foil over the edges of the pan. Lightly grease foil. Press the Ginger Crumb Crust evenly and firmly onto the bottom of the prepared pan.

2 In a large bowl stir together the pumpkin, brown sugar, cinnamon, ginger, salt, and cloves. Add eggs; beat lightly with a fork until combined. Gradually stir in half-and-half just until combined. Pour pumpkin mixture over crust in pan.

3 Bake for 40 to 45 minutes or until a knife inserted near the center comes out clean. Immediately sprinkle top with toffee pieces and pecans. Cool in pan on a wire rack.

4 Use the foil to lift the uncut bars out of the pan. Place on a cutting board; cut into bars. Cover and chill for 2 hours.
MAKES 32 BARS

Ginger Crumb Crust: In a medium bowl combine 2 cups crushed gingersnaps (about 35 cookies), ¼ cup sugar, and ¼ cup all-purpose flour. Add ½ cup melted butter; stir until well combined.

TO MAKE AHEAD AND STORE: Place bars in a single layer in an airtight container; cover. Store in the refrigerator for up to 2 days. Do not freeze.

Pumpkin Bars

PREP **25 MINUTES**   BAKE **25 MINUTES**   COOL **2 HOURS**   OVEN **350°F**

2   cups all-purpose flour
1½   cups sugar
2   teaspoons baking powder
2   teaspoons ground cinnamon
1   teaspoon baking soda
½   teaspoon salt
¼   teaspoon ground cloves
4   eggs, lightly beaten
1   15-ounce can pumpkin
1   cup cooking oil
1   recipe Cream Cheese Frosting

1 Preheat oven to 350°F. In a large bowl stir together the flour, sugar, baking powder, cinnamon, baking soda, salt, and cloves. Stir in the eggs, pumpkin, and oil until combined. Spoon batter into an ungreased 15x10x1-inch baking pan, spreading evenly.

2 Bake for 25 to 30 minutes or until a wooden toothpick inserted near the center comes out clean. Cool in pan on a wire rack for 2 hours. Spread Cream Cheese Frosting evenly over bars. Cut into bars. MAKES 36 BARS

Cream Cheese Frosting: In a large mixing bowl combine two 3-ounce packages cream cheese, softened; ⅓ cup butter, softened; and 1½ teaspoons vanilla. Beat with an electric mixer on medium speed until light and fluffy. Gradually beat in 4½ to 5 cups powdered sugar to make a frosting of spreading consistency.

Applesauce Bars: Prepare as directed, except substitute one 15-ounce jar (1¾ cups) applesauce for the pumpkin.

TO MAKE AHEAD AND STORE: Place bars in a single layer in an airtight container; cover. Store in the refrigerator for up to 3 days. Or freeze unfrosted bars for up to 3 months. Thaw bars; frost as directed.

In a *twinkling*

Turn these bars into dessert-worthy treats by drizzling them with caramel-flavor ice cream topping just before serving.

231

TOFFEE-PUMPKIN PIE BARS

GIANT NUTMEG COOKIES, PAGE 242

simply spiced

These recipes delight twice!
First, when they bake in the oven, filling
your house with the unmistakably seasonal aromas
of cinnamon, ginger, nutmeg, and more. Then, when
they bring the rich and warming spices to your
festive platter of home-baked
goodness.

★

Two-Tone Cinnamon Cookies

PREP **35 MINUTES**   CHILL **1 HOUR**   BAKE **8 MINUTES PER BATCH**   COOL **1 MINUTE PER BATCH**   OVEN **375°F**

- ½   cup butter, softened
- 1   3-ounce package cream cheese, softened
- 1   cup powdered sugar
- ½   teaspoon baking powder
- ½   teaspoon salt
- ½   teaspoon ground cinnamon
- 1   egg
- 1½   teaspoons vanilla
- 2¼   cups all-purpose flour
- 1   recipe Cinnamon Glaze
- 1   recipe White Glaze

1 In a large mixing bowl beat butter and cream cheese with an electric mixer on medium to high speed for 30 seconds. Add powdered sugar, baking powder, salt, and cinnamon. Beat until combined, scraping sides of bowl occasionally. Beat in the egg and vanilla until combined. Beat in as much of the flour as you can with the mixer. Using a wooden spoon, stir in any remaining flour. Cover and chill dough about 1 hour or until easy to handle.

2 Preheat oven to 375°F. On a lightly floured surface roll out dough to ¼-inch thickness. Using a 3½-inch fluted round cookie cutter, cut out dough. Place cutouts 1 inch apart on an ungreased cookie sheet.

3 Bake for 8 to 10 minutes or until edges are very light brown. Cool on cookie sheet for 1 minute. Transfer cookies to a wire rack and let cool.

4 Spoon Cinnamon Glaze into a heavy resealable plastic bag. Seal bag and snip a small hole in one corner. Spoon White Glaze over tops of cookies, spreading almost to the edges. Place cookies on a wire rack set over waxed paper. Drizzle Cinnamon Glaze over cookies. If desired, gently swirl a knife through the glazes to marble. Let cookies stand until glazes are set. **MAKES ABOUT 14 COOKIES**

Cinnamon Glaze: In a small saucepan combine 1 cup cinnamon-flavor pieces, bittersweet chocolate pieces, or semisweet chocolate pieces and 2 teaspoons shortening. Cook and stir over low heat until pieces melt.

White Glaze: In a small saucepan combine 1 cup white baking pieces and 2 teaspoons shortening. Cook and stir over low heat until melted.

TO MAKE AHEAD AND STORE: Place cookies in a single layer in an airtight container; cover. Store at room temperature for up to 3 days or freeze for up to 3 months.

Spicy-Sweet Cinnamon Chips

Cinnamon-flavor pieces work much the same way as chocolate chips—they add little pockets of delightful flavor here and there in your baked goods, but with spicy (rather than chocolaty) appeal. And like chocolate chips, they're gooey when warm and firm when cool.

Try substituting cinnamon chips for other kinds of chips in your recipes; they're a natural in oatmeal cookies and can also be used in scones, biscotti, muffins, and bread pudding or any recipe that could benefit from a little cinnamon boost. Also try them in your morning granola or oatmeal.

Store baking chips in a cool, dry place in your pantry and use them by the "best before" date given on the package.

Spice Windmills

PREP **45 MINUTES**   CHILL **4 HOURS**   BAKE **8 MINUTES PER BATCH**   OVEN **350°F**

⅓ **cup butter**

⅓ **cup shortening**

¾ **cup packed brown sugar**

1 **teaspoon baking powder**

¾ **teaspoon pumpkin pie spice**

¼ **teaspoon baking soda**

¼ **teaspoon salt**

1 **egg**

2 **teaspoons vanilla**

2 **cups all-purpose flour**

1 **3-ounce package cream cheese, softened**

¼ **cup packed brown sugar**

1 **teaspoon all-purpose flour**

½ **teaspoon vanilla**

¾ **cup salted dry-roasted sunflower kernels**

1 **tablespoon granulated sugar**

½ **teaspoon ground cinnamon**

Salted dry-roasted sunflower kernels

1 In a large mixing bowl beat butter and shortening with an electric mixer on medium to high speed for 30 seconds. Add the ¾ cup brown sugar, the baking powder, pumpkin pie spice, baking soda, and salt. Beat until combined, scraping sides of bowl occasionally. Beat in the egg and the 2 teaspoons vanilla until combined. Beat in as much of the 2 cups flour as you can with the mixer. Using a wooden spoon, stir in any remaining 2 cups flour. Divide dough in half. Cover and chill dough about 4 hours or until easy to handle.

2 Meanwhile, in a medium mixing bowl combine cream cheese, the ¼ cup brown sugar, the 1 teaspoon flour, and the ½ teaspoon vanilla. Beat with an electric mixer on medium speed until smooth. Stir in the ¾ cup sunflower kernels.

3 Preheat oven to 350°F. Lightly grease a cookie sheet. On a lightly floured surface roll each dough half into a 10-inch square. Using a pastry wheel, cut each dough square into sixteen 2½-inch squares. Place squares 2 inches apart on the prepared cookie sheet. Make 1-inch-long slits from the corners toward the centers of each square.

4 Spoon about 1 teaspoon of the cream cheese mixture onto the center of each dough square. Bring four alternating corners of each square up over filling to the center to form a windmill; lightly press to seal.

5 In a small bowl stir together the granulated sugar and cinnamon; sprinkle lightly over cookies. Press additional sunflower kernels in centers of cookies. Bake for 8 to 10 minutes or until edges are light brown. Transfer cookies to a wire rack and let cool. **MAKES 32 COOKIES**

TO MAKE AHEAD AND STORE: Place cookies in a single layer in an airtight container; cover. Store in the refrigerator for up to 3 days or freeze for up to 3 months.

Gingerbread Cutouts

PREP 35 MINUTES **CHILL 3 HOURS** **BAKE 5 MINUTES PER BATCH** **COOL 1 MINUTE PER BATCH** **OVEN 375°F**

½ cup shortening
½ cup sugar
1 teaspoon baking powder
1 teaspoon ground ginger
½ teaspoon baking soda
½ teaspoon ground cinnamon
½ teaspoon ground cloves
½ cup molasses
1 egg
1 tablespoon vinegar
2½ cups all-purpose flour
1 recipe Royal Icing (optional)
Decorative candies (optional)

1 In a large mixing bowl beat shortening with an electric mixer on medium to high speed for 30 seconds. Add sugar, baking powder, ginger, baking soda, cinnamon, and cloves. Beat until combined, scraping sides of bowl occasionally. Beat in the molasses, egg, and vinegar until combined. Beat in as much of the flour as you can with the mixer. Using a wooden spoon, stir in any remaining flour. Divide dough in half. Cover and chill dough about 3 hours or until easy to handle.

2 Preheat oven to 375°F. Grease a cookie sheet. On a lightly floured surface roll each dough half to ⅛-inch thickness. Using a 2½-inch cookie cutter, cut out dough into desired shape. Place cutouts 1 inch apart on the prepared cookie sheet.

3 Bake for 5 to 6 minutes or until bottoms are light brown. Cool on cookie sheet 1 minute. Transfer cookies to a wire rack and let cool. If desired, decorate cookies with Royal Icing and candies. **MAKES 36 TO 48 COOKIES**

Royal Icing: In a large mixing bowl stir together 4 cups powdered sugar, 3 tablespoons meringue powder, and ½ teaspoon cream of tartar. Add ½ cup warm water and 1 teaspoon vanilla. Beat with an electric mixer on low speed until combined, then on high speed for 7 to 10 minutes or until very stiff. Beat in 2 to 4 tablespoons additional water, 1 teaspoon at a time, to make an icing of spreading consistency. If desired, tint portions of icing with food coloring.

Gingerbread People Cutouts: Prepare as directed, except roll dough to ¼-inch thickness. Using a 4½- to 6-inch people-shape cookie cutter, cut out dough. Bake for 6 to 8 minutes or until edges are light brown. Cool on cookie sheet for 1 minute. Makes about 18 cookies.

TO MAKE AHEAD AND STORE: Layer cookies between sheets of waxed paper in an airtight container; cover. Store at room temperature for up to 3 days or freeze for up to 3 months.

gift It

Hit Singles!

Use paper CD envelopes to give these greatest hits to friends and co-workers. Cut a square of colored scrapbooking paper to fit inside a CD envelope; slide the paper inside. Cut a piece of ribbon the width of the envelope and attach it across the front using a glue stick. Affix a snowflake adornment to the ribbon with crafts glue. Be sure the icing is dry on the cookie, then carefully slide it into the envelope.

Spiced Oatmeal Shortbread Wedges

PREP **20 MINUTES** BAKE **31 MINUTES** COOL **5 MINUTES** OVEN **325°F**

- ½ **cup regular rolled oats**
- 1 **cup all-purpose flour**
- 3 **tablespoons packed brown sugar**
- ½ **teaspoon ground cinnamon**
- ¼ **teaspoon ground ginger**
- ⅛ **teaspoon ground cloves**
- ½ **cup butter, cut into small pieces**
- 2 **teaspoons milk**
- 1 **tablespoon coarse sugar or granulated sugar**

1 Preheat oven to 325°F. Spread oats in a 15x10x1-inch baking pan. Bake for 6 to 8 minutes or until light brown. Cool completely.

2 In a food processor combine ⅓ cup of the cooled, toasted oats; the flour; brown sugar; cinnamon; ginger; and cloves. Cover and process until oats are ground. Add the butter pieces to the food processor. Cover and process with on-off pulses until the mixture just comes together. Form dough into a ball and knead until smooth.

3 On an ungreased cookie sheet pat the dough into an 8-inch circle. If desired, make a scalloped edge. Brush the dough circle lightly with milk. Sprinkle with the remaining toasted oats and the coarse sugar; press down lightly.

Cut circle into 10 wedges, leaving wedges in place.

4 Bake for 25 to 30 minutes or until center is set. Cut circle into wedges again while warm. Cool on cookie sheet for 5 minutes. Transfer cookies to a wire rack and let cool. **MAKES 10 COOKIES**

TO MAKE AHEAD AND STORE: Layer cookies between sheets of waxed paper in an airtight container; cover. Store at room temperature for up to 3 days or freeze for up to 3 months.

In a *twinkling*

For an extra drizzle of sweetness and spice, melt ⅔ cup cinnamon-flavor pieces and 1½ teaspoons shortening together; drizzle over shortbread wedges.

Ginger-Sesame Balls

PREP **25 MINUTES**   BAKE **15 MINUTES PER BATCH**   OVEN **325°F**

1 **cup butter, softened**
½ **cup powdered sugar**
¾ **teaspoon vanilla**
½ **teaspoon ground ginger**
2 **cups all-purpose flour**
¾ **cup coarsely ground macadamia nuts (3 ounces)**
1 **tablespoon finely chopped crystallized ginger**
⅓ **cup sesame seeds**

1 Preheat oven to 325°F. In a large mixing bowl beat butter with an electric mixer on medium to high speed for 30 seconds. Add powdered sugar, the vanilla, and ground ginger. Beat until combined, scraping sides of bowl occasionally. Beat in as much of the flour as you can with the mixer. Using a wooden spoon, stir in any remaining flour, the nuts, and crystallized ginger.

2 Shape dough into 1-inch balls. Roll each ball in sesame seeds to coat. Place balls 2 inches apart on an ungreased cookie sheet.

3 Bake about 15 minutes or until bottoms are light brown. Transfer cookies to a wire rack and let cool. **MAKES ABOUT 48 COOKIES**

TO MAKE AHEAD AND STORE: Layer cookies between sheets of waxed paper in an airtight container; cover. Store at room temperature for up to 3 days or freeze for up to 3 months.

A Bit about . . . Crystallized Ginger

Crystallized ginger is made by cooking ginger in sugar syrup, then coating it with a dusting of sugar. The result is a tender confection that adds a layer of exotic sweetness and spice to recipes.

To chop crystallized ginger without having it stick to the knife, spray the knife blade with nonstick cooking spray or dip the blade in flour.

Look for crystallized ginger in organic and health food stores and in the spice aisle of supermarkets.

With Best
Christmas Wishes

BLACK-AND-WHITE
MOLASSES COOKIES

Black-and-White Molasses Cookies

START TO FINISH **35 MINUTES**

2 cups powdered sugar

2 tablespoons light corn syrup

1 to 2 tablespoons milk

½ to 1 teaspoon vanilla

1 tablespoon unsweetened cocoa powder

1 to 1½ teaspoons milk (optional)

8 to 10 packaged molasses, sugar, chocolate chip, or other flat, soft cookies (3-inch diameter)

1 For white icing, in a medium mixing bowl combine powdered sugar, corn syrup, 1 tablespoon of the milk, and the vanilla. Beat with an electric mixer on low speed until combined. Stir in additional milk, 1 teaspoon at a time, to make an icing of piping consistency. Transfer half of the white icing to a small bowl.

2 For cocoa icing, stir the cocoa powder into the remaining white icing. If necessary, stir in additional milk, 1 teaspoon at a time, to make an icing of piping consistency.

3 Place cookies on a wire rack over waxed paper. Spoon the white icing into a pastry bag fitted with a small round tip. (Or spoon icing into a heavy resealable plastic bag; seal bag and snip a small hole in one corner.) Pipe icing in a very thin line down the center of each cookie; pipe icing to outline half of each cookie. Let stand until outlines are slightly firm.

4 Pipe white icing into the centers of the white icing outlines; use a thin metal spatula and/or a toothpick to spread icing to edges. Repeat piping process with the cocoa icing on the other half of each cookie. Let cookies stand until icing is firm. **MAKES 8 TO 10 COOKIES**

TO MAKE AHEAD AND STORE: Place cookies in a single layer in an airtight container; cover. Store at room temperature for up to 3 days.

Spicy Ginger Crinkle Cookies

PREP **35 MINUTES**   BAKE **10 MINUTES PER BATCH**   OVEN **350°F**

¾ cup butter, softened

1 cup packed brown sugar

2 teaspoons baking soda

2 teaspoons ground ginger

1 teaspoon ground cinnamon

¾ teaspoon salt

¼ teaspoon ground cloves

¼ teaspoon ground allspice

1 egg

¼ cup full-flavor molasses

1 teaspoon vanilla

2¼ cups all-purpose flour

2 tablespoons finely chopped crystallized ginger

Granulated sugar, pearl decorating sugar, and/or colored sugar

1 In a large mixing bowl beat butter with an electric mixer on medium to high speed for 30 seconds. Add brown sugar, baking soda, ginger, cinnamon, salt, cloves, and allspice. Beat until combined, scraping sides of bowl occasionally. Beat in the egg, molasses, and vanilla until combined. Beat in as much of the flour as you can with the mixer. Using a wooden spoon, stir in any remaining flour and the crystallized ginger. If necessary, cover and chill dough for 1 to 2 hours or until easy to handle.

2 Preheat oven to 350°F. Place granulated sugar, pearl sugar, and/or colored sugar in separate small bowls. Shape dough into 1¼-inch balls. Roll balls in desired sugar to coat. Place balls 2 inches apart on an ungreased cookie sheet.

3 Bake about 10 minutes or until tops are crackled and edges are firm. Transfer cookies to a wire rack and let cool. **MAKES ABOUT 42 COOKIES**

TO MAKE AHEAD AND STORE: Layer cookies between sheets of waxed paper in an airtight container; cover. Store at room temperature for up to 3 days or freeze for up to 3 months.

Giant Nutmeg Cookies

PREP **30 MINUTES**   BAKE **13 MINUTES PER BATCH**   COOL **2 MINUTES PER BATCH**   OVEN **350°F**

1½   cups shortening

2   cups sugar

2   tablespoons freshly grated nutmeg or 1 tablespoon ground nutmeg

2   teaspoons baking soda

1   teaspoon ground cinnamon

¼   teaspoon salt

2   eggs

½   cup molasses

4½   cups all-purpose flour

⅓   cup sugar

1   teaspoon freshly grated nutmeg or ½ teaspoon ground nutmeg

1 Preheat oven to 350°F. In a large mixing bowl beat shortening with an electric mixer on medium to high speed for 30 seconds. Add the 2 cups sugar, 2 tablespoons nutmeg, the baking soda, cinnamon, and salt. Beat until combined, scraping sides of bowl occasionally. Beat in the eggs and molasses until combined. Beat in as much of the flour as you can with the mixer. Using a wooden spoon, stir in any remaining flour.

2 In a small bowl stir together the ⅓ cup sugar and 1 teaspoon nutmeg. Shape dough into 2-inch balls.* Roll balls in the sugar mixture to coat. Place balls 2½ inches apart on an ungreased cookie sheet.

3 Bake about 13 minutes or until tops are cracked and edges are firm (do not overbake). Cool on cookie sheet for 2 minutes. Transfer cookies to a wire rack and let cool. **MAKES ABOUT 24 COOKIES**

*note *Use a ¼-cup measure or scoop to easily measure out enough dough for 2-inch balls.*

TO MAKE AHEAD AND STORE: Layer cookies between sheets of waxed paper in an airtight container; cover. Store at room temperature for up to 3 days or freeze for up to 3 months.

Molasses Matters

Molasses is a by-product of the sugar-making process; the thick brown syrup is made from the boiled juices of sugar beets or sugarcane, after the sugar crystals have been extracted.

Light molasses is milder in flavor and lighter in color; dark molasses, which has undergone a second boiling, is darker, thicker, and more strongly flavored.

When a recipe would benefit from a more delicate molasses flavor, mild-flavor (light) molasses is called for over full-flavor (dark) molasses. If neither dark nor light is specified, either style of molasses can be used interchangeably, depending on how strong of a molasses flavor you desire.

A third product, blackstrap molasses, is the deepest of them all; more bitter than sweet, it's generally not used for baking.

Spicy Molasses Waffle Squares

PREP **25 MINUTES**   BAKE **1 MINUTE PER BATCH**

⅔   cup all-purpose flour
½   cup whole wheat flour
½   cup sugar
½   teaspoon baking powder
¼   teaspoon salt
¼   teaspoon ground
      cinnamon
⅛   teaspoon ground ginger
      Pinch ground cloves
1   egg, lightly beaten
¼   cup butter, melted
2   tablespoons molasses
1   tablespoon milk
¼   cup finely chopped
      toasted walnuts
1   recipe Vanilla Glaze
1   recipe Spiced Sugar

1 Lightly grease a waffle iron; preheat waffle iron according to manufacturer's directions. In a medium bowl stir together the all-purpose flour, whole wheat flour, sugar, baking powder, salt, cinnamon, ginger, and cloves. In a small bowl stir together egg, butter, molasses, and milk. Add the egg mixture and walnuts all at once to flour mixture. Stir just until moistened.

2 Drop batter by rounded teaspoons 3 inches apart onto grids of the waffle iron. Close lid. Bake for 1 to 1½ minutes or until cookies are golden brown. Using a fork, lift cookies from waffle iron. Transfer cookies to a wire rack and let cool. Repeat with remaining batter.

3 Drizzle Vanilla Glaze over cooled cookies. Sprinkle cookies with Spiced Sugar. MAKES 24 COOKIES

Vanilla Glaze: In a small bowl stir together ¾ cup powdered sugar, ¼ teaspoon vanilla, and enough milk (2 to 3 teaspoons) to make a glaze of drizzling consistency.

Spiced Sugar: In a small bowl stir together 1 tablespoon powdered sugar and ⅛ teaspoon pumpkin pie spice.

TO MAKE AHEAD AND STORE: Layer cookies between sheets of waxed paper in an airtight container; cover. Store in the refrigerator for up to 3 days or freeze for up to 3 months.

In a *twinkling*

Instead of the Vanilla Glaze, chop 2 ounces white baking chocolate in the microwave on 50 percent power (medium) for 1½ to 2 minutes or until melted and smooth, stirring once. Drizzle cookies with melted chocolate.

Buttermilk Cookies with Nutmeg

PREP **45 MINUTES**   BAKE **8 MINUTES PER BATCH**   COOL **1 MINUTE PER BATCH**   OVEN **375°F**

1   cup butter, softened
2   cups sugar
2   teaspoons freshly grated
        nutmeg or 1 teaspoon
        ground nutmeg
1   teaspoon baking soda
½   teaspoon salt
2   eggs
5   cups all-purpose flour
1¼   cups buttermilk
1   recipe Sour Cream
        Frosting
        Freshly grated nutmeg
        or ground nutmeg
        (optional)

1 Preheat oven to 375°F. Line a cookie sheet with parchment paper; set aside.

2 In an extra-large mixing bowl beat butter with an electric mixer on medium to high speed for 30 seconds. Add sugar, the 2 teaspoons nutmeg, the baking soda, and salt. Beat until combined, scraping sides of bowl occasionally. Beat in the eggs until combined. Add the flour alternately with the buttermilk, beating on low speed after each addition just until combined.

3 Drop dough by rounded teaspoons 2 inches apart onto the prepared cookie sheet. Bake about 8 minutes or until cookies are set. Let cool on cookie sheet for 1 minute. Transfer cookies to a wire rack and let cool. Spread Sour Cream Frosting on cookies. If desired, sprinkle with additional nutmeg. **MAKES ABOUT 75 COOKIES**

Sour Cream Frosting: In a medium mixing bowl combine ½ cup sour cream, ⅓ cup softened butter, and 1 teaspoon vanilla. Beat with an electric mixer on low speed until smooth. Gradually beat in 2¾ to 3¼ cups powdered sugar to make a frosting of spreading consistency.

TO MAKE AHEAD AND STORE: Layer unfrosted cookies between sheets of waxed paper in an airtight container; cover. Store at room temperature for up to 3 days or freeze for up to 3 months. Thaw cookies, if frozen. Frost cookies as directed.

Cinnamon-Sugar Roll Cookies

PREP **40 MINUTES**   FREEZE **2 HOURS**   BAKE **8 MINUTES PER BATCH**   COOL **2 MINUTES PER BATCH**
OVEN **375°F**

¼   cup butter, softened
¼   cup shortening
2   ounces cream cheese, softened
1   cup packed brown sugar
½   teaspoon baking powder
½   teaspoon salt
½   teaspoon ground cinnamon
½   teaspoon ground nutmeg
1   egg
2   teaspoons vanilla
2½   cups all-purpose flour
½   cup salted roasted mixed nuts, finely chopped
¼   cup packed brown sugar
½   teaspoon ground cinnamon
2   tablespoons butter
1   recipe Vanilla Glaze

1 In a large mixing bowl beat butter, shortening, and cream cheese with an electric mixer on medium to high speed for 30 seconds. Add the 1 cup brown sugar, the baking powder, salt, ½ teaspoon cinnamon, and the nutmeg. Beat until combined, scraping sides of bowl occasionally. Beat in the egg and vanilla until combined. Beat in as much of the flour as you can with the mixer. Using a wooden spoon, stir in any remaining flour.

2 In a medium bowl combine the chopped nuts, the ¼ cup brown sugar, and ½ teaspoon cinnamon. Using a pastry blender, cut in butter until mixture clings together. Roll dough between two sheets of lightly floured waxed paper into a 16x9-inch rectangle. Remove top sheet of waxed paper. Sprinkle nut mixture evenly over dough. Starting from a long side, roll up dough tightly using the waxed paper to help lift and guide the roll. Wrap in plastic wrap. Freeze dough about 2 hours or until firm

3 Preheat oven to 375°F. Line a cookie sheet with parchment paper. Cut roll crosswise into ¼-inch-thick slices. Place slices 2 inches apart on the prepared cookie sheet.

4 Bake about 8 minutes or until edges are light brown. Cool on cookie sheet for 2 minutes. Transfer cookies to a wire rack and cool. Drizzle Vanilla Glaze over cookies. Let stand until glaze is set. **MAKES ABOUT 60 COOKIES**

Vanilla Glaze: In a small bowl stir together 1 cup powdered sugar and 1 teaspoon vanilla. Stir in enough milk (3 to 4 teaspoons) to make a glaze of drizzling consistency.

TO MAKE AHEAD AND STORE: Layer cookies between sheets of waxed paper in an airtight container; cover. Store at room temperature for up to 3 days or freeze for up to 3 months.

In a *twinkling*

After glazing the cool cookies with the Vanilla Glaze, sprinkle with additional chopped mixed nuts.

Gingersnaps in a Snap

PREP **25 MINUTES**   BAKE **10 MINUTES PER BATCH**   COOL **1 MINUTE PER BATCH**   OVEN **375°F**

1   **17.5-ounce package sugar cookie mix**
½   **cup butter, melted**
¼   **cup granulated sugar**
1   **egg**
1   **tablespoon mild-flavor molasses**
1   **teaspoon ground ginger**
1   **cup finely chopped pecans**
     Powdered sugar

1 Preheat oven to 375°F. In a large bowl stir together sugar cookie mix, melted butter, granulated sugar, egg, molasses, and ginger until well mixed.

2 Place pecans in a shallow dish. Shape dough into 1-inch balls. Roll balls in pecans to coat. Place balls 2 inches apart on an ungreased cookie sheet; flatten slightly.

3 Bake about 10 minutes or until cookies are light brown. Cool on cookie sheet for 1 minute. Transfer cookies to a wire rack and let cool. Dust cooled cookies with powdered sugar. **MAKES 48 COOKIES**

TO MAKE AHEAD AND STORE: Layer cookies between sheets of waxed paper in an airtight container; cover. Store at room temperature for up to 3 days or freeze for up to 3 months.

gift It

A Win-Win Presentation

When looking for ways to present cookies, head downstairs to your (or your mother's) basement and see what's there. You may just come up with some long-forgotten wide-mouth jars or canisters that would be perfect for presenting cookies to friends. Simply tie with a ribbon, and you're set.

Striped Ginger Cookies

PREP **30 MINUTES**   BAKE **6 MINUTES PER BATCH**   OVEN **375°F**

½   of a 16.5-ounce package refrigerated sugar cookie dough

2   tablespoons all-purpose flour

½   of a 16.5-ounce package refrigerated gingerbread cookie dough

2   tablespoons all-purpose flour

1 Preheat oven to 375°F. In a medium bowl combine sugar cookie dough and 2 tablespoons flour; stir until well mixed. In another medium bowl combine gingerbread cookie dough and 2 tablespoons flour; stir until well mixed.

2 Shape both doughs into 1-inch balls. To shape cookies, roll one ball of each color into a 4-inch-long rope. Lay ropes side by side, then twist and roll together to make an 8-inch-long rope. Cut each rope into six pieces. Place pieces on an ungreased cookie sheet. Repeat with remaining balls of dough.

3 Bake for 6 to 8 minutes or until edges are set. Transfer cookies to a wire rack and let cool.

MAKES ABOUT 96 COOKIES

TO MAKE AHEAD AND STORE: Layer cookies between sheets of waxed paper in an airtight container; cover. Store at room temperature for up to 3 days or freeze for up to 3 months.

247

Spiced Brownies with Cream Cheese Swirl

PREP **20 MINUTES**   BAKE **25 MINUTES**   COOL **1 HOUR**   OVEN **350°F**

1   3-ounce package cream cheese, softened
¼   cup sugar
1   egg yolk
1   tablespoon all-purpose flour
1   19.5-ounce package traditional fudge brownie mix
½   teaspoon ground cinnamon
½   teaspoon ground ginger
¼   teaspoon ground nutmeg
⅛   teaspoon ground cloves

1 Preheat oven to 350°F. Line a 13x9x2-inch baking pan with foil, extending the foil over the edges of the pan. Lightly grease foil; set pan aside.

2 In a small mixing bowl beat cream cheese and sugar with an electric mixer on medium to high speed until combined. Beat in the egg yolk and flour.

3 In a large bowl combine the brownie mix, cinnamon, ginger, nutmeg, and cloves. Prepare brownie mix according to package directions, except substitute melted butter for the vegetable oil. Spoon batter into the prepared baking pan, spreading evenly. Spoon cream cheese mixture in small mounds over brownie batter. Using a table knife, swirl cream cheese mixture into brownie batter.

4 Bake for 25 to 30 minutes or until center is set and cream cheese swirl is light brown. Cool in pan on a wire rack for 1 hour. Use the foil to lift the uncut brownies out of the pan. Place on a cutting board; cut into bars. **MAKES 32 BROWNIES**

TO MAKE AHEAD AND STORE: Place brownies in a single layer in an airtight container; cover. Store in the refrigerator for up to 4 days or freeze for up to 3 months.

Easy Gingerbread Bars

PREP **15 MINUTES**   COOL **1 HOUR**   BAKE **15 MINUTES 350°F**   OVEN **350°F**

1   14.5-ounce package gingerbread mix
¾   cup water
1   egg
¾   cup raisins
¾   cup snipped dried apricots
¾   cup chopped pecans
1   cup powdered sugar
1   to 2 tablespoons milk

1 Preheat oven to 350°F. Grease a 13x9x2-inch baking pan; set aside.

2 In a medium bowl, stir together gingerbread mix, water, egg, raisins, apricots, and pecans just until blended. Spread batter into prepared pan.

3 Bake for 15 to 20 minutes or until a toothpick inserted near the center comes out clean. Cool completely on a wire rack.

4 For glaze, in a small bowl, stir together powdered sugar and enough milk to make a drizzling consistency. Drizzle glaze over top. Cut into bars. **MAKES 24 BARS**

index

Metric Information

The charts on this page provide a guide for converting measurements from the U.S. customary system, which is used throughout this book, to the metric system.

PRODUCT DIFFERENCES

Most of the ingredients called for in the recipes in this book are available in most countries. However, some are known by different names. Here are some common American ingredients and their possible counterparts:

- Sugar (white) is granulated, fine granulated, or castor sugar.
- Powdered sugar is icing sugar.
- All-purpose flour is enriched, bleached, or unbleached white household flour. When self-rising flour is used in place of all-purpose flour in a recipe that calls for leavening, omit the leavening agent (baking soda or baking powder) and salt.
- Light-colored corn syrup is golden syrup.
- Cornstarch is cornflour.
- Baking soda is bicarbonate of soda.
- Vanilla or vanilla extract is vanilla essence.
- Green, red, or yellow sweet peppers are capsicums or bell peppers.
- Golden raisins are sultanas.

VOLUME AND WEIGHT

The United States traditionally uses cup measures for liquid and solid ingredients. The chart, top right, shows the approximate imperial and metric equivalents. If you are accustomed to weighing solid ingredients, the following approximate equivalents will be helpful.

- 1 cup butter, castor sugar, or rice = 8 ounces = ½ pound = 250 grams
- 1 cup flour = 4 ounces = ¼ pound = 125 grams
- 1 cup icing sugar = 5 ounces = 150 grams

Canadian and U.S. volume for a cup measure is 8 fluid ounces (237 ml), but the standard metric equivalent is 250 ml.

1 British imperial cup is 10 fluid ounces.

In Australia, 1 tablespoon equals 20 ml, and there are 4 teaspoons in the Australian tablespoon.

Spoon measures are used for smaller amounts of ingredients. Although the size of the tablespoon varies slightly in different countries, for practical purposes and for recipes in this book, a straight substitution is all that's necessary. Measurements made using cups or spoons always should be level unless stated otherwise.

Common Weight Range Replacements

Imperial / U.S.	Metric
½ ounce	15 g
1 ounce	25 g or 30 g
4 ounces (¼ pound)	115 g or 125 g
8 ounces (½ pound)	225 g or 250 g
16 ounces (1 pound)	450 g or 500 g
1¼ pounds	625 g
1½ pounds	750 g
2 pounds or 2¼ pounds	1,000 g or 1 Kg

Oven Temperature Equivalents

Fahrenheit Setting	Celsius Setting*	Gas Setting
300°F	150°C	Gas Mark 2 (very low)
325°F	160°C	Gas Mark 3 (low)
350°F	180°C	Gas Mark 4 (moderate)
375°F	190°C	Gas Mark 5 (moderate)
400°F	200°C	Gas Mark 6 (hot)
425°F	220°C	Gas Mark 7 (hot)
450°F	230°C	Gas Mark 8 (very hot)
475°F	240°C	Gas Mark 9 (very hot)
500°F	260°C	Gas Mark 10 (extremely hot)
Broil	Broil	Grill

Electric and gas ovens may be calibrated using Celsius. However, for an electric oven, increase Celsius setting 10 to 20 degrees when cooking above 160°C. For convection or forced air ovens (gas or electric) lower the temperature setting 25°F/10°C when cooking at all heat levels.

Baking Pan Sizes

Imperial / U.S.	Metric
9×1½-inch round cake pan	22- or 23×4-cm (1.5 L)
9×1½-inch pie plate	22- or 23×4-cm (1 L)
8×8×2-inch square cake pan	20×5-cm (2 L)
9×9×2-inch square cake pan	22- or 23×4.5-cm (2.5 L)
11×7×1½-inch baking pan	28×17×4-cm (2 L)
2-quart rectangular baking pan	30×19×4.5-cm (3 L)
13×9×2-inch baking pan	34×22×4.5-cm (3.5 L)
15×10×1-inch jelly roll pan	40×25×2-cm
9×5×3-inch loaf pan	23×13×8-cm (2 L)
2-quart casserole	2 L

U.S. / Standard Metric Equivalents

⅛ teaspoon = 0.5 ml	⅓ cup = 3 fluid ounces = 75 ml
¼ teaspoon = 1 ml	½ cup = 4 fluid ounces = 125 ml
½ teaspoon = 2 ml	⅔ cup = 5 fluid ounces = 150 ml
1 teaspoon = 5 ml	¾ cup = 6 fluid ounces = 175 ml
1 tablespoon = 15 ml	1 cup = 8 fluid ounces = 250 ml
2 tablespoons = 25 ml	2 cups = 1 pint = 500 ml
¼ cup = 2 fluid ounces = 50 ml	1 quart = 1 liter